HUMANITY
IN THE
THOUGHT OF
KARL BARTH

HUMANITY IN THE THOUGHT OF KARL BARTH

BY
STUART D. McLEAN

T.&T. CLARK LTD.
36 GEORGE STREET, EDINBURGH

Copyright © T. & T. Clark Limited 1981
PRINTED IN THE U.S.A. BY
WILLIAM B. EERDMANS COMPANY
FOR
T. & T. CLARL LIMITED, EDINBURGH
0 567 09304 2
First Printed..........1981

All Rights Reserved. No part of this publication may be reproduced, stored in a retrieval system, or transmitted, in any form or by any means, electronic, .mechanical, photocopying, recording or otherwise, without the prior permission of T. & T. Clark Limited.

CONTENTS

Foreword	vii
I. *Introduction*	1
II. *Background of III/2.*	11
A. *General Aids to Interpretation.*	11
B. *The Placement of III/2 in Barth's Theology as a Whole.*	14
III. *III/2 The Creature.*	23
A. §43 *Man as the Problem of Dogmatics.*	24
B. §44 *Man as the Creature of God.*	25
C. §45 *Man in His Determination as the Covenant-partner of God.*	34
D. §46 *Man as Soul and Body.*	43
IV. *Criticisms of Barth.*	55
V. *Conclusion.*	71
Indexes	
I. *Scripture References*	195
II. *Names*	196
III. *Subjects*	197

This book is dedicated to my
mother and father, Ruth Shuman
and Milton Duncan McLean

FOREWORD

One purpose of this essay is to introduce social scientists to Karl Barth. It is unfortunate that their universes of discourse makes interchange between the social sciences and theology unusual. My contention, that Barth's discussion of humanity is among the most profound in Western literature, coupled with my commitment to the inquiry into the nature of man carried on in contemporary social science, leads me to believe that the one holds a unique contribution for the other. Whether or not a student of social science can agree with all of Barth's ideas and assumptions, he is bound to be struck immediately by language and concepts which often parallel his own. The potential fruitfulness of this dialogue rests on common use of interactional and relational language.

An additional purpose is to rectify distorted images of Barth's theology, as they exist especially in American theological circles. Translation lag is further aggravated by scholars' acceptance of his earlier material as normative. Barth has rectified this initial one-sidedness in his later major work, *The Church Dogmatics*. Rereading the earlier Barth, it is understandable how many were innoculated against him and were, consequently, unable to receive the new input when a change in his theological orientation occurred. After the original impact of commentary on *The Epistle to the Romans*, which I read in 1954, I left his writing until 1962 when I again entered his world through *The Church Dogmatics* III/4 (on Special Ethics). Barth's thought conformed to few of the caricatures then free-floating in the American scene. Many of these distortions I had accepted from authors I am now convinced had received them second hand or through casual reading. There are major differences between Barth and other major contemporary theologians which should not be overlooked, but the argument should be made not from caricature but from an understanding of the completed Barth corpus. I want to attempt to rectify a distorted image.

Third, and more specifically, I hope to clarify his method of dialogical-dialectical thinking which is pivotal for an understanding of: (1) the actional/relational categories of his thought and (2) his concept of the independence and freedom of the human actor. Misinterpretation of these areas leads to the accusation that Barth's theology absorbs man[1] into God. I hope, on the contrary, to show that for Barth true individuality and personhood emerge as the consequence of relationship between God and man, and man and man. I will in the process offer my own critiques of his thought.

The section developing the man-man relationship, III/2/45, Man in His Determination as the Covenant-partner of God, reproduced in entirety as the body of this text, is an excellent point of entry into the Barth corpus for those new to his work—both theologians and social scientists. Here he discusses what most directly relates to the social sciences—his understanding of humanity. Here also are set forth some key theological/anthropological insights which can unlock the remaining volumes of Barth's thought. In order to understand adequately this section on humanity—its insights and limitations—it is important to place it in the context of all of III/2, Chapter X, "The Creature," and to set forth some of the controlling theological insights from the whole *Dogmatics*.

The introduction which follows does not pretend to be exhaustive. Through it I hope that readers are drawn into Barth's larger work, to experience its scope and to make judgments of their own.

Notes

1. I will use throughout this introduction the term "man" in the way Barth uses it—generically. Though recognizing the sexist distortion associated with this custom, I have had to be content with the terminology he chose for the purposes of clarity and faithfulness to his discussion. The deeper question, whether the use of the term necessarily implies a prejudicial concept of woman, is beyond the scope of this paper.

CHAPTER I

INTRODUCTION

The development of Barth's thought took place in what can be seen as four phases. In the first — the liberal phase — he shared in some measure the theological insights of 19th Century Protestantism — Harnack, Ritschl, Schleiermacher, Herrmann, Troeltsch. But preaching weekly at Safenwil, Switzerland, sermons based on the study of scripture, and confronted with the gathering crisis of Western society through World War I, he saw liberalism's deficiencies and sought a different starting place for his theology.

The publication of *Der Römerbrief* in 1919, a study of The Epistle to the Romans, marked the beginning of the second phase of his theological life. This work ". . . fell like a bomb on the playground of the theologians."[1] As the first phase was represented by theology's too close identification with high European culture, the second was characterized by the proclamation of God as "wholly Other," by the radical separation of God from the cultural and human interpretations of the 19th and 20th centuries. Barth stressed the discontinuity between God and man — man as sinner, wholly dependent upon God's judgment and grace.

In the third phase, Barth shifted from dialectical to dogmatic[2] thinking. No longer was he writing to let the "No" of God's judgment and the distance of God from man prevail. Increasingly the Word of God as revealed in Jesus Christ took center stage, leading him to focus on revelation, the trinity, and the character of the God-man. His emphasis shifted toward a positive Christian dogmatics centered in Jesus Christ and away from the polemics of *Der Römerbrief*.

His theological development reached its final phase, characterized first by a clear statement of the relationship of philosophy and theology, in his book on Anselm, *Fides Quaerens Intellectum*. God in Jesus Christ determined his methodology. He saw philosophy providing important tools of analysis and construction but thought that it should not shape the content of the theology. The Word of God was understood as shaping its own response. And, second, theology was seen as the reflective activity of the church on its own life and its center, Jesus Christ. Thus, his emphasis shifted from *Christliche Dogmatik* to *Kirchliche Dogmatik* (1932), from a focus on Jesus Christ himself to Jesus Christ *and* the community which had responded to the Word and action of God. This phase, especially as it developed during and after World War II in the writing of the third volume, stressed the "humanity of God" and the relationship of God *with* and *for* man. The distance, God as "wholly other," was still present but now complemented by an equal emphasis on the manhood of Christ and on the relationship between them. The question repeatedly addressed was the relationship between God and man in Jesus Christ as the prototype for the relationship of God and man. This is the period of emphasis on *analogia fidei* and *analogia relationis*. From 1932 until his death in 1968 he wrote the massive volumes of *The Church Dogmatics*.³

Such a review of Barth's development reveals major shifts in his understanding of theology and, consequently, verifies that judgments made of his work based on the earlier theology alone are bound to be partial. The section reproduced here, from *The Church Dogmatics* III/2, published after World War II in 1948, is part of the culmination of his theological development.

Scanning the Barth landscape, five scenes strike me as apt for a thumbnail sketch of Karl Barth, the man.

The Patmos Circle (1915-1930). Barth was an original member of the Patmos Circle, a group gathered by Rosenstock-Huessy to ponder the problem of Western culture as:

... characterized by an absence of real personal encounter, together with a lack of a common language able to bridge the cultural and academic compartmentalization which prevailed, not only in academic circles, but at every level of European, and especially German, culture. According to Kurt Ballenstedt's comments on the situation: 'How can a human being teach credibly of history, society or language in monologues? Only a human being who has lived and experienced the *thou* and the *we* in their fullness can reveal the secret of the university.' The Patmos circle was founded in response to this dilemma, the name serving as a symbol of their need for a common speech, as well as providing both a sense of the past and a vision of their responsibility to shape a common future.'⁴

The name "Patmos" is specially appropriate since it was associated with the "Incarnate Word" written by John in the Prologue of the Fourth Gospel and the vision of the future by "the other John" of the Book of Revelation. The primary concern of the Patmos group was interdisciplinary dialogue in the service of the future of society.

The original Circle expanded through the publication of a magazine, called *The Creature*, to include Martin Buber, Franz Rosenzweig, Hans and Rudolf Ehrenberg, Joseph Wittig, Victor Von Weizsäcker, Leo Weismantel, Werner Picht, Nicholas Berdyaev, Ferdinand Ebner, Theodore Litt, Friedrich Gogarten, Karl Löwith, Eberhard Grisebach, and Gabriel Marcel. "What the editors of *The Creature* discovered, were the spiritually nourishing processes experienced by genuinely speaking and existentially thinking persons."⁵

Although the Patmos Circle is not mentioned in any of the biographical material on Barth with which I am acquainted,⁶ I suggest that the dialogue within such a network of people was important in shaping the most innovative structure of Barth's theology: the central place of the I-Thou relationship, of the word as dialogue. It is difficult to characterize the core of Barth's re-understanding of the traditional doctrines of the church without a deep appreciation for this influence.[7]

Preaching in Prison. Throughout Barth's life, his associations were predominately with the cultural and educational elite of Western Europe. He was from a middle class Basel home. When he was three years old, his father was appointed Professor of New Testament and Early Church History at the University of Bern. His educational experience was the typical peripetetic journey through German universities, absorbing the best of Western education and culture. In many ways he appeared to remain isolated in his cultural and academic ivory tower; yet he took two directions away from this circumscribed existence: in his study of the scriptures with their description of a God who revealed himself in those outcast by society, and by his visits to the prisons, where it was his custom to go to preach regularly, listening and experiencing life from a very different perspective. Had Barth lived at a later date, he would have been present among and listening to the outcasts from the Black and Third World communities.

Post-Capitalist. In Barth's early days, he identified with Christian socialist movements which criticized capitalism and strongly identified with the dispossessed. Later he saw that the problem was more general than the distortion of an economic system. In addition, he was never thoroughly conversant with the intricacies of economics, neither Marxist nor capitalist. Nevertheless, out of his understanding of the gospel, he criticized any system that elevated the narrow concerns of profit or technological efficiency to god-like status. This critique included systems which had little concern for the oppression of the poor by the rich. In retrospect, his stance might or might not lead to what is called democratic socialism; however, it did include a significant critique of certain aspects of capitalism.

Perhaps he was insufficiently aware of the exploitative nature of Russia's occupation of Hungary (although he opposed Soviet totalitarianism), but the severe attack leveled by Reinhold Niebuhr against Barth's supposed inability to choose between relative goods — communist totalitarianism and modified capitalist democracy — is somewhat tempered through our present awareness of Niebuhr's own theological support of the cold war and of a modified capitalism with its dual expressions of Third World exploitation and the misbehavior of multinational corporations. Barth said, in effect, a plague on both your houses; both systems have major flaws. Upon reflection, his reticence, or blindness, in judging Russia's occupation of Hungary seems no worse than Niebuhr's blindness to and implicit support of a political system controlled by gigantic corporations.

But basically there is no comfort in juxtaposing Barth's inadequacy in judging current political and economic phenomena against Niebuhr's. From my perspective both made errors of judgment which may or may not call into question the theological stance from which each man worked. Both also consistently supported the poor, weak, and alienated. Both make the point that political and economic judgments must be arrived at only after asking what they do to persons for whom Christ died and with the recognition that all social-economic-political systems stand under judgment.

Roman Catholicism. Stimulating dialogue between Roman Catholics and Protestants has been perhaps his most creative contribution to the future of the Christian church. The initial distance between Rome and Barth, expressed in the juxtaposition of *analogia entis* and *analogia fidei* (and *analogia relationis*), was later modified through lively conversation with many Roman Catholic scholars; prominent among them Jerome Hamer, Henri Bouillard, Hans Ur Balthasar, Yves Congar, and Hans Küng. Hans Küng and Hans Ur Balthasar declared that the distance was not so great as it originally appeared. Their judgment was upheld in the acceptance of many of Barth's themes at Vatican II. Hans Küng, along with other Catholic theologians who were also in touch with Barth, made a significant contribution to the new Roman Catholic position. Barth's imprint on Vatican II is unmistakable, especially his insights regarding the authority of scripture, the doctrine of justification, and the church as community, the People of God. Although significant differences remain between Barth and official Roman Catholic interpretation on many questions, these insights — his discourse on the freedom of God and man — have stimulated many Catholic theologians to new formulations beyond official doctrine. It is hard to argue that conversations with Barth were not important components in the current new freedom of the Roman Catholic church.

Mozart. Each morning Barth played a Mozart record. In him, Barth found an incomparable musician. In praise of Mozart he said,

. . . "beautiful" is not a fitting epithet: music which for the true Christian is not mere entertainment, enjoyment or edification but food and drink; music full of comfort and counsel for his needs; music which is never a slave to its technique nor sentimental but always "moving," free and liberating because wise, strong and sovereign.
Why is it[?]. . . . He had heard, and causes those who have ears to hear, even today, what we shall not see until the end of time — the whole context of providence. As though in the light of this end, he heard the harmony of creation to which the shadow also belongs but in which the shadow is not darkness, deficiency is not defeat, sadness cannot become despair, trouble cannot degenerate into tragedy and infinite melancholy is not ultimately forced to claim undisputed sway. Thus the cheerfulness in this harmony is not without its limits. But the light shines all the more brightly because it breaks forth from the shadow.
The sweetness is also bitter and cannot therefore cloy. Life does not fear death but knows it well. . . . Mozart saw this light no more than we do, but he heard the whole world of creation enveloped by this light. Hence it was fundamentally in order that he should not hear a middle or neutral note, but the positive far more strongly than the negative. He heard the negative only in and with the positive. Yet in their inequality

he heard them both together, as, for example, in the Symphony in G-minor of 1788. He never heard only the one in abstraction. He heard concretely, and therefore his compositions were and are total music. Hearing creation unresentfully and impartially, he did not produce merely his own music but that of creation, its twofold and yet harmonious praise of God. He neither needed nor desired to express or represent himself, his vitality, sorrow, piety, or any programme. He was remarkably free from the mania for self-expression. He simply offered himself as the agent by which little bits of horn, metal and catgut could serve as the voices of creation, sometimes leading, sometimes accompanying and sometimes in harmony. . . . Mozart has created order for those who have ears to hear, and he has done it better than any scientific deduction could.[8]

In Mozart's music Barth saw the shadow-accented glory and order of creation. But more; he embodied a "moving," "liberating" form: not sentiment, but joy.

Contrary to some reports, Barth was not a dour theologian, critical of all man-made constructs; rather, he embodied distinct pleasure and joy in man's constructions. His "No" against culture was not against the joy of life, but against its presumption to be more than it is, to be more than a human product.

In preparation for an overview of the major themes of *The Church Dogmatics*, and more specifically III/2, *The Creature*, to attempt to overcome some distortions and to further orient the reader, several observations need to be set forth.

Whether or not one agrees with Barth's fundamental assumptions, it has been a long time since the theological world has witnessed such careful articulation of the basic Christian assumptions. Elegance of style wedded to content, fruitful interpretation of traditional doctrines, a humanistic bias (appealing even to those who disagree with his points of conclusion and beginning), and sheer magnitude of creative energy further characterize him. Comparisons to Augustine, Thomas Aquinas, Calvin, and Luther are not uncommon.

Twelve black bound volumes, entitled *Church Dogmatics*, put the reader off initially. Yet this response soon succumbs to fascination and even joy in the reading of his exposition. Those seeking shortcuts in excerpted texts or compiled summaries cheat themselves of the writing's rich texture. This style, nuanced thought, knowledge of the tradition, and fresh interpretation of scripture impact unforgettably one's own thought and life. Whoever has read him firsthand will not be able to dismiss him lightly or accept one-dimensional renditions of his ideas.

For most, limitations of time preclude reading the whole *Church Dogmatics*; but reading some portion of his later writings is essential for the theologically literate. It is my hope that blatant caricatures of his theology will be put to rest in those who read this republication of his work on humanity. Furthermore, an understanding of the excerpt included here is a key to the major portion of his theological thought.

Devastating criticism has intended to bury Barth. Some claim he reserves no place for the individuality and freedom of man; others, that he has no respect for the evidence of social and psychological sciences; and still others, that some of his ethical views clash with evolving humanistic insights. But the casket lid refuses to stay closed. Careful study of even a portion of his major work contradicts the caricature. A more nuanced understanding of the social sciences shows his sophistication regarding their scope and limits. Many will disagree with his starting point and basic assumptions; but no one can score him for lack of sophistication. And much of the creative work in social science confirms his insights. When the evidence is in, I believe that he will be judged a "peculiarly modern theologian," in tune with what is enduring in humanistic and social thought.

This is not to argue that Barth is complete and totally accurate in certain historical or ethical judgments, in interpretations of the biblical text, or in all his theological statements. He cheerfully admitted his limitations. He was, at the same time, both radically open to new insights and aware of the limitation and sinfulness of human knowledge. He constantly moved beyond and corrected his previous theological positions. I believe the adequacy of his theology will rest finally on the direction he chose to take and on the degree to which his dialogical-dialectical thought captures the dynamics of the God-man and man-man relationships.

In addition, acceptance of Barth's interpretation of reality will come through recognition of the viability of the root metaphor, covenant, found in the Old and New Testaments and basic to Barth's theology. The use of the concept of covenant does not imply that other metaphors are not important in explicating human existence. Perhaps there is a hierarchy, or plurality, of metaphors which intersect all the social sciences, more than one of which is important for an adequate understanding of man. If a multiplicity of metaphors is involved, the question then becomes which is most adequate to describe one or another dimension of human existence, and which governs most appropriately the overall context of understanding?

For Barth, the context-giving metaphor is the covenant. Hence it would shape the appropriate ordering and use of other metaphors. For example, Barth would undoubtedly challenge B. F. Skinner's insight where it claims to be sovereign. For describing some levels of human behavior, however, Skinner's analysis seems most appropriate. It seems to "work" in clarifying certain behavioral and psychological problems in a way superior to other forms of analysis.[9]

Rather than opposing anthropological metaphors and arguing the case for exclusiveness, I am suggesting that a multi-metaphor approach be used, that no metaphor be relied upon to describe all aspects of the human phenomenon. But I further contend that the covenantal metaphor is the significant key to the context for our fulfillment as human beings, vis-a-vis God and man.

Introduction

Thomas F. Torrance has taken the baton in the area of Barth's understanding of *time* and *space* and carried forward the conversation with theoreticians and practitioners of the physical sciences.[10] A similar discussion needs to proceed in relationship to the social sciences. Robert Willis[11] faults Barth for not taking the "facts" of the empirical social sciences seriously. However, he underestimates Barth's awareness of the methodological issues involved in organizing data into facts. In fact, Barth reveals a profound understanding of the function of the social sciences. More and more social scientists are becoming aware of the implicit assumptions governing the theories which in turn shape what are called "facts." Increasingly, they themselves realize that the fact-value dichotomy is overly simplistic, that values or value assumptions influence the very ordering of data into facts. The social scientist's failure to acknowledge the presuppositional structure of his science opens him up to the pejorative use of the label "dogmatic." But "dogmatic" can also be understood in a positive way, that is, as a thinker/scientist acknowledges the presuppositions of his thought. Barth is dogmatic in this non-pejorative sense when he accepts and identifies as his starting point the testimony of a community to the God-man, Jesus Christ. At the same time, he acknowledges that this starting point comes in a finite form, that the objective referent of this testimony can never be totally captured by the dogma of the church and, beyond this, some aspects of the dogma itself are open to developing insight about the nature of reality. There are apparently more paraphernalia associated with theological than with social scientific dogma, but this situation may in fact testify to the naivete of social scientists rather than to the closedness of theologians. The critical question is not dogma, but the spirit and awareness with which the inquiry proceeds. Recognition of one's presuppositions, awareness of the limitations of human constructs, and openness to impinging "newness"—all three—characterize the scientific spirit, whether in social, physical, or theological thought.

Thomas F. Torrance sets forth four characteristics which convey the spirit of Barth's inquiry.[12] He says, "Barth has the most searching, questioning mind I have ever known. Never have I heard or read of anyone who asks questions so relentlessly or who engages in such ruthless criticism, not with any negative intention, but *in order to let the truth bespeak itself clearly and positively*."[13] Barth's presupposition is that God is, that he communicates himself to man, and that getting at this truth requires a vigorous questioning of all the human constructs used to understand him.

Second, "Barth has an uncanny ability to listen which is accompanied by an astonishing humility and childlikeness in which he is ready to learn."[14] He embodies one of his crucial theological assumptions—that truth itself is genuinely dialogical, and dialogue means openness to listen as well as willingness to speak.

Third, "Another typical characteristic of Barth to which we must give attention is his sheer creative power, his ability to produce something new."[15] The number of words (6,000,000) in the *Church Dogmatics* testifies to his mammoth energy. This could signal merely the working out of fixed theological ideas into a massive system. Basic themes do hold the *Church Dogmatics* together, but in him innovation and freedom are constantly present. This is especially evident as he comments on the humanity of man in the text reproduced here.

Fourth, he is also, and maybe most crucially, a theologian of joy and humor. One is reminded of Gerhard Von Rad's definition of man as "the thanksgiving animal." "Thanks" results from love of God which frees as it relates (unites); joy, from the inner secret of man's humanity as he is related to "the other." But humor there is also. "That is something that runs through all his writing and preaching, though certain passages leap immediately to mind: the sparkling prefaces to the different volumes of *The Church Dogmatics*, the discussion of the phenomena of the human in volume three where he cannot repress his chuckles at the frightful seriousness with which too many theologians have set forth their picture of *homo sapiens* —'What a pity that none of these apologists consider it worthy of mention that man is apparently the only being accustomed to laugh and smoke'!"[16]

After reading in his *Church Dogmatics*, one may disagree with him, but one can never again simply categorize him as a dour, dogmatic, inhumane theologian. Joy is the inner secret of the dialogue between God and man, and between man and man, and dialogue is questioning and listening and creativity spawned by the liberating word.

Notes

1. J. McConnachie, *The Significance of Karl Barth* (London: Hodder and Stoughton, 1931), p. 43.
2. "Dogmatic" means starting from the story of God's and man's interaction (the Word of God), set forth in the Old and New Testament, and communicated through the Christian community, in preference to submitting to the judgment of systematic theology or philosophical systems.
3. The definitive and fascinating exposition of these phases is found in *Karl Barth: An Introduction to His Early Theology, 1910-1931*, by Thomas Torrance (London: SCM Press, 1962).
4. Harold Stahmer, *Speak that I May See Thee!: The Religious Significance of Language* (New York: Macmillian Co., 1968), pp. 121-22.
5. Rosenstock-Huessy, "Ruehblick auf die Kreature," *Deutsche Beitrage* (Chicago: University of Chicago Press, 1947), p. 210.
6. Except in Eberhard Busch's recent book *Karl Barth: His Life From Letters and Autobiographical Texts* (Philadelphia: Fortress Press, 1976), pp. 112, 135, and 141.

Introduction

7. He withdrew from this group in 1922 saying that they wanted to overwhelm him with gnosticism.

8. *Church Dogmatics*, III/3, pp. 297-99.

9. However, some reasons for this success may be not intrinsic to Skinner's mechanistic model. For example: (1) behaviorists give extreme care and attention to observing the concrete details of human action; (2) they take seriously the need to proceed by incremental, not global steps; and (3) they take a hopeful approach to the patient (subject). I suggest that these attributes may be as important to the behaviorists' success as the operation of a strict cause-and-effect mechanistic model.

10. This discussion is most clearly set forth in *Space, Time, and Incarnation* (London: Oxford Press, 1969).

11. *The Ethics of Karl Barth* (Leiden, Netherlands: E. J. Brill, 1971).

12. *Karl Barth: An Introduction to His Early Theology, 1910-1931* (London: SCM Press, 1962), pp. 19-25.

13. Ibid., p. 19.

14. Ibid., p. 21.

15. Ibid., p. 23.

16. Ibid., p. 24. Inner quote is from *Church Dogmatics*, III/2, p. 83.

CHAPTER II

BACKGROUND OF III/2

Outlining or summarizing the whole of *The Church Dogmatics* to set the context for III/2 is difficult in any introduction, no matter what the length. It has been well-done already in a number of places.[1] However, I do want to state some of the principles of interpretation which aid my own understanding. In addition, I will place the section on humanity, III/2/45, in the overall discussion of III/2, *The Creature*. As the discussion of humanity proceeds, many of Barth's theological insights, more fully developed in other volumes, will be set forth.

A. GENERAL AIDS TO INTERPRETATION

Barth denies that his theology is "systematic," if one understands system to mean ". . . a self-contained and fully established coherence of principles and deductions, constructed on the basis of the presupposition of a certain fundamental perspective and with the rise of certain sources of knowledge and axioms."[2] Rather, the theologian must bring to his task no presuppositions, no established knowledge or axioms. He must simply unfold and present the content of the Word of God as a way of checking the authenticity of the preaching of the gospel. Even this act will not be an "objective exhibition and analysis" because the content has the character of a ". . . conversation, a process, an active struggle, an act of guidance."[3] Barth acknowledges that a theologian does have his pre-formed philosophies, theologies, mythologies, sociologies, and psychologies; but he should not impose, but should try to avoid imposing them on the content of the Word in order to systematize it. While one may argue with Barth about how successful he has been in letting the Word shape his theology, it is hard to argue that he has not attempted to do so. I find several interpretative clues implied in his theology that can be said to flow out of his attempt to listen to the Word.

Key to his theological method is the principle that the object should generate or determine the method. For Barth the object of theology is God, the Word of God, and its revelation in Jesus Christ. Any other method imposes, in principle, man-made constructs on that which transcends man. Clearly, there are problems with this approach. For example, there is no independent means of verification. There is a long history of interpreters who have claimed to do just this, but who, in retrospect, primarily reflected the world view and social concepts of their age. Barth, however, benefited from such historical awareness and, striving to overcome this tendency, succeeded better than most — in many people's eyes, to a remarkable degree. Nevertheless, if this starting point is valid, it indicates an acute awareness of the problem of controlling our understanding of the transcendent with categories shaped by human finitude.

A second key is that form and content are bound up together and should be separated only for the purpose of speech. Even then, speech itself must constantly attempt to reveal that they are together. This is one reason Barth's expositions use so many words. It is another way of saying that concrete reality precedes its analysis into its various aspects. In the doctrine of creation, for example, we will find it impossible to discuss just the created form (relationship) of man, which shows his connection with God and with other men, without understanding the content (action) that constitutes these relationships.

A third key is an adequate understanding of dialectical-dialogical thought. When Torrance says that Barth moves from dialectical to dogmatic thinking, he is speaking of only one kind of dialectic.[4] I contend that Barth continues to use dialectical thought, and no real understanding of him will be gained without seeing *how* he uses it.[5]

His earliest use of the dialectic stressed saying "No" to the identification of the Christian faith with culture, with feeling, with the finite constructs of man. As such, and in that context, it was a much needed and important "No." By it he focused on the mystery of God and the paradoxes of love and judgment, of time and eternity. Barth used it in clear opposition to Hegel's resolution of the dialectic into a higher synthesis and against the Neo-Protestants' "instinctual abhorrence of all discontinuity."[6] He felt discontinuity should have an equal place with continuity. If God was to be God, and not domesticated by current cultural and human constructs, His priority, His reality, His objectivity must be accepted as a starting point. However, dialectical theology often overstated the issue to make the case more powerfully.[7] After the 19th Century landscape had been sufficiently cleared, Barth was able to consider the "Yes" as strongly as the "No."

Barth still uses dialectical-dialogical language to describe the relationships and actions between God-man, man-man, and body-soul. The synthesis, however, the usual third step of the dialectic, is not a necessary part of his use of this thought-form. Rather, it refers to the interactional structure of life, thought, and speech. A ping-pong game or a conversation is a better model than the more linear billiard game. In conversation there is speaking and listening. There is separation of the speakers and hearers; yet, in the give-and-take of conversation, there is also union. In good conversation an *event* takes place which can't be fully or adequately described in cause-and-effect or linear language. Barth uses dialectical-dialogical language as the most appropriate to describe the event and the relational character of life in its differentiation and unity. One needs to evaluate the adequacy of this method of thought very carefully because his whole theology stands on the assumption that this thinking reflects the structures of relationship between God-man and man-man.

A fourth key follows. Some argue that dialectical-dialogical thought is an alien presupposition imposed on theological subject matter. Although both visual/spatial and auditory/temporal analogies are important to theology, Barth implies that the auditory and the temporal analogies more faithfully depict the essential character of the relationships between God and man, and man and man. It is not incidental that Barth's thought stresses the importance of the Word and preaching and Roman Catholic thought, substance and the beatific vision. At their roots these theologies employ different metaphors and have different emphases: tongue and ears on the one hand, and sight on the other. Each of these senses implies a form of relationship — dialectical-dialogical on the one hand, and linear on the other. In spite of the receptivity to Barth in Roman Catholic circles, the prevailing and residual difference will remain for some time because of the relative importance of these alternative ways of thought and experience in the two major Christian groupings.

A fifth key is Barth's insistence on treating the *part* in relationship to and from the perspective of the *whole*. Atomistic language treats the whole as composed of the total of its individual parts, or it implies that wholes can be adequately understood by analyzing them into their component parts. Barth would agree that atomistic language is useful for describing a certain range of reality. However, he dissents when the subject or object to be understood has to do with the community and the person, or with man's and God's freedom, or with salvation and creation. For him, part and whole, part and part are dialectically related. For example, the individual Christian cannot be understood outside the community of the church, nor the church without the personhood of Jesus, nor Jesus without relation to his fellow human beings. Again, unity and differentiation are functions of one another. Another expression of the whole-part principle, and perhaps the key one, is that the "lower" reality, man, cannot be understood outside the context of the "higher" reality, God, the God-man, Jesus Christ. So Barth does not proceed by finding the smallest unit out of which all else is constructed or understood (e.g., B. F. Skinner's method in psychology); rather, he starts with more comprehensive reality — God as He makes himself known in Jesus Christ, the church, the creation, etc. This analytical principle is closer to the holistic approach of ecology and organic sociology than to mechanistic and technological thought.[8]

These five keys — (1) the object generates the method, (2) form and content need to be understood together, (3) dialogical-dialectical thought is based on the model of conversation, (4) auditory and temporal analogies are more adequate than visual and spatial ones in understanding God and his relationship to man, and (5) whole and part are dialectically related — aid in the understanding of Barth. Some argue that he imposes these on the religious phenomena. Barth replies that they emerge from the basic encounter with the subject/object of theology, God, as he reveals himself in Jesus Christ through the community of faith.

B. THE PLACEMENT OF III/2 IN BARTH'S THEOLOGY AS A WHOLE

The previous section set forth general aids to interpretation of Barth's theology. These emerged from his central theological assumptions. In this section, I discuss aspects of his overall theology and show the place of III/2 in the larger plan.

The controlling reality in *The Church Dogmatics* is God's revelation in Jesus Christ. He is God and man, Son of God and Son of man. Scriptures attest to this reality through human words. The church as a community continually attempts to live this witness and respond to God's inbreaking judgment, freedom, and love.

But one does not understand Barth's meaning of these traditional words unless one understands that for him *action* and *being* define each other. What God has done and is doing is critical! Although Barth sets forth his understanding of God's action and being in Volume IV, the substance of reconciliation is present, as well as controlling, throughout the whole *Dogmatics*, including the section presently under consideration. But reconciliation itself has dialectically-related phases reflecting this action: (1) justification by grace — Jesus Christ, the Lord as Servant (IV/1), (2) sanctification — Jesus Christ, the Servant as Lord (IV/2), and (3) vocation (the calling) — Jesus Christ, the True Witness (IV/3). These movements describe the double action of God in Jesus Christ through the Holy Spirit. In justification the sovereign love of God (as servant) enters into man's sinful condition, pride, *with* and *for* man. In sanctification God's love (as Lord) elevates man from his dehumanized state, sloth. The act of Jesus Christ reveals man's pride and sloth wherein man has made himself into a god or dehumanized himself. It also makes available to man through the Christian community the resources of reconciliation — love and freedom.

The presupposition of reconciliation is the covenant. At this point we are driven back further to God's act of creation and providence (the continuation of creation). The creation is the *external basis* of the covenant and the covenant is the *internal meaning* of creation. Further, logical and temporal regression indicates that this covenantal-reconciling meaning is God's initial meaning and purpose. It reflects his choice (election) of man and man's response in eternity, in the Godhead itself (the election and response of the man, Jesus Christ). God's intent from the beginning is seen in the creation where he sets forth a place and time for the unfolding of the relationship between the Father and the Son, between God and man. The meaning is set forth as covenant which is the basic relationship between God and his people. Therefore, men don't choose whether or not to be related to God. Rather, God actively chooses man to be in relationship with him. It is Barth's fundamental assumption that "in the nature of things" there is a relationship between God and man, and man and man, whether or not particular men acknowledge it. Reconciliation, then, is God's free and ever-renewed action of judgment and love of men. It presupposes the covenant. In Jesus Christ, both God's choice and man's response to that choice is present. In him the covenant is already fulfilled. It remains only for men to participate in it and acknowledge it. Our involvement in the community of Jesus Christ through the action of the Holy Spirit effectively engages us with this reality.

Thus creation is the external context of the covenant. Reconciliation enacts the fulfillment of the internal covenantal relationship, not only between God and man, but also between man and man; first in Jesus Christ, but also as other human beings participate in this reality.

We have moved from God's action of reconciliation, justification, sanctification, and vocation back to the creation, the external basis of the covenant, and then to covenant, the internal basis or meaning of the creation. To complete the cycle, reconciliation is the fulfillment of the covenant.

Barth communicates the essence of covenant and reconciliation in yet another way. He uses the word history to speak of the relationship between God and man. History is the word which refers to God's choice *for* man out of love. This is grace. Man's response to God's choice is thankfulness. Thus grace (God's action) and thanksgiving (man's action) describes the dialectical-dialogical interplay between God and man which Barth calls *history*. Only in this *history* is man free to act anew.[9] This happens archetypically and essentially in Jesus Christ, but secondarily in ourselves.

The covenantal reality (its action and relationship) is also the pattern for the relationship between Jesus Christ and ourselves. This covenantal form is repeated in the relationship between man and man. One of Barth's contributions to theology is the analogical connection of these three covenantal patterns: between man and man, God and man, and the Father and Son in the Godhead itself. This is *analogia relationis* (the analogy of relations).[10]

The *imago Dei* needs to be understood within this context. While

KARL BARTH'S CHURCH DOGMATICS

WORD OF GOD	GOD	CREATION	RECONCILIATION	REDEMPTION
I:1 Introduction	II:1 Ch. 5 *The Knowledge of God*	III:1 Ch. 9 *The Work of Creation*	IV:1 Ch. 13 *The Subject and the Problems of the Doctrine of Reconciliation*	
1. The Task of Dogmatics	25. The Knowledge of God in its Consummation	40. Faith in God the Creator	57. The Work of God the Reconciler	
2. The Task of Prolegomena to Dogmatics	26. The Knowability of God	41. Creation and Covenant	58. The Doctrine of Reconciliation	
Ch. 1 *The Word of God as the Criterion of Dogmatics*	27. The Limits of the Knowledge of God	42. The Yes of God the Creator	Ch. 14 *Jesus Christ, the Lord as Servant*	
3. Church Proclamation as the Material of Dogmatics	Ch. 6 *The Reality of God*	III:2 Ch. 10 *The Creature*	59. The Obedience of the Son of God	
4. The Word of God in its Threefold Form	28. God's Being as the One Who Freely Loves	43. Man as a Problem of Dogmatics	60. Man's Pride and Fall	
5. The Nature of the Word of God	29. God's Perfections	44. Man as God's Creature	61. Man's Justification	
6. The Knowability of the Word of God	30. The Perfections of the Divine Loving	45. Man in His Appointment to Be God's Covenant-Partner	62. The Holy Spirit and the Assembly of the Christian Congregation	
7. The Word of God, Dogma, and Dogmatics	31. The Perfection of the Divine Freedom	46. Man as Soul and Body	63. The Holy Spirit and Christian Faith	
Ch. 2 *The Revelation of God*	II:2 Ch. 7 *God's Gracious Election*	47. Man in His Time	IV:2 Ch. 15 *Jesus Christ, the Servant as Lord*	
Part I. *The Triune God*	32. The Task of a Correct Doctrine of God's Gracious Election	III:3 Ch. 11 *The Creator and His Creature*	64. The Exaltation of the Son of Man	
8. God in His Revelation	33. The Election of Jesus Christ	48. The Doctrine of Providence, Its Ground and Structure	65. Man's Indolence and Wretchedness	
9. God's Three-in-Oneness	34. The Election of the Congregation	49. God the Father as Lord of His Creature	66. Man's Sanctification	
10. God the Father	35. The Election of the Individual		67. The Holy Spirit and the Upbuilding of the Christian Congregation	
11. God the Son			68. The Holy Spirit and Christian Love	
12. God the Holy Spirit			IV:3 Ch. 16 *Jesus Christ, the True Witness*	

KARL BARTH'S CHURCH DOGMATICS
(Continued)

WORD OF GOD	GOD	CREATION	RECONCILIATION	REDEMPTION
I:2 Part 2. *The Incarnation of the Word*	Ch. 8 *God's Commandment*	50. God and the Nihil	69. The Glory of the Mediator	
13. God's Freedom for Man	36. Ethics as a Task of the Doctrine of God	51. The Kingdom of Heaven, God's Messengers & their Adversaries	70. Man's Lie	
14. The Time of Revelation	37. The Commandment as God's Claim	III:4 Ch. 12 *The Commandment of God the Creator*	71. Man's Calling	
15. The Secret of Revelation	38. The Commandment as God's Decision	52. Ethics as a Task of the Doctrine of Creation	72. The Holy Spirit and the Sending of the Christian Congregation	
Part 3. *The Outpouring of the Holy Spirit*	39. The Commandment as God's Judgment	53. Freedom before God	73. The Holy Spirit and Christian Hope	
16. The Freedom of Man for God		54. Freedom in Community	IV:4 Ch. 17 *The Commandment of God the Reconciler*	
17. God's Revelation as the Annulment of Religion		55. Freedom to Live		
18. The Life of the Children of God		56. Freedom within Limitations		
Ch. 3 *The Holy Scripture*				
19. God's Word for the Church				
20. Authority in the Church				
21. Freedom in the Church				
Ch. 4 *The Proclamation of the Church*				
22. The Commission of the Church				
23. Dogmatics as a Function of the Listening Church				
24. Dogmatics as a Function of the Teaching Church				

(The overall outline of Karl Barth's *Church Dogmatics*).

traditional theology sees the image of God in man's reason, will, individuality, or freedom, Barth understands it as constituting the dialogical/interactional structure of man and man. This bi-polar reality is the essence of our humanity. Thus, humanity, covenantally understood, is analogous to the God-man covenantal action-relationship and to the intra-divine bi-polarity. Dialectical-dialogical language is essential to the proper understanding of these relationships. It is the key to understanding what Barth means by covenant. But resting with this covenantal relationship is inadequate unless the "content" or "material" aspect of the covenant as "event" or "act" is also understood. <u>Thus, covenant points, not only to relationships, but also to an act or event which is normative: God's act in Jesus Christ. This event is God's freedom and love, his being *with* (relationship) and *for* (action/event) man. The key event is his radical love for man which is freely given.</u>

This covenantal understanding of relationship and action also helps us understand the doctrine of the Trinity. Its early location in *The Church Dogmatics*, in the section on Revelation,[11] and even in The Word of God,[12] preceding the doctrine of God, clearly conveys its fundamental importance in the overall structure of *The Church Dogmatics*. The discussion starts with Jesus Christ, ". . . the creature form which God has assumed in His revelation,"[13] not from analogies to nature, history, or man's soul-life. The Trinity refers both to the dynamics and structure of God in and of Himself (in eternity) and to His operations in the world (in revelation, creation, reconciliation, and redemption). This dynamic life of the Trinity is bi-polar and covenantal. The Father and the Son are two "poles," defined in relationship to each other, the Father having functional priority, but not priority in essence and dignity. The Holy Spirit is the communion in being and action which happens between the two "poles."[14]

In revelation, creation, reconciliation, and redemption, the same covenantal dynamic-form is the structure-event: the action-relationship of God's relating with, for, to man and creation, as well as between men. While still maintaining the essential oneness of God, God the Father is primarily understood as the God of Creation, God the Son primarily as God the Reconciler, and God the Holy Spirit primarily as God the Redeemer; while at the same time in creation, as well as in reconciliation and redemption, God is always at work in the unity of His three modes of being. The work of the Father in creation cannot be understood as simply a prelude to the work of reconciliation, but rather as the consequence of a God whose inner life is mutual communion, whose intent is reconciliation, and who freely binds Himself with it (creation/creature) from the beginning in covenant. The work of reconciliation in Jesus Christ is senseless without the presupposition of creation and covenant, or without our efficacious engagement with it through the operation of the Holy Spirit. Jesus Christ, Himself, prior to our participation in Him, is an expression of Father and Holy Spirit, as well as the Son. Similar analysis obtains for the work of the Holy Spirit. No part of Christian theology, from Barth's perspective, is adequately understood without the dynamic unity of the Trinity. Again, covenant, dialogically and dialectically understood, gives us some clues to the kind of unity which is entailed. At the same time, it is necessary to acknowledge the incapacity of our categories to adequately grasp this mystery.

Jesus Christ is central to Barth's theology. In him both of these covenants — between God and man, and between man and man — are conjoined and set forth as the normative understanding of real man and humanity.[15] From this perspective, Barth listens to what is being said about man and God. The basic assumption is not only that Jesus reveals the nature of man as well as God, but that participation in him makes persons whole because of God's liberating love *to*, *with*, and *for* man. Barth invites us to listen to this authority (Jesus) and to shape our categories of thought and action by him. He uses philosophy, history, and social science to understand the meaning of Jesus Christ, but he is wary of their power to distort the message. Rather, the message, the reality of God's action, should determine how aspects of philosophy, history and social science should be used. History testifies to the ease with which Christian theology is assimilated by dominant cultural categories. A theologian who resists this tendency is refreshing. Barth assumes God is an objective reality, transcendent to creature and culture. He reverses our customary way of knowing and assumes the priority of God's positing a relationship to the creation. Barth's corrective was badly needed, albeit at times overdone and single-focused.[16]

Perhaps his theology will be shown to be one more culture-bound attempt, stating who God is and what his actions are, in twentieth century German thought-patterns. No doubt, to some extent this will be true, and he would be the first to admit the danger. Yet three themes lead me to suggest that his general thrust will find an unusual kind of permanence. First, he submitted himself to the tutelage of the objectivity of God's revelation and this carries with it a self-corrective. Second, the category, covenant, is increasingly supported by the empirical evidence from social science. I think this rediscovery of covenant, and understanding it dialogically-dialectically, will be an enduring contribution of Barth's theological investigations. Third, he rescued love (eros and agape) from sentimentality, paternalistic charity, and joyless obedience by understanding it within a dynamic structure, with dialogical action and a core of joy.

Notes

1. Arnold Come, *An Introduction to Barth's "Dogmatics" for Preachers* (Philadelphia: Westminster Press, 1963); Herbert Hartwell, *The Theology of Karl Barth* (Philadelphia: Westminster Press, 1964); Hans Un Von Balthasar, *The Theology of Karl Barth* (Garden City, New York: Anchor Books, Doubleday and Co., 1972); Robert E. Willis, *The Ethics of Karl Barth* (Leiden, Netherlands: E. J. Brill, 1971); G. C. Berkouwer, *The Triumph of Grace in the Theology of Karl Barth* (Grand Rapids, Michigan: Eerdmans, 1956); Thomas C. Oden, *The Promise of Barth* (New York: J. B. Lippincott Co., 1969); Thomas Torrance, *Karl Barth; An Introduction to His Early Theology 1910-1931* (London: SCM Press, 1962).
2. *Church Dogmatics*, I/2, p. 861. Cited by Arnold B. Come, *An Introduction to Barth's "Dogmatics" for Preachors, p.* 81.
3. Ibid., p. 858.
4. T. Torrance, *Karl Barth: An Introduction to His Early Theology*, 1910-1931, pp. 48-105.
5. It is wise to be suspicious of dialectical thought, since it has been used by a variety of thinkers in various ways to paste over contradictions and to join irreconcilables. There is a genuine need for a careful study of its uses, attempting to separate the legitimate from the illegitimate. However, this only argues for its more careful use. Later on I will attempt to show why it describes certain aspects of human activity more accurately than other forms of thought.
6. Ibid., p. 83.
7. One can continue to argue whether this strong stress on the "No," the wholly Other, was necessary at this time. Now both supporters and critics agree that it was only part of the dialectic and hence a distortion of the truth.
8. Ecology sees life linked in a complex organic whole. This point is important to make over against technological and atomistic thinking. However, Barth moves beyond the organic to the covenantal metaphor. While agreement in rejecting an atomistic-mechanistic metaphor exists between Barth and theologians operating out of an organic metaphor (e.g., Hartshorn, Cobb), they disagree on the alternative. Process theologians opt for a complex organic model; Barth and H. R. Niebuhr choose a covenantal model. Disagreement over basic metaphors is at the heart of contemporary theological controversy.
9. *Church Dogmatics*, III/2/44, pp. 157-63.
10. This point will be developed further in Chapter III. §45 *Man in His Determination as the Covenant-partner of God.*
11. *Church Dogmatics*, I/1, pp. 339-560.
12. Ibid., pp. 98-212.
13. H. Hartwell, *The Theology of Karl Barth*, p. 74.
14. The richest discussion of this kind of relationship, of unity and difference, of communion and distinctiveness, as functions of one another, is found in *Church Dogmatics*, III/2/45, pp. 250-74, in the section reprinted in this volume.
15. Further on I will detail more precisely Barth's understanding of real man and humanity.
16. I employ, for example, as I believe he did, other criteria for making theological and ethical judgments. For example, one cannot help but be influenced by negative or positive consequences which seem to stem from a particular faith, even though correlations between faith and consequences

are tenuous and uncertain. Early in his theological journey Barth judged Schleiermacher's and other 19th century theologies by consequences he observed in 19th and 20th century political and cultural life. He drew the conclusion that practiced Christianity had led to devastating consequences in personal and corporate existence. Perceived negative consequences led him to be skeptical about certain theological approaches. He also observed positive consequences in those who found themselves related to a particular experience of Jesus Christ: persons were liberated, made new; they identified with each other; they learned to love more freely; they became more joyful and thankful human beings. This new way of life and thought evolved from listening and responding to the Word. It had positive consequences in Barth's life as well as in the lives of others. In other words, one basis by which alternative religions are evaluated are the consequences in personal and corporate existence, however difficult it is to make these evaluations.

CHAPTER III

III/2 THE CREATURE

If time allows only one volume of *The Church Dogmatics* to be read, it should be III/2. In it Barth places the doctrine of the creature, man, in the context of the creation, but also defines men in relationship to Jesus Christ. Thus, the doctrine of reconciliation, while not fully developed, is present also. In addition, the discussion of *real man* (the relationship of God *to*, *with* and *for* man), of *humanity* (the relationship of man with other men), and of the *whole man* (the relationship of Spirit to man's soul and body) is also present.

The developmental order of these topics is crucial. By it Barth makes a central point. Most theologies start with man, then demonstrate how he is related to God, and finally show how he is related to other men. But Barth begins with God's freely-given relationship to man which can be ignored or forgotten by man, but not destroyed. For Barth, this relationship constitutes the most essential aspect of man's being. Man is linked with God from the beginning. Within that context, man is seen as also related to others (III/2/45, the section here republished). <u>Man is structurally and essentially, not secondarily or accidentally, related to others. One can forget or ignore this reality, but in so doing man contradicts his humanity.</u> *Within* these God-man and man-man relationships, Barth speaks of the individual person with his soul and body. Thus, psychology is not separated from theology and sociology. Nor can society be understood as separated from theology or psychology. In addition, neither a person's relationship with God nor his relationship with his fellowman can be understood as man's achievement. In this, Barth makes room for man's individuality (I will support this point against his critics later), but it is an individuality that emerges from relationship with God and other persons.

His thought is powerful, nuanced, but "repetitive." However, the repetition is not pure redundancy but performs an important function. In speaking of each different aspect of his theology, it is important to remind one of the whole. The parts can be understood only by their relationships to other parts (the gestalt).

One section of III/2/45 is being reproduced so that the nuances and power of his argument can be seen first hand, but also because of the particular importance of this section both in illuminating the rest of his theology and in providing the most lively interface with the social and human sciences.

One reason for an introductory summary is to separate the trees from the forest. Another is to lift up key and oft repeated thought-patterns as a help in identifying what Barth is doing.

A. §43 MAN AS THE PROBLEM OF DOGMATICS

Creation and covenant are reciprocally related. The covenant is the internal meaning of creation, and the creation the external basis of the covenant.[1] But Barth has few specific references to the creation in general, the cosmos and the other animals; rather, he focuses attention almost entirely upon the creature, man. Barth implies that theology and anthropology should not be determined by the changing paradigms of physics, biology, and social science.[2] He limits his statements about creation. God created the cosmos. He is Lord over the creation, and the creation praises Him in return. He doesn't comment on *how* the cosmos was created nor how the non-human aspects of creation praise Him. He avoids the problem of other theologies which attach themselves to a specific cosmology and subsequently allow it to influence their theologies. The Christian faith does not contain a specific cosmology. At this point, it should be non-commital and seek to free itself from any particular paradigm of physics. Thus, he is only secondarily concerned with the cosmos itself, affirming that it is fundamentally good, the creation of a good and loving God.

For Barth, theology should reflect on the Word of God. Its primary focus is the relationship of God and man, and man and man. Jesus Christ reveals these relationships and thus becomes normative for understanding both man and God. Consequently, anthropology, the center of III/2, is based on Christology. Each section of III/2 will treat its special emphasis in terms of the God/man Jesus Christ.

After distinguishing man from the cosmos and other creatures (animals), Barth distinguishes his understanding of man from non-theological anthropologies. Scientific approaches to man (through physics, biology, psychology, and sociology) are faulted because their concern is not with the being of man but with appearances. Theological anthropology, on the other hand, does not deal merely with man as a phenomenon but with man himself. This means that if God is and is essentially related to man (and for Barth both are true), this relationship undergirds and conditions *all* other dimensions in understanding man. Thus, taking his holistic principle of interpretation seriously, any interpretation which excludes this basic relationship is flawed. The same rationale applies to man's relationship to man and the soul's relationship to the body. If man is essentially related to man, to view man atomistically, and community as an aggregate of individuals, distorts the perception of man. If man's body and soul are dialectically related, to interpret the body or soul without the other fundamentally distorts. These three sets of relationships — God-man, man-man, and body-soul — form an essential gestalt which, in the nature of our human ways of knowing, can't be empirically understood. At least the basic relationship, relationship with God, can't be empirically demonstrated, and the other relationships are distorted if not seen within this context. In principle, then, "scientific understanding" screens out the most crucial aspect of the gestalt. Exact sciences can not know man as "creature of God."

Philosophical theories of man are also faulted in that they proceed from certain speculative ideas. They are not grounded in a reality which includes the *actual* relationship between God and man. For Barth, this relationship is not secondary, nor accidental, but a primary and essential dimension of man, and thus conditions all other aspects of understanding him. He claims that understanding man in Christological terms is not speculative but based on the concrete manifestation of a man — who is normative for all and who starts from "the other side" with the presupposition that *God is*, and *God and man are related essentially*. "It [theological anthropology] has the responsibility to make the claim of truth. We repeat that this does not mean that it can not err, that it does not need continually to correct and improve itself."[3] Having shown why both the sciences and speculative philosophy are incomplete and uncertain clues to our manhood (personhood), Barth has to face the question of how Jesus Christ can be normative for man when he is distinguished from man by his godhood, and man is distinguished from Jesus by his sin.

B. §44 MAN AS THE CREATURE OF GOD

One difficulty understanding Barth's anthropology lies with failing to notice major distinctions between the phrases real man, humanity, and whole man. Real man refers to the God-man relationship, humanity to the man-man relationships, and whole man to the unity of soul and body in the individual person. This section and the next two sections will summarize Barth's understanding of these three phrases, so that section §45 on humanity (reproduced in its entirety) can be seen in its proper context, and so that certain criticisms posed by interpretations of Barth's theology might be more adequately answered (Chapter IV). In each section Barth first discusses Jesus Christ, and then man in general.

Christology: Basis for Defining Real Man

Barth begins this discussion with a statement about the *real man*, Jesus Christ, who is man *for* God and God *for* man. He sets forth six criteria of the real man, Jesus.[4] Then he applies these six criteria to man *in general*.

Next Barth explores the formal and material bases of the real man, Jesus. The *material* basis of man's being is a "history" which is the election of God and the response of man. More particularly, man in this history is defined as a being-in-gratitude. A further step shows that this being-in-gratitude has the character of responsibility. Finally, "as human life is a being-in-responsibility before God," it has the character of the knowledge of God, obedience to God, invocation of God, and the freedom which God imparts to it. Thus the being of real man is seen as the history of the God-man relationship.

These six criteria emerge from an analysis of the God-man, Jesus Christ. Since, for Barth, anthropology is based on Christology, the implications of these criteria are necessary for understanding man in general. However, there are two differences between the man Jesus and ourselves: (1) the mystery of our sin, and (2) the mystery of His identity with God; so there can be no *direct* knowledge of the nature of real man in general. In addition the man Jesus and man in general have two things in common: (1) living in the same world, and (2) having the same humanity; so there can be an indirect knowledge of our real nature from an understanding of the real man Jesus. Thus the six criteria which were used to define the nature of the man Jesus apply in an indirect way to the definition of the real man in general. Let us look at this step in detail. Barth says that

1. If it is the case in relation to the man Jesus that in His humanity we are confronted immediately and directly with the being of God,

    then necessarily, assuming that there is similarity between Him and us in spite of all dissimilarity, *every man is to be understood,* at least mediately and indirectly, to the extent that he is conditioned by priority of this man, *in his relationship* with God, i.e., in the light of the fact that he comes *from* God and, above all, that God moves *to* him.

2. If it is the case in relation to the man Jesus that the presence and revelation of God in Him is the history of the deliverance of each and every man,

4. If it is the case in relation to the man Jesus that He exists in the lordship, i.e., in the fulfilling of the lordship of God, and not otherwise, not outside this occurrence

    then . . . *it must be said of every man that it is essential to him that as he exists, God is over him as his Lord, and he himself stands under the lordship of God the Lord.*

5. If it is the case in relation to the man Jesus that His being consists wholly in the history in which God is active as man's Deliverer,

then . . . *every man is a being which is conditioned by the fact that this deliverance is for him, that every man as such must exist and have his being in a history which stands in a clear and recognizable relationship to the divine deliverance enacted in the man Jesus.*

3. If it is the case in relation to the man Jesus that in the divine action in favor of each and every man in Him, it is also a matter of the freedom, the sovereignty, and the glory of God,

   then . . . *the being of every man, insofar as this history essentially concerns it, is not an end in itself, but has its true determination in the glory of God. . . .*

   then . . . *the being of every man must consist in this history. Not only his actions but his being will consist in his participation in what God does and means for him. His freedom will be his freedom to decide for God, for what God wills to do and be for him in this history. The proper action of real man can then be understood only in the light of the fact that it may correspond to the divine action in his favor, doing justice to the grace addressed to him.*

6. If the man Jesus is *for* God, and surpasses all other creatures in the fact that He *is* only in order that God's work may be done, His kingdom come, and His Word be spoken in Him,

   then . . . *the being of no other man can be understood apart from the fact that his existence too, as an active participation in what God does and means for him, is an event in which he renders God service, in which he for his part is for God,* because God first willed to bind Himself to man, and in so doing has bound man to Himself.[5]

Why six criteria? They seem important since Barth gives considerable space to them and repeats them in one form or another on pages 68-71, 73-74, and 214-218. They seem to reflect or express various aspects of the dialectical-dialogical relationship between God and man in Jesus Christ: presence and Lordship (revelation) (points one and four), deliverance (reconciliation) (points two and five), and glory (redemption) (points three and six). Further analysis reveals that points one and four refer to the *relationship* between God and man, points two and four to the *action* within the relationship, and points three and six to *fulfilled* or *completed action*. The three sets of two recapitulate the three moments of the "history" of Jesus Christ and in effect summarize Barth's whole theological "system."

But why six and not just three? In each use of the six points a different distinction obtains between the first three and the second three which reflects the relationship between the entities involved—God and man in Jesus Christ (real man, pp. 68-71), Jesus Christ and us (pp. 73-74), or Jesus and man (humanity, pp. 214-218). In the

III/2 The Creature

above section the second three all involve participation in the first three descriptions or facts. Two and five reflect the distinction most clearly: (2) ". . . every man is conditioned *by the fact* that this deliverance is for him. . . ." (p. 73) and (5) ". . . the being of every man must consist in this history. Not only man's actions but his being will consist *in his participation* in what God does. . . ." (p. 74)

These criteria are the minimal requirements by which other definitions of man's nature are evaluated. Barth says:

> No definition of human nature can meet our present need if it is merely an assertion and description of immediately accessible and knowable characteristics of the nature which man thinks he can regard as that of his fellows and therefore of man in general . . . [Man's self-knowledge is to be regarded as a vicious circle. The point at issue as Barth states it, is] . . . . How does he [man] reach the platform from which he thinks he can see himself? . . . Who is the man who to know himself first wishes to disregard the fact that he belongs to God?[6]

If man attempts to understand himself from a perspective which is not based on Jesus Christ, he misses real man, for the immediately knowable phenomena are (1) neutral, (2) relative, and (3) ambiguous. Whether or not those "immediately knowable phenomena" are genuine symptoms depends on whether they correspond to the criteria of real man. In themselves, the phenomena are silent.[7]

Barth clearly starts with a Biblical definition of the nature of man, but even more clearly, a definition that is centered in the God-man, Jesus Christ. From the perspective of contemporary social science, this is an outrageous starting point. While not denying the outrageousness of his position, it is important to assess the point he is making, and also to indicate what he is not saying. First, he is claiming that if God is real, and is related to human beings, then it follows that any definition of man (persons) without this dimension present would be deficient. In addition, if, for the Christian, the character and nature of God is defined through Jesus Christ, then it follows that Christology is central for understanding man's nature.

Second, he is not denying that the social sciences have not or cannot discover something or even much about man. They have and they can. After all it is God's creation and it would be strange if investigation of it did not yield insights into whom man is. The fact, however, is that the sciences of man and philosophical anthropology have set forth a wide spectrum of views of man's nature — all the way from B. F. Skinner to the existentialists, each with "convincing" evidence and large followings. The question for Barth is *what* norm or criteria should be used to judge among them. In this section[8] he establishes one major criteria — that man is essentially a God-connected entity. This criterion, by definition, screens out the methods used by the empirical sciences. Therefore, any approach to this dimension of man's nature depends on some method which starts from

III/2 The Creature

revelation or involves faith assumptions. In later sections, especially the section on humanity, another criterion enters—that man is essentially social, i.e., dyadic. These criteria are then used to judge whether the empirical sciences, however useful they may be in discovering particular aspects of man's nature and function, adequately understand the nature of man. From this perspective, then, certain symptoms of man discovered by the empirical sciences can be viewed as adequate or inadequate. This, indeed, may seem an outrageous method, but certain aspects of the man-man relationship set forth by Barth find impressive support among some social scientists. This doesn't "prove" Barth is right, but it does blunt the edge of outrage.

The Formal and Material Dimensions of Real Man

In *Church Dogmatics*, Vol. III, Part 1, Barth established two propositions: that the creation is the external basis of the covenant, and that the covenant is the internal basis of creation. Here Barth assumes the external basis and proceeds to explicate the *formal* and *material*[9] dimensions of the covenant—the internal basis of creation, the relationship and action between God and man.

The *formal* dimension of real man is the *relationship* between God and man—the fact that man is *from*, *to*, and *with* God. But this *formal* dimension is ensconced within the *material* dimension. Both are made known to us in Jesus Christ, the God-man.

Barth analyzes the *material* definition of real man in four stages. First, the being of man as the being *with* Jesus rests on the call (election) of God and the hearing of the Word of God. Secondly, this relationship is understood as "history." Thirdly, the being of man is more precisely defined by thanksgiving—as being-in-gratitude. Finally, the nature of real man is defined as responsibility—further understood as knowledge, obedience, invocation, and freedom.

The Call and the Hearing of the Word

On the first level,

> ... the two material and therefore primary statements in our exposition are: [1] that the being of man as a being with Jesus rests upon the election [the call] of God; and [2] that it consists in the hearing of the Word of God.[10]

It is *first* the man Jesus who is elected or called by God.[11]

Here the *formal* definition of real man is given its first *material* content. To be a man is to be *with* the One who is the true and primary chosen (elect) of God. Thus man is *with* God because he is *with* Jesus. And "To the extent that he [man in general] is with Jesus and therefore with God, man himself is a creature elected [chosen, called] in the divine election of grace."[12]

The second *material* statement is that the being of man as being with Jesus consists in *listening to the Word of God*. Who is the one who has heard? We know only that the man Jesus has heard, and, therefore, that it is the being and existence of all men to be addressed and summoned. Because Jesus has *received* the Word of God, He is the sum of the divine address to the created cosmos. He is not merely the bearer of the divine address, but is Himself the divine address and summons. Man is the creature whose being is from the first addressed, called, and summoned by God. Man isn't first a kind of nature, which then has a relationship with God, and finally is addressed by God. Rather, he is from the beginning in the Word of God. Thus, "Men are those who are summoned by this Word."[13] But, "To be summoned means to have heard, to have been awakened. . . ."[14]

Since Jesus Christ is *real man*, since He is *in* our sphere, since it appears that we have been, as men, already fundamentally determined by our relationship with God in creation, the material dimension of the covenantal relationship is "objectively" already the determination and destiny of all men. However, "subjectively," the fact that man is *real man*, and has been summoned by God, is *known* only by some.

The Being of Man as a History

On the second level of explanation, Barth sums up all that he has said with the statement, ". . . *the being of man is a history* [not *has* a history, but *is* a history]."[15] The contrast between the concept "history" and the concept "state" (or "condition") may clarify this distinction. Even when a "state" is very much in flux, it is never open to more than certain particular movements. History occurs when something happens to a being in a certain state, i.e., when something *new* befalls it, when something takes place upon and to the being as it is, when its circular movement is broken from without. In this instance, that which breaks in is the decision of God (God's freedom). The being of the man Jesus lies in the fact that God is *for* Him in this way and He is *for* God. God gives Himself to Jesus as the deliverance in order that He may Himself be the deliverance. Thus, apart from the eternal will and counsel of God (apart from the inner Godhead), Jesus exists only in this history, i.e., in the particular history of the covenant, salvation, and revelation inaugurated by God. "Jesus *is*, as this history takes place."[16]

Again, let us consider man in general in the light of these statements about "history." Man is the being (1) whose kinsman or brother is the man Jesus and (2) in whose sphere, therefore, this "history" takes place. "He [man] is with God, confronted and prevented and elected and summoned by Him, in the fact that this history takes place

III/2 The Creature

in his own sphere."[17] "Man is what he is as a creature, as the man Jesus, and in Him God Himself, moves towards him, and as he moves towards the man Jesus and therefore towards God.",[18] i.e., he is real man in this history which is the new (God's freedom) breaking into man's sphere.

The Being of Man as a Being in Gratitude

On the third level, Barth says that a more precise *material* definition of man is "a being in gratitude."[19] For,

If the Word of God in which man is, and is therefore historical, is a Word of divine grace, if he is thus summoned to hear and obey this Word . . . then the being of man can and must be more precisely defined as a being in gratitude.[20]

Gratitude is the precise creaturely counterpart to the grace of God. In daring to cast himself upon God, he corresponds to the Word without which he would not be this human creature. "To be grateful is to recognize a benefit,"[21] a benefit which is a good which one has received. A benefit presupposes the action of a benefactor, an action which one could not perform for oneself but which, nevertheless, happens to one. But the true Benefactor is God, the Creator of all benefits. He transcends the limits of the human condition and makes the being of man a history so that the being of man is a being open to the benefits of God.

However, "As it [the being of man] cannot be gracious to itself, it cannot tell itself that God is gracious to it. This it can only hear,"[22] can only receive. But as it does this, as it is content to be what it is by this Word, as it exists by its openness toward God, the question is decided that it is a being in gratitude. "It has not taken the grace of God, but the latter [grace of God] has come to it; it has not opened itself but God has opened it and made it this open being."[23]

When we see man as a being in gratitude we see him for the first time *in his own act*. It is the act in which he *accepts* the validity of the act which not he but God has done. "To see this acceptance as such is to see real man in his *own* action, not merely as the object but as the subject of the history in which his being consists."[24] God is a subject, and man can be considered an object. On the other hand, man is subject, having been addressed by God, distinguished from Him, and given His grace, as He responds to God as object. Thus both God and man are subject in one sense and object in another. The intersubjectivity of the interaction of grace (charis) and thanksgiving (eucharistia) is the history of the God-man relationship and constitutes the content of the being of man. However, what we are speaking of here is the being of the man Jesus, real man, upon which the being of man in general depends by participation. He (Jesus Christ) participates in our life and, consequently, we participate in His life, and hence in the life of God.

Barth is not defining man in general or "natural man," but Jesus Christ and the saved man who *consciously* participates in Christ. Certainly Barth argues that all men in general are saved by God, yet many are not aware of it or ever reject it. So far so good. Here one is led to expect that Barth will indicate some incomplete forms of gratitude capable of being experienced by men in general even though they don't know the name of the Benefactor. But Barth doesn't proceed in this direction.

The Being-of-Man-as-Responsibility

We have discussed the "material" dimensions of the being of man as God's election, and man's hearing; as "history"; and, more precisely, man as a being-in-gratitude. We go further now to discuss responsibility, the fourth level of Barth's understanding of man's being.

"Deriving from God, it [man's being] is an object in pure receptivity."[25] As object of the grace of God, in its pure receptivity. "It opens itself to God as God first opened *it* to Himself. . . . And opened to God it [man's being] is subject in pure spontaneity."[26] Barth understands the being of man seen in this second sense as spontaneity, rather than receptivity, under the concept of responsibility. "Being, human thanksgiving, has the character of responsibility."[27]

Human being consists in thanksgiving, or response to God, and, therefore, in responsibility. In its own place and way, man's response is itself a word, a human word which is to the Word of God. It is the word of thanks rather than the Word of grace. The being of man is an answer, a response, a being lived in the *act* of answering the Word of God. Thus, Barth says:

Man is, and is human, *as* he performs this act of responsibility, offering Himself as the response to the Word of God, and conducting, shaping and expressing himself as an answer to it.[28]

What makes him *real* man is that he is engaged in active responsibility to God.

Barth further develops this theme, "man's being-in-responsibility before God," as "inner notes:" (1) man's knowledge of God, (2) his obedience to God, (3) his invocation of God (call), and (4) the freedom which God imparts to him.

Barth has asserted that God decides for man by creating and sustaining him as man; in love He delivers him from sin as he works through His Son and Spirit. There is no question of a special *state* in which man finds himself placed. It is always a question of his act, as he thanks the God who tells him that He is gracious to him, as he moves to the God from whom he comes.

However, these decisions of God do not assure that man chooses his only possibility — he may not choose at all but simply be involved in sloth and pride resulting in a life which is "impossible" — because God has created man as a being who is not mechanical, but who is genuinely personal, from whom God's Word *may* evoke, but does not necessitate, a response. Barth says, God ". . . has not therefore made obedience physically necessary or disobedience physically impossible."[29] To have protected man from transgression in this way would have been the expression of an inferior love. Thus the "causal" connection between God and man is not a straight cause-and-effect schema but the peculiar interaction, analagous to the complex occurrence when words are used, when a person is called or named. This interpersonal, interverbal, and interactional nexus establishes the basis for subjectivity and spontaneity of the "call" and "answer" more characteristic of an exchange of words than anything else. This makes the spontaneity no less spontaneous but places it within a context which acknowledges the dimensions preceding man's spontaneity.

However Barth is discussing here, not man who has opted for his impossibility, but *real man*, the man who uncoercively responds to God's free grace in this nexus, and consequently, in his freedom knows, obeys, and invokes God. In the first place, this is Jesus Christ; secondarily, and indirectly, it is man in general who participates in Jesus Christ.

It seems to me, however, the meaning of real man is limited, when it is defined only as one *fully* and *consciously* engaged with God in Jesus. This formulation fails to make sufficient use of one of Barth's main points — that man's nature, *in general*, needs to be defined as linked with a gracious God, whether he is conscious of it or not, whether he denies it or not. Although Barth is concerned with action and relationships, at this point his concern with specific Christian terminology gives us insufficient help in discerning the action of God and the response of man in experiential and relational terms. While Christian language and categories may be unknown, the experience of receptivity, spontaneity, gratitude, response, etc., to God's gracious actions may be present. Or stating it another way, some persons may have "the Christian tune" but not know "the specific Christian words." Barth's highly significant contribution calls for further development. This is *not* inconsistent with his major theological thrust. If this implication were developed, one could see the theological reality in actions and relationships which are not consciously understood by the actor. In this way, the term "real man" could apply, at least incompletely and partially, to those who respond to God's gracious presence and action in thanksgiving, yet do not have the proper language with which to identify it; to those maintained by "the Spirit," even though they are ignorant of it; or even to those who may know it, yet reject its terminology.

The major thrust of Barth's contribution, however, remains—that "real man," as applied to men in general, relates to the God-man linkage enacted and revealed in Jesus Christ. Without consideration of this dimension, we don't know man as assumed in Biblical thought.

C. §45 MAN IN HIS DETERMINATION AS THE COVENANT-PARTNER OF GOD

This section is reproduced in full as the second part of this text. The following analysis summarizes the argument of Barth's understanding of humanity. In conjunction with material that precedes, real man, the discussion of the relationship of man with God; and that follows, whole man, the discussion of the individual person, it gives a full view of Barth's understanding of man. Without this discussion of covenant-partnership, of humanity, the deeper levels of Barth's understanding of Christ's manhood (and Godhood) are glossed over. Lack of understanding at this point obscures understanding of his later discussion of reconciliation and redemption.

In addition, the relational and actional character of Barth's thought most clearly manifests itself in this discussion. At this point we can also see why I have been bold to suggest that Barth, more than most contemporary theologians, uses language that closely parallels, overlaps, and intersects the language of some major schools of social science. This statement surprises us, for Barth is known as the theologian who focuses on the "wholly other" and rejects social science. He does neither. While his early writings did stress the "wholly other" aspects of God, rectifying theology's near identification with cultural criteria of truth, later writings dialectically balanced the transcendent and immanent theological thrusts. While he rejects the findings of social science, used as the source of norms of human nature, he accepts social science when it functions within its limits and when the norm of anthropology is theology. Since Barth shares the language of interaction and relationship with some schools of social science, this makes the potential overlap between them suggestive and fruitful.

Jesus as Man for Man, the Basis for Understanding Humanity

According to Barth our natural knowledge of humanity is uncertain and "arbitrary,"[30] thus we need the Word of God in Jesus Christ to know ourselves. Hence, Christology is the key. In order to properly understand humanity in general, it is necessary to investigate the humanity of Jesus.

Jesus is true man and true God. The humanity of the man Jesus means that He is the true creaturely *form* of man, i.e., the form of I-Thou human relationship.

If the divinity of the man Jesus is to be described comprehensively in the statement that He is *man for God*, His humanity can and must be described no less succinctly in the proposition that He is *man for man*, for other men, His fellows.[31]

The distinctions between His manhood and those of others are two. 1) He is referred to other men, not partially, incidentally, or subsequently, but originally, exclusively, and totally. "In the light of the man Jesus, man is the cosmic being which exists absolutely *for* its fellows."[32] 2) In addition, he is human in the specific sense that *His special activity* is to be *for* God, i.e., be *the deliverer* of man.

The relationship in which Jesus binds Himself to man is wholly real. He is affected by the existence of His fellows. This relationship is not a "stoic calm," untouched by the problems and the fate of men. He is not passive; rather, He *actively* makes the cause of other men His own. He suffers, His vitals are affected. He sacrifices Himself to the need of men. He gives Himself to them. He puts Himself in their place. He makes their state and fate His own cause. However, man also needs something more than this suffering with; he needs a new beginning. Jesus Christ delivers man. He gives him freedom through His activity. Thus, the humanity of Jesus means that He is *for* man in a radical way.

From this basic affirmation Barth develops the following implications:

1. *Jesus is from his fellows*. ". . . Jesus has to let His being, Himself, be prescribed and dictated and determined by an alien human being (that of His more near and distant fellows), and by the need and infinite peril of this being."[33] Here Barth points to the I-Thou relationship. The "I" of the selfhood of Jesus is not found in isolation from others but in relationship to the "Thous" who are rebels from God. The self or "I" of Jesus is given its meaning by them; his "I" as determined by these alien beings means that he becomes ". . . the Representative and Bearer of all the alien guilt and punishment transferred from them to Him."[34]

2. *Jesus is to His fellows*. "He moves towards the Thou from which He comes [i.e., his fellow-man]."[35] He is active only in the fact that he makes the deliverance of this alien being His exclusive task. He gives Himself freely to His fellows for their salvation. He offers Himself up for them. He, therefore, serves them.

3. *Jesus is with His fellows*. ". . . His being is both *from* and *to* His fellows, so that He is *with* them."[36] Thus, if we see Jesus at all, we see Him *with* His disciples, the people, His enemies, and ". . . the countless millions who have not yet heard His name."[37] We see Him determined by them and for them. In this way, He is supremely Himself. In this way, He is human.

4. *There is no alienation, distance, or neutrality between this human definition and the divine.* Although there is no distance between this human definition and the divine definition, His humanity is not His divinity. His divinity is from and to God; His humanity is from and to human persons. But His humanity is in closest correspondence with His divinity; they are in harmony with one another. "There is here a *tertium comparationis* which includes His being for God as well as His being for man. . . ."[38, 39]

5. *His saving work not His own choice.* "The saving work in which He serves His fellows is not a matter of His own choice or caprice, but the task which He is given by God."[40] The activity and work of Jesus is not first His own work, but the choice and will of God, because God first, and not the man Jesus, is *for* man. Since Jesus is *for* God, it is not an accident that He is *for* man because God is *for* man. Jesus exists and lives in God's saving work. He is only Jesus because and as He is doing God's work.

6. *There is freedom in God but no caprice.* "If 'God for man' is the eternal covenant revealed and effective in time in the humanity of Jesus, in this decision of the Creator for the creature there arises a relationship which is not alien to the Creator, to God as God, but we might almost say appropriate and natural to Him."[41] God repeats *ad extra* a relationship which is proper to Himself, His own inner essence. He makes a copy of Himself. He imparts to the relationship between Jesus and Himself, and thus to the relationship between Jesus and man, the freedom and eternal love which is the inner essence of God. Thus, this freedom becomes the true, yet ultimately mysterious, basis of Jesus which makes legitimate the designation of the term "divine" to Him.

Barth establishes a theological basis for understanding man in *general* from these six criteria. He sees the connection in the "fact" that Jesus Christ is both man and God.

When he refers to the correspondence and similarity between God and man, Barth points to a set of actions and relationships central to his theology. If this correspondence and similarity (*analogia relationis*) is understood, a crucial door is opened into the mansion of Barth's theology.

First, let us focus on the "form" which is the I-Thou relationship before we focus on the "dynamics" or "material content" of the relationship. The correspondence and similarity is between three different relationships: the I-Thou relationship *within* God Himself; the I-Thou relationship *between* God and man in Real Man (variously referred to as God's eternal covenant, man's being for God, the Divinity of Jesus); and the I-Thou relationship *between* man and man (or person and person), the humanity of man. So let us speak of the I-Thou *relationship*, the element of "form."

Barth says,

> If "God for man" is the eternal covenant [God-man] revealed and effective in time in the humanity of Jesus [man-man] . . . there arises a relationship which is not alien to the Creator, . . . but we might almost say appropriate and natural to Him. God repeats Himself in this relationship *ad extra* [God-man], a relationship proper to Himself in His inner divine essence [God-God]. Entering into this relationship, He makes a copy of Himself.[42]

But what is copied? It is the *relationship* between Father and Son. "There is in Him a co-existence, co-inherence and reciprocity . . . [But further] in this triunity He is the original and source of every I and Thou, of the I which is eternally from and to the Thou and therefore supremely I."[43] It is this *relationship* in the inner divine being (Father-Son) which is reflected in God's eternal covenant with man (God-man). This eternal covenant (God-man) is revealed and operative in time together with and through the humanity of Jesus (man-man).

We have seen above that there is a necessary correspondence and similarity between the being of the man Jesus for God (His Divinity; God-man) and His being for his fellows (His humanity; man-man).[44] However, "The humanity of Jesus is not merely the repetition and reflection of His divinity, or of God's controlling will; it is the repetition and reflection of God Himself. . . ."[45] It is the *imago Dei*.[46]

He speaks of the image as the "plurality in man," or "being man means being in togetherness: [as] man and wife."[47] Thus the image for Barth is the togetherness, the plurality of the I-Thou relationship.

Barth goes further and says that the

> Image has a *double meaning*: God lives in togetherness within Himself [the Original], then God lives in togetherness with man [first image], then men live in togetherness with one another [a second image].[48]

To say that the "image has a double meaning" adds another innovative dimension to the traditional understanding of the *imago Dei*. Thus Barth sees the I-Thou-ness of our humanity not only as a reflection of the inner Godhead, but also as a reflection of the I-Thou form of real man (God-man). Both I-Thou relationships are the *imago Dei* and because they are both images they are signs of one another. Thus, humanity (man-man) reflects and points to man's destiny which is to realize that we are covenant-partners of God (man-God).

Up to this point we have focused on the *form* of the *analogia relationis*.

Second, let us consider the same three relationships, but from the perspective of the correspondence and similarity between the "content" or "material" or "dynamic" dimension. This has to do with the actional dimension of the relationship, here referred to as the freedom and love of God. Barth says:

> This is not a correspondence and similarity of being, an *analogia entis*. . . . but it is not a question of this twofold being. It is a question of the relationship within the being

of God on the one side and between the being of God and that of man on the other. Between these two relationships as such — and it is in this sense that the second is the image of the first. . . . There is an *analogia relationis*. . . . The correspondence and similarity of the two relationships *consists in the fact that the eternal love in which God as the Father loves the Son, and as the Son loves the Father, and in which God as the Father is loved by the Son and as the Son by the Father, is also the love which is addressed by God to man.*[49]

But how do we know about the image of God in man? Barth says,

The humanity of Jesus, His fellow-humanity, His being for man as the direct correlative of His being for God, indicates, attests, and reveals this correspondence and similarity. It [His humanity] is not oriented and constituted as it is in a purely factual and perhaps accidental parallelism, or on the basis of a capricious divine resolve, but it follows the essence, the inner being of God. It is this inner being which takes this form, *ad extra* in the humanity of Jesus, and in this form, for all the disparity of sphere and object, remains true to itself and therefore reflects itself. Hence the factuality, the material necessity of the being of the man Jesus for His fellows, does not really rest on the mystery of an accident or caprice, but on the mystery of the purpose and meaning of God, who can maintain and demonstrate His essence even in His work, and in His relation to this work.[50]

The analysis of *analogia relationis* shows how Barth establishes his understanding of the *imago Dei* and the humanity of Jesus. By it Barth sets forth both relational (formal) and actional (material) aspects of the basic metaphor of covenant, the I-Thou dyad, present between Father and Son in the Godhead, between God and man, and between man and man. Dialectical-dialogical language is used to describe these relationships because for Barth this language reflects the nature of reality — both human and divine. I argue that the *key* to understanding Barth rests in an adequate understanding of *analogia relationis*.

The Basic Form of Humanity

In the attempt to understand our humanity, we turn from the humanity of Jesus, man *for* other men, to the humanity of man *in general*. But it is difficult to see man in his real humanity because we observe him as a sinner, hence in contradiction to himself. Thus, there are fundamental *differences* between Jesus and ourselves: first, he is *for* man from the beginning; and second, He acts on behalf of man as his deliverer.

On the other hand, there are *similarities* between the humanity of Jesus and our own which is given and revealed in the fact that the man Jesus *can be for man*. Barth says, "Where one being is for others, there is necessarily a common sphere or form of existence in which the 'for' can be possible and effective."[51] Also, God is the Creator not just of the man Jesus, but of all men, so that in all men there is a *basic creaturely form*, a creaturely essence which is given them by God. Further, being able to enter into the covenant revealed in Jesus implies a basic form *in common* between the humanity of Jesus and the humanity of man in general.

What then is the common form basic to our humanity? Barth says that the criterion for determining this human form is Jesus Christ, the humanity of Jesus. Accordingly, many definitions of humanity are inadequate. For example, any definition of man in which man is abstracted from the co-existence with his fellowman is false. Any definition of man as a being in and for himself, as a being opposed to or neutral about his fellowman, or wherein his humanity is subsequently or secondarily determined rather than seen as an essential and primary aspect of being with fellowmen, is false or inhuman. Positively stated, ". . . the humanity of each and every man consists in the determination of man's being as a being with others, or rather with the other man."⁵² "It is not as he is for himself but with others, not in loneliness but in fellowship, that he is genuinely human, that he achieves true humanity, that he corresponds to his determination to be God's covenant-partner."⁵³ Thus, through the criterion of the humanity of Jesus, Barth establishes a boundary line beyond which man exists in contradiction to his nature, i.e., in inhumanity.⁵⁴

The Humanity of Man as the Being-With-the-Other

The background has been laid for an analysis of the humanity of man as *the being-with-the-other*. From my perspective Barth sets forth the most careful development of the basic form of humanity, the I-Thou relationship, available in theology, philosophy, or the social sciences. It is to be noticed that this definition does not necessarily depend on theology, for much of it has been arrived at by non-theologians or non-Christians, e.g., Buber and Confucius. However, *the criterion of its adequacy and its validity*, Barth says, depends upon theology.⁵⁵

Barth develops an analysis of the "I" proceeding to an analysis of the "I am," to "I am in encounter with the other," to "I am in encounter essentially," to "I am as Thou art." Then he discusses four elements of the history of being-in-encounter.

But, first, Barth discusses what he does *not* mean by humanity. Things which might be said about man as an "empty subject," as he is man *without* his fellowman, have no "categorical" significance in the description of humanity for Barth. For example:

> . . . . the fact that I am born and die; that I eat and drink and sleep; that I develop and maintain myself; that beyond this I assert myself in the face of others, and even physically propagate my species; that I enjoy and work and plan and fashion and possess; that I acquire and have and exercise powers; that I take part in all the works of the race either accomplished or in process of accomplishment; that in all this I satisfy religious needs and can realize religious possibilities; and that in it all I fulfill my aptitudes as an understanding and thinking, willing and feeling being—all this as such is *not* my humanity.⁵⁶

This is the "field" in which human being either takes place or does not take place, but it is not humanity. Rather, to be human one must exist in this field according to the categories of humanity, as a being *with* his fellowman, and in the encounter of the I and Thou. If man denies himself as essentially with his fellowman, all man's "participation in scholarship and art, politics and economics, civilization and culture"[57] will not reveal his humanity. The crucial question for man's humanity is the *enactment* of this history, i.e., the realization of the encounter in which "I am as Thou art."

There are four elements of the "I am as Thou art," or "being in encounter": (1) the being in which one man looks another man in the eye; (2) the fact that there is mutual speech and hearing; (3) the fact that we render mutual assistance in the act of being; and (4) the fact that all this is done, on both sides, with gladness.

The discussion of these four elements[58] is the core of the discussion of humanity. Attempts to summarize it suffer greater distortion than most summaries of Barth's theology. The nuanced discussion of dialogical-dialectical relationships between persons, while building on Martin Buber's discussion, goes beyond it and forms the most perceptive and profound discussion of the meaning of humanity that I have seen in Western literature, theological or non-theological. Let me explicate these four elements in greater detail.

"*Being in encounter is (1) a being in which one man looks the other in the eye*. The human significance of the eye is that we see one another eye to eye."[59] (Man, not things or the cosmos, sees and is seen. We don't know about animals). A man who is visible to another man is distinct from the one who sees him. There is an over-against-ness of two men as they see one another. When one man looks another in the eye, he lets the other look him in the eye. "To see the other thus means directly to let oneself be seen by him."[60]

More generally, being in encounter is a being in *openness* of the one to the other with a view to and on behalf of the other. In other words, the "I" doesn't hide himself or refuse to be seen by the other but rather the I and the Thou are *open* to one another. As one man is open to another, we give each other something, ". . . an insight into our being."[61] Therefore, as I see you and you see me and we are no longer closed to one another, I am not *for* myself, but *for* thee and thou *for* me. Where openness obtains, humanity begins to occur. This two-sided openness is the first element of humanity.

"*Being in encounter consists (2) in the fact that there is mutual speech and hearing*."[62] Although seeing the other and being open in turn to his seeing me is a necessary first step in my humanity, it is only the beginning. In seeing the other we are limited in our knowing him because we interpret him through our own concepts and by our own standards. Something more than separately formed views and arbitrary conclusions is required on both sides if we are to be in real

III/2 The Creature

communication with the other. <u>Unless there is something more than the mutual look, we can still enter into this intercommunication *without* the other.</u>[63]

This step in the I-Thou interaction is speech and hearing, which consists in both the *self-expression* of the I to the thou and its *reception*, as well as the *address* of the I to the thou and its *reception*.

<small>Humanity as encounter must *become* the event of speech. And speech means comprehensively reciprocal *expression* and its reciprocal *reception*, reciprocal *address* and its reciprocal *reception*. All . . . four elements are vital.[35]</small>

"*Being in encounter consists (3) in the fact that we render mutual assistance in the act of being.*"[65] The third step is being *for* one another, however limited. In the strictest sense Jesus is *for* us, living *for* us, accepting responsibility for us. But in this respect, acting as the Son of God, he differs from us. Therefore, our *for* one another, our assistance to each other in the basic form of our humanity, is not this kind of *for*. Nevertheless, our *forness* corresponds to His *forness* so that we can say that humanity is constituted by rendering mutual assistance to each other. <u>Our humanity cannot be less than *giving* and *receiving* assistance.</u> We are inhuman if we withhold or reject this assistance. What is assistance? For one thing, it is actively standing by the other, standing so close that one's own action means help and support to him.

It also means that one does not leave him to his own being and action, but rather takes part in his anxiety and burden, accepting concern for his life. It means to live with the other. "As we see one another and speak and listen to one another, we call to one another for assistance."[66] <u>We can't be *for* him in the strictest sense, only God can be that, but we can be at his disposal. We can assist in meeting his needs. We can support but not carry him, give him encouragement but not victory, alleviate but not liberate. Thus, ". . . humanity consists in the fact that we need and are capable of mutual assistance."</u>[67] By his very being man calls for assistance that only fellow-man can give, so when he calls for assistance he calls for fellow-man.

However, if I refuse to let myself be helped, others cannot help me, however much they would like to do so. Thus,

<small>My humanity depends on the fact that I am always aware, and my action is determined by the awareness, that I need the assistance of others as a fish needs water. It depends upon my not being content with what I can do for myself, but calling for the Thou to give me the benefit of his action as well.[68]</small>

This notion of humanity is not idealistic, but ultimately realistic. Man is not alone, but *with* his fellowman. He needs his help and is pledged to help him. "To be human, and therefore to act accordingly, confessing both the need of assistance and the willingness to render it, is supremely natural and not unnatural."⁶⁹ It is an obvious thing to do. Not to do so, to be by oneself, not assisting the fellowman, or calling for his assistance, is artificial. All man has to do is to see himself in the situation in which he actually finds himself and not try to construct another alien situation for himself.

<u>"Being in encounter consists (4) in the fact that all the occurrence which we have so far described as the basic form of humanity stands under the sign that it is done on both sides with gladness."</u>⁷⁰ We *gladly* see and are seen. We *gladly* speak and listen. We *gladly* receive and offer assistance. This last and final step of humanity, the *gladly*, is the secret of the preceding three stages. Without it, humanity suffers an essential lack and is empty. <u>If man is only human *externally* in the I-Thou interrelationship of seeing, speech, and assistance, but does not do them "gladly," then he is *internally*, and thus essentially, inhuman. The real substance and soul of humanity is in the secret of the gladly."</u>

Is not Barth actually referring to the freedom and gladly of the God-man covenant partnership? Apparently not. Barth says, that man belongs to God is the *great secret* of man. However, in this section he is not speaking of that secret but of a lesser one, the secret of man's creatureliness, his humanity. Even for the person who has not become aware of the covenant-partnership with God, there can be some realization of this human "gladly;" a freedom which is based on man's creaturely form.⁷¹

However, this lesser secret, the secret of humanity, remains a mystery. It can be indicated, pointed to, but not solved. The "gladly" does not penetrate the secret before which it stands, but stands as the *conditio sine qua non* of humanity.

This "gladly" cannot be grounded or deduced from elsewhere but can only be affirmed as the living center of the whole. One can say that a *discovery* takes place. But a discovery implies that something is posited and given, not created by man's activity and/or ability. What is it? The gift consists in the fact

> . . . that the one has quite simply been given the other, and that what he, for his part, has to give is again himself. It is in this being given and giving that there consists the electing and election, the mutual acceptance, the common joy, and therefore the freedom of this encounter.⁷²

<u>Barth disavows the implication that this elaborate description of humanity with its "gladly" is Christian love or *agape*.</u> Too frequently it has been the custom of Christian theologians to depreciate the fullness of humanity in order to contrast it with Christian love. In the process, Christian love has been identified as nothing more than the good humanist would also set forth. As a result the humanist cannot understand the real content of Christian love, and consequently, does not take it seriously. Thus Barth says, "At this final level of the concept of humanity we have *not* been speaking about Christian love."⁷³,⁷⁴

On the contrary, we have been speaking of the nature of the human creature. The same man who in the course of his history with God, in the fulfillment of his fellowship with Jesus Christ, *will also* participate in and be capable of Christian love for God and fellow-men as brothers, is as such this creature . . . we have come to know as humanity. Humanity, even as we finally spoke of it in the secret of that free co-existence of man and man, is *not Christian love*, but only the natural exercise and actualization of human nature—something which *formally is on the same level as the corresponding vital functions and natural determinations of other beings which are not men.*[75]

The fact that a man is a man involves the co-existence of man and man ". . . in which the one may be, and will be, the companion, associate, comrade, fellow and helpmate of the other."[76] This is human nature, humanity. The man who is determined "from above" to be the covenant-partner of God, is determined "down below" to the the creature—fellow-man. "For all the difference in detail, he always lives with varying degrees of consistency and perfection the life characterized by this nature."[77] Again, "*What we have called humanity can be present and known in varying degrees of perfection and imperfection even where there can be no question of a direct revelation and knowledge of Jesus Christ.*"[78] Thus the reality of human nature (humanity) and its recognition are not restricted to the Christian community.

The totality which we have described as humanity is the determination of human being as such irrespective of what may become of man in the course of his history with God. We cannot, therefore, expect to hear about Christian love when the reference is to humanity in the Christian doctrine of the creature.[79]

In the discussion of humanity I have addressed myself primarily to the "form" of the human relationship. Even though humanity has a relative independence outside of redemption, its I-Thou form corresponds and reflects the I-Thou reality of the God-man and God-God relationships. (Barth speaks of this as the *analogia relationis*.) Humanity, as the image of God, is a "sign" pointing to man's fulfillment in the covenant relationship with God. Although it is known with clarity through the revelation of God in Christ, humanity does not depend upon that *revelation* for its reality. Since Jesus Christ is the ontological form of *all* humanity in creation, whether or not it is *recognized* as such, he is the reality of our humanity and can be and has been described by non-Christian thinkers.

The form of our humanity is the dialogical structure of the I-Thou relationship, of being-in-relationship-to-the-other, of mutually seeing, speaking, and listening, assisting, and doing all this "gladly."

In this section we have seen the expression of the dialectics of man-being-in-encounter-with-man. Here the dialectical-dialogical mode of thought is used to capture the reality of interaction.

D. §46 MAN AS SOUL AND BODY

Barth's understanding of the individual person, whole man, is also dependent on Christology. To see whole man properly one must see him in the context first of real man, the God-man relationship, and second of humanity, the man-man relationship, both set forth in Jesus Christ. The discussion of the person then proceeds from the "outer" relationship with God (Spirit) to the "inner" relationships of soul and body. Finally the particular operations of the soul and body (perceiving, thinking, desiring and willing) are described. As usual, the "parts" are dialectically-dialogically related, no part can be understood without the other, although distinctions are made and priorities given. There is unity, difference and order.

A key to understanding is 1) the relationship of the Spirit to whole man and 2) the distinction between the function of the Spirit in creation, providence (preservation), and redemption. Confusion at these points leads to the accusation that man's independence is absorbed into God. Arnold Come puts the issue in the following way. Barth seems ". . . to reduce man as created by God to an empty and impotent vessel into which God later pours his grace, a purely animal substructure to which God later adds a totally new and unrelated spiritual superstructure."[80]

The function of the Spirit in redemption brings man into a salvatory relationship with God where whole man is in the process of fulfillment. This has to do with participation in Jesus Christ through the Christian community. But the function of the Spirit *in creation and providence* (preservation) has to do with the relationship between the Creator and the creature, as such, and applies to all persons. <u>Whereas, for Barth, the Spirit *in creation and providence* is most clearly known through Jesus Christ, creation and providence are *not* redemption. They precede it, and are preparatory to it. Jesus Christ is the normative revelation of God's meaning and purpose even in creation and providence.</u>

A further distinction, between creation and providence (preservation), clarifies the critical issue regarding man's independence.

> In creation God acts directly, i.e., without the intervention of other things, for other things could enter in only as the product of His creative activity. . . . But when it is a matter of the preservation of creation as such, when it is a matter of that which *succeeds creation but precedes redemption*, there is need of a free but obviously *not of a direct or immediate* activity on the part of God.[81]

Does this mean that this is less the act of God because it is indirect? Barth says "No!"

> Its actual preservation is not less the free act of God because in this case He acts *indirectly*. . . . Hence, it is not really the creature which sustains the creature. It is not the context of the whole which guarantees the continuance of the individual, nor is it the individual which guarantees the continuity of the whole. . . . It is God alone who does everything according to His own free good pleasure. But He does it by maintaining this relationship and therefore by maintaining **the creature** *by means of* the creature.[82]

III/2 *The Creature* 45

... it takes place wholly and utterly as a free act of God, but in such a way that creation itself is the means by which it is preserved in being: the human body by the soul which directs it; the human soul by the body which serves it; the race as a whole and all the species of beasts and plants by natural propagation; the individual by his human and cosmic environment; and every creaturely thing by its environment and according to the particular order of that environment. God Himself sustains the creature, but He sustains it in the context in which He has created it and ordains that it should exist.[83]

Thus in preservation (providence) there is a "natural man," maintained by God's active and free relationship to this context. This relationship is designated as Spirit. Man is not absorbed. God created him, maintains him, and is constantly relating to him, *indirectly*, through the context of his life.

This interpretation differs significantly with natural theology, not only in that it is revealed through Jesus Christ, but also in that the relationship and action in Christ sets forth the meaning of creation and preservation. They are seen in the context of covenant. In addition He reveals that men in general are *essentially linked with God and with fellowman* preceding redemption. Neither of these insights can be reached by reason or empirical methods.

Further, when Barth says that man *has* Spirit, it means that God is there *for* him. Every moment that he breathes and lives he has a witness that God turns to him in His free grace as Creator and Preserver, that He has willed him again and again *as a living being*, and that He has allowed him to become whole soul of his body.[84]

Since man *has* Him, the Spirit is certainly *in* man—in his soul and through his soul in his body too.... But [Spirit] ... is not identical with him ... [Spirit] does not merely become the human subject.... [Spirit] *is the principle which makes man into a subject*. The human subject is man as soul, and it is this which is created and maintained by the Spirit. But ... the Spirit lives His own superior ... life over against the soul and the human subject. He is not bound to the life of the human subject.[85]

Barth makes a clear distinction between Spirit and soul, so that God is not identified with man, but the Spirit is efficacious in maintaining the soul in creation, however indirectly.

There are many questions regarding how the Spirit functions indirectly (in preservation) which it is not possible to examine at this point. Putting that issue aside, let us focus on the significance of Barth's position. It affirms the independence of whole man, thus refuting interpretations of Barth that accuse him of absorbing man into God. Secondly it affirms the significance of all normal functions of man described by philosophical and psychological anthropology such as thought, will, desire, and awareness, but at the same time places these within a larger context of meaning. Thus, the ordinary meaning of freedom as choice among options, or freedom as self-determination, is affirmed.[86]

Now we are prepared to discuss that which is within the "brackets," the soul and body in their interconnexion and particularity.

Soul and Body in Their Interconnexion — Man's Nature

Man is constituted as a unity within which there is an antithesis. There is creaturely *life* and creaturely *being*.[87] The former refers to the soul and the latter to the body, each in its interconnexion. Creaturely *life* is a *living* being, an individual *life* of a body which emphasizes man's *temporal existence*. Creaturely being is a living *being*, an individual life of the body which emphasizes *spatial form*. Man is one, i.e., an inwardly united and self-enclosed subject; therefore with man we speak not only of interconnexion, but also of unity.[88] This understanding of the soul and body relationship eliminates false spiritualization and false materialization. It also eliminates the dualistic interpretations of body and soul that have plagued Christian thought and had such devastating consequences for ethics.

<u>The soul, as movement *in time*, as inner, fulfills itself in specific perceptions, experiences, thoughts, feelings, and resolutions, but it needs the body as movement *in space*, as outer, as means to execute the functions of the soul. Therefore, every trivializing of the body, or removal of the body from the soul, jeopardizes the soul. Every denial of the body is a denial of the soul.</u>

The soul is life, the independent life of a corporeal being. Life in general means *capacity* for action, self-movement, self-activity, self-determination.[89] Independent life, the life of a specific subject, does not emerge except where the capacity for action of a corporeal being is not bound to a specific point in space. The function of the soul is related to time, hence the soul and its functions are not spatially bound. This is one basis for Barth's affirmation of freedom as *self-determination* in "natural man."

However, the process whereby we become conscious of ourselves as independent and self-determining is not merely an act of the soul; it also involves the body. As I live, I find myself able to become conscious that I am a soul.

And as I make use of this ability, my life itself and therefore my soul, executes a return movement to itself. I come to myself, discover myself and become assured of myself. It belongs to my capacity for action that I continuously do this. . . .[90]

This life I live is the independent life of my physical body. This act is performed by the material body as well as my soul. Without the material body, I cannot be aware of objects different from myself, "I cannot distinguish myself from others as the object identical with myself, and cannot therefore recognize myself as a subject."[91] Consequently, I have need of the corporeal senses to determine myself as an object of my knowledge, which is decisive for my self-consciousness and is presupposed in my self-knowledge as subject. If the act, in which we become conscious of ourselves, is not both a soulful and corporeal act, the one within the other, then it does not happen at all.

III/2 The Creature

The soul and body can be distinguished but not separated, for I cannot answer for myself without at the same time answering for my body. Thus there is an interconnexion and unity between soul and body of the human being. Barth says that all rejection of this interconnexion, or attempts to deny it, can only mean a distortion of nature of man.

Soul and Body in Their Particularity — Their Operations

As man is in *this* relationship with God, i.e., in providence or preservation, as he has Spirit, two presuppositions emerge in regard to his creaturely nature. First, man is a *percipient being*, and second, he is an *active being*. But these operations refer to the functions of the whole self (body and soul) rather than to the distinction between the soul and body.

Initially, perception (percepient being) is understood as a compound act of two functions: *awareness*, which is external and related to the body; and *thought*, which is internal and related to the soul. However, the situation is more complicated than this, for the act of perception is single and the act of the whole man.[92] Thus not only the body but also the soul has *awareness*, and not only the soul but also the body *thinks*. Therefore, awareness is not only with the body. The body is the body of man's soul, yet he does not execute this act as soul, but as body, i.e., by means of his organs. Again, *thinking* is not only with the soul but with the body, the brain, nerves, and the whole organism. As man thinks, he leads the life of his body and is disturbed by what disturbs it, and when he dies, thinking ceases. So both awareness and thinking are functions of the soul *and* the body. There is a distinction without separation.

However, Barth says, the acts of awareness and thought, though they involve both soul and body, are *primarily* of the soul and *secondarily* of the body. An order exists between the functions. There is a special relationship of the body ascribed to the act of awareness (the outside of perception), although the soul also has awareness. This awareness of the soul is only possible as the body in its outer form is open to the other. "Body is the openness of soul. Body is the capacity in man in virtue of which another *can come to* him and *be for* him. Man has awareness, therefore, insofar as he is the soul of his *body*."[93]

On the other hand, there is a special relation of the soul to *thinking* (the inner side of perception). "When I think, the other which I perceive *comes into* me, after it has come to me."[94] But the soul is man's self-consciousness taking place in and essentially related to the body, for the soul does not think without the body.

The soul is the capacity in virtue of which he can make another his own, in virtue of which the other can be not only *for him* but *in him*. Man thinks, therefore, insofar as he is the *soul* of his body.

Now Barth proceeds to the discussion of man as *active being*. As there is an inner and outer aspect to perception, so too there is an inner and outer aspect to action. The outer side of action is *desire* and the inner side is *will*. But, as soon will be seen, these are only functional distinctions within an essential unity. Finally, it will be seen that the same kind of dialectical-dialogical relationship which characterizes most of Barth's thought, wherein he speaks of relationships in terms of unity, differentiation, and order, will relate perception to action.

These functions of desiring and willing are differentiated for the purpose of understanding them as separate, yet related, having the same kind of relationship between them as we saw when Barth spoke of sensing and thinking. Although there is no partition between desiring and willing — both are soulful and bodily, and both are primarily of the soul and secondarily of the body — there is a *special relationship* of *desiring* to the *bodily* nature and *willing* to the *soulful* nature.

In the operation of *desire* the nerves of the brain and body participate. (Awareness is also involved [external bodily action] because particular sensible experiences [awareness] release in man particular desires and urges.) Thus, there is a special relation between desiring and the body. However ". . . the urge as such . . . does not constitute the desire or aversion. If I am to desire or shun, it is necessary that I not only be *aware* of the *urge* concerned but that I affirm it, making it my own and committing myself . . . to it [as a particular desire]."[95] That a man can do this or not do this, that he can accept or shun the material (urge) is not merely the response of his nerves, although it is that, it is also his "own affair."[96] This is where his will, as a function of his soul, participates in his desiring. This is what constitutes the most decisive participation of man's soul in his desiring. This indicates how desiring is not strictly a function of the body, but also a function of the soul (the will).

It is a matter of willing (and thus primarily a matter of the soul) that man is not only the object of desire, but also an object of man's will. Barth says, ". . . that I have a certain intention and come to a resolution with respect to it or to my relation to it; that I set it before me and put myself into the corresponding movement in relation to it,"[97] is a matter of my will. Desiring is presupposed. By the operation of the will a choice is made among several desires, so the self does not will everything it desires. To will means *to make up one's mind* (involving thought and awareness as well as desire) in respect to a desire. To will means that the "I" chooses. The "I" determines itself and its activity for the execution or the non-execution of its desiring. (What Barth describes as "will" is the process of the soul, but it can be realized only because the soul is the *soul* of the *body*.) It is the "I" who decides and determines the relation to the desiring of the body. When it elevates itself above, it becomes aware of itself only when it realizes the distinction between its desires and makes use of the power of will over them. When the "I" wills, it abandons its neutrality to itself and its desiring and takes a position over against them both. This is the act of the soul, the man's act. Once again Barth affirms freedom as self-determination or choice.

In summary, man is the percipient and active soul of the body which puts into effect his perception and action. Soul and body, and perception and action cannot be seen without each other, although they are not interchangeable. They have different functions, and one precedes the other. On both sides of perception and action there is a primacy of the soul, but at no level is the soul found without the body. Although there is a primacy of the soul, at no level can it be said that the soul only thinks and wills; it also senses and desires. Barth says,

> ... [man] does not think without sensing [awareness], nor will without desiring. But when he thinks and wills, he stands at a distance from his sensing [awareness] and desiring. . . . He becomes an object to himself. In this freedom to stand at a distance, pass under review and become object, he conducts himself as soul of his body. The body lacks this freedom. It can only participate in it.[98]

Although Barth's method for arriving at his description of whole man ("natural man") differs significantly from the physical and social sciences, his conclusions overlap with some basic insights of humanistic psychology. He affirms, with humanistic psychology, the interdependence and unity of body and soul. He refuses both materialistic and spiritualistic reductionistic temptations. At the same time he affirms the distinctive functions of the body-soul complex — thinking, awareness, willing, and desiring, but always dialectically related and with a concern for the priority of certain of the functions — thinking and willing.

Biology, psychology, sociology, and philosophical anthropology are currently in a state of disarray regarding these questions. However, if they were to reach a convincing consensus which significantly differed with Barth, it would be important to look again at Barth's understanding of whole man.

This focuses a critical issue regarding Barth's theology — how open is it to discoveries from the human sciences? Would one continue to accept Barth's theological psychology even though it were rejected by newly discovered empirical "facts?" Or would one change one's viewpoint in relationship to the facts? One way to respond to this question is by yielding to current social science on the understanding of whole man (psychology), yet still affirming his understanding of the man to man and God to man relationships. One could still affirm Barth's placement of the individual person in the context of others (humanity), and God (real man), preserving Barth's whole-part dialectic-dialogic whatever the particular psychology. Or, one could continue with Barth's psychology in spite of discoveries in psychology and sociology, arguing that the particular data is insignificant regarding this aspect of man.

Or, one could argue that if his theological psychology is at wide variance with psychological discoveries, it not only invalidates his theological psychology, but his entire theological system.

I would predict, however, that the outlines of Barth's general position are on target, and that empirical research and philosophical studies may contribute refinements, but will not overturn his basic position. In addition it must be remembered that Barth's theological position places man in a context in which man is understood as essentially social, and as essentially related to God, even though man may be blind to both these relationships. Beyond this, however, is Barth's theological assumption and affirmation that the context itself, and the persons within the context, are purposed by God's freely-given love.

These latter affirmations are based on revelation, not empirical verification. Since they form the critical context of Barth's understanding of man, Barth's method will always use social science in a critical way, not allowing its discoveries to determine the basic understanding of man, but only to supplement and confirm. <u>Theology, as understood through Christology, is "sovereign."</u> If one strays from this fundamental assumption, one no longer accepts Barth's theology. However, a final comment may soften this theological imperialism. In recapturing an actional-relational understanding of human reality, and in reasserting a modified dialectical and interactional method of thinking, his thought provocatively overlaps many movements of current theory and research of the social sciences and suggests that both revelation and the empirical methods are dealing with a common reality.

Notes

1. III/1, pp. 94ff, pp. 228ff.
2. Cf. Thomas S. Kuhn, *The Structure of Scientific Revolutions* (Chicago: The University of Chicago, 1962).
3. These arguments are too lengthy to be made here. See III/2, p. 25ff.
4. Karl Barth, *Church Dogmatics*, III/2, pp. 68-71.
5. Ibid., pp. 73-74. Italics mine.
6. Ibid., p. 75.
7. Some characteristics of man defined by non-Christians are true symptoms, but we do not know which are true except as they are viewed from the perspective of real man. Barth discusses these other anthropologies (naturalistic, ethical, idealistic, existentialistic, and theistic) in the light of these six criteria. The discussion follows at this point in the text (pp. 76-132). It is a fascinating and important discussion. Unfortunately, it cannot be summarized in the space available.
8. In the next two sections other criteria are set forth that give Barth more leverage in critiquing "the wide spectrum of views of human nature."
9. For Barth, "material" refers to God's grace and man's response to this grace, the actional dimension of the relationship. Formal=relationship; ma-

terial=action for Barth. This is a bit strange upon first sight, but if we recognize that action defines being, then the "matter" of life is actional. Also, if we recognize that action (God's freedom) is superordinate to form (relationship) and defines relationship, we can understand the shift Barth has made from Platonic ontology where form was superordinate to matter.

10. Ibid., p. 142.
11. Election means a special *decision* (of God) with a special *intention* (the delivery of man) in relation to a special *object* (man). The decision is God's free choice as an expression of His love.
12. Ibid., p. 145.
13. Ibid., p. 150.
14. Ibid.
15. Ibid., p. 157. Italics mine.
16. Ibid., p. 160. Italics mine.
17. Ibid.
18. Ibid., pp. 161-62.
19. Ibid., p. 166.
20. Ibid.
21. Ibid., p. 167.
22. Ibid.
23. Ibid., p. 168.
24. Ibid. Italics mine.
25. Ibid., p. 174.
26. Ibid. Italics mine.
27. Ibid. Barth distinguishes between the phrases "to act responsibly" and "to be a responsible being." The former is *act* and the latter is *potentiality*. Barth means to point to the act and event of man's answer to the Word of God, and not to a state of being which can be characterized by a particular potentiality.
28. Ibid., p. 175. Italics mine.
29. III/1, p. 266.
30. III/2, p. 207.
31. Ibid., p. 208. Italics mine.
32. Ibid. Italics mine.
33. Ibid., p. 214.
34. Ibid., p. 215.
35. Ibid.
36. Ibid., p. 216. Italics mine.
37. Ibid.
38. Ibid.
39. See following discussion on *analogia relationis*.
40. Ibid., p. 217.
41. Ibid., p. 218.
42. Ibid.
43. Ibid.
44. The crucial link between the inner Godhead (Father-Son) and the humanity of Jesus (man-man, hence our humanity) is the being of the man Jesus for God. Since action and being define each other, for Barth, God's act or action of deliverance in Jesus Christ means His being and reality *ad extra*. Ensconced within action is the form of the relationship. This link establishes the relationship between God in Himself and humanity.

45. Ibid., p. 219.

46. The *imago Dei* has both dynamic (material, as defined by Barth) and form (structural) elements. Although we are lifting up the aspect of *form* for consideration at this point, he is also speaking of the material, actional, or dynamic dimension of the relationship. Common definitions of the *imago Dei*, "reason," "personality," "responsibility," or "original righteousness," are not shared by Barth.

47. John D. Godsey, ed., *Karl Barth's Table Talks* (Richmond, Va.: John Knox Press, 1962), p. 57.

48. Ibid. Italics mine.

49. *Church Dogmatics,* III/2, p. 220. Italics mine.

50. Ibid. Parentheses added.

51. Ibid., p. 223.

52. Ibid., p. 243.

53. Ibid.

54. Barth elucidates this statement: <u>Humanity is described as a being of man *with the other*. But only the humanity of Jesus can be absolutely described as being *for* man</u>. The extent to which the being of the one man with the other also includes a certain being of the one *for* the other will have to be shown.

Barth describes ". . . humanity as a being of the *one* man with the other." (Ibid. Italics mine.)

"Fundamentally, we speak on both sides in the singular and not in the plural. We are not thinking here in terms of individualism. <u>But the basic form of humanity . . . is a being of the one man with the other</u>. And where one is with many, or many with one, or many with many, the humanity consists in the fact that in truth, in the basic form of this occurrence, one is always with another, and this basic form persists. Humanity is not in isolation, and it is in pluralities only when these are constituted by genuine duality, by the singular on both sides.

The singular, not alone but in this duality, is the presupposition without which there can never be humanity in the plural." (Ibid., p. 244.)

55. "We need not be surprised that there are approximations and similarities. Indeed, in this very fact we may even see a certain confirmation of our results — a confirmation which we do not need and which will not cause us any particular excitement, but of which, in view of its occurrence, we shall not be ashamed. Why should there not be confirmation of this kind? *In this context we are not speaking of the Christian in particular but of man in general*, and therefore of something which has been the object of all kinds of 'worldly,' i.e., non-Christian wisdom. And surely it need not be, and is not actually, the case, that this worldly wisdom with its very different criteria has always been mistaken, always seeking humanity in the direction of Idealism and finally of Nietzsche, and therefore establishing and describing it as humanity without the fellow-man, the humanity of man in isolation. It would be far more strange if not the slightest trace had ever been found of fellow-humanity, of the humanity of I and Thou." (Ibid., p. 277. Italics mine.)

56. Ibid., p. 249. Italics mine.

57. Ibid.

58. Ibid., p. 250-274.

59. Ibid., p. 250.

60. Ibid.

III/2 The Creature

61. Ibid., p. 251.
62. Ibid., p. 252.
63. The complexity of Barth's thought is at most points difficult to summarize without doing it injustice; however, the problem is especially acute when dealing with his analysis on the very complex interactional phenomena of speech and hearing.
64. Ibid., p. 253. Italics mine.
65. Ibid., p. 260.
66. Ibid., p. 262.
67. Ibid.
68. Ibid., p. 263.
69. Ibid., p. 264.
70. Ibid., p. 265.
71. This is not redemption, but neither is it independent from God's constant action; rather, it is related to God's activity operating in creation and providence.
72. Ibid., p. 272.
73. Ibid., p. 274. Italics mine.
74. Christian love or agape "... is the action and attitude of the man who only *becomes* real and can only be understood in the course of his history with God. Love is the new gratitude of those who *have come to know* God the Creator as the merciful Deliverer. As such it is the gracious gift of the Holy Ghost shed abroad in the hearts of Christians convicted of sin against God and outrage against themselves. ... In love they respond to the revelation of the covenant fulfilled in Jesus Christ, in which God comes to them as their merciful Father, Lord and Judge, and they see their fellow-men as brothers and sisters, i.e., as those who have sinned with them and found grace with them." (Ibid., p. 275. Italics mine.)
75. Ibid. Italics mine.
76. Ibid., p. 276.
77. Ibid.
78. Ibid. Italics mine.
79. Ibid.
80. Arnold Come, *An Introduction to Barth's "Dogmatics" for Preachers* (Philadelphia: Westminster Press, 1963), p. 152.
81. III/3, p. 64. Italics mine.
82. Ibid., p. 65. Italics mine.
83. Ibid., p. 63.
84. III/2, p. 363.
85. Ibid., p. 364. Italics mine.
86. Confusion regarding definitions of freedom is allayed if one recognizes that Barth uses the term *freedom* for a special use of will—when thought, will, desire, and awareness are efficaciously related to the reality of God's redemptive action, as well as for freedom as self-determination. A more appropriate term for self-determination is *life* (p. 374).
87. III/2, p. 367.
88. Ibid., p. 371.
89. Ibid., p. 374.
90. Ibid., p. 375.
91. Ibid.
92. Ibid., p. 400.

93. Ibid., p. 401. Italics mine.
94. Ibid. Italics mine.
95. Ibid., p. 408. Italics mine.
96. Ibid.
97. Ibid.
98. Ibid., p. 419-20.

CHAPTER IV

CRITICISMS OF BARTH

It is the rare book in contemporary theology that does not refer to Karl Barth. While this recognition frequently is an occasion for criticism or rejection, it testifies to the difficulty of ignoring him. Whether appreciatively or not, those writing in the field of theology must take him seriously. Unfortunately, most commentators are well acquainted only with secondary sources which, in many instances, demonstrate an inadequate grasp of his thought. In short, the field of Barth commentary is extensive and strewn with misconceptions. Predominant among these are distortions of his understanding of the Word of God, of his view of the individualism and freedom of man, and of his political posture. The following discussion addresses these areas.

The Problem of the Understanding of the Word of God

Commentary on Barth's understanding of the Word of God encounters problems less with interpreting his thought in *Church Dogmatics* I/I (on the Word of God) than with understanding how the discourse found there relates to the content of the later volumes. From this opening section the reader easily forms the impression that, from Barth's perspective, the major tasks of the church are Bible study and preaching. On careful reading, Barth himself must be accused of leaving that impression. It is necessary, therefore, to look first at what he says in *Dogmatics* I/I and then relate it to his thought in later volumes.

Proclamation, scripture, and revelation are the three forms of the Word of God. Revelation is the primary event; the Bible and proclamation, secondary. "In revelation we are concerned with Jesus Christ to come, who ultimately in the fulness of time did come."[1] Jesus Christ is Immanuel, God with us. He came into ". . . the deepest depth of our plight. . . ."[2] He is one of us. "Revelation in fact does not differ from the person of Jesus Christ, and again does not differ from the reconciliation that took place in him. To say revelation is to say, 'the Word became flesh. . . .' "[3] Further, a proper understanding of Jesus Christ is Trinitarian. Thus, <u>the Word of God is primarily revelation, and that understood as Jesus Christ, and, secondarily, the Bible and proclamation.</u>

This much is readily understood by reading *Church Dogmatics* I/I. A deeper understanding of the Word of God, meaning Jesus Christ, is explicated in the rest of the *Dogmatics*. For example, the idea of *logos* (John 1:14-18) provides a crucial link in Barth's theology. "The logos became flesh and dwelt among us. . . ." (John 1:14) has two dimensions. It is dynamic, actional: "The Word of God is God's act . . . in that it is a decision."[4] And "<u>Decision means choice, freedom used.</u>"[5] It is also relational form: *Logos*, while meaning word, also means form, reason, pattern, and structure. Thus *logos* combines the dynamic-actional element with form-meaning-pattern, a wedding exemplified best by the structure and dynamics of conversation as well as the content of speech. There is the address by an actor to someone and its reception by that other; there is also the content, meaning, pattern of the message spoken. Conversation presupposes a dyadic form, two persons exchanging words and meanings. Jesus Christ, for Barth, involves this dyadic *logos*.

But a particular understanding of action and relationship was conveyed through Jesus Christ. It is my thesis that this particular content can best be summarized by the root metaphor "covenant." According to this thesis, <u>scripture can be understood basically as variations on the theme of logos-covenant.</u> The final norm for understanding the dynamic/form of covenant is the revelation of Jesus Christ. One aspect of the unity of the Old and New Testaments is based on the common sharing of this metaphor. The Old Testament expresses this theme — a community living according to and in violation of various interpretations of covenant. On the one hand, the Old Testament records occasions of deep understanding and participation in the covenant; on the other, misunderstanding and violations of it, both conjoined with hope of fuller realization of this peculiar relationship with God.

But the meaning of covenant is not self-evident. Alternative meanings gather under the umbrella of the one concept. Pious appeals to "covenant faith," as if the term signifies one clear idea, further confuses theological discourse. Barth contributes to clarification, but his definition is not set forth in full in *Church Dogmatics* I/1, but rather in III/2.

<u>The alternative root metaphors,[6] contract and organic, which frequently pass for "covenant," differ in significant ways from it. The contract metaphor is conditional; covenant, unconditional. The organic metaphor stresses harmony; covenant not only includes, but gives positive value to struggle and "conflict" as normative ingredients.</u>

It is helpful to dissect and analyze the various root metaphors into their component elements as an aid to seeing differences and similarities. For example, in reading Karl Barth seven elements of the covenantal metaphor emerge:

1) The relationship is dyadic, ego-alter, or I-thou in structure (whether between man and man, and/or God and man).

2) The relationship is interactional; more specifically, it is dialogical-dialectical[7] (either term, used singly, has flaws; together, they describe the kind of interaction of which Barth speaks). There is choice

and freedom on both sides, although in biblical thought one side initiates, leads, and basically establishes the relationship. Negatively, one can say it is *not* a unilateral form of relationship.[8]

3) The occurrence of harmony and unity between the two actors is important, and probably to be stressed, but there is a significant place for struggle and conflict. Instead of being considered pathological, as in the organic metaphor, struggle and conflict (of a certain kind) are viewed as healthy and essential for the growth of persons and communities. At this point, covenantal thought, in Karl Barth's explication of it, breaks with organic thought, the metaphor with which it most closely contends for understanding the meaning of the Word of God.

4) Because man violates the covenant (is sinful), and when, in addition, struggle and conflict are normative, the need for forgiveness is acutely real. The line between healthy and pathological conflict is narrow; going over the line is the risk involved in its affirmation. This risk is compensated for by greater emphasis on unconditional forgiveness. In the contract metaphor, forgiveness is conditional. In the organic metaphor, unconditional forgiveness is present, but less stressed. Another way of stating this point is that if we know we are bound to God and to one another, we are freed to struggle and risk creatively and, hence, to grow.

5) The time dimension is taken seriously, especially in terms of the future. The metaphor is eschatological. Promise-making and promise-keeping, by God with man and man with man, are essential dimensions. In the contract metaphor, time is an important factor, but again it is conditional. The organic metaphor affirms the present and the past, but there is little eschatological consciousness.

6) The importance of law, rules, and structures are included. Law is understood as ensconced within covenant, just as Sinai occurred within the Abrahamic covenant and God's action of liberation from Egypt. Man needs structures, laws, rules to live — personally and communally — but law is understood as relative to other elements of the covenant. It is not absolutized — neither rigidly nor legalistically understood. It is absolutely necessary, but also absolutely relative to the purposes, relationships, and dynamics of covenant.

7) Finally, covenant involves loyalty to and trust in God and others. Persons in covenant see that relationships involve loyalty to and trust in persons, causes, communities, and God. The theological-ethical issues come to focus in the following questions: a) To whom or to what does one give loyalty; in whom or in what does one trust? and b) How does one order trusts and loyalties, and subordinate them to the ultimate "subject-object" of loyalty?

While Barth does not set forth covenant in this analytical way or with this exact terminology, it is my contention that a deeper investigation of his thought depends on and develops out of seeing this distinctive mataphor at work. I am persuaded that part of the difficulty in approaching his thought exists because the covenantal metaphor is inadequately understood or is not seen as unique and distinctive, different from its organic and contract relatives.

To return to Barth: In the discussion of *analogia relationis*, we saw that the covenantal relationship between persons was analogous to that between God and man. Jesus Christ was understood as the normative expression of both these covenants. In other words, he is the incarnation of both covenantal relationships — relationship to God and relationship to man.

The next step is to look again at the four aspects set forth under the humanity of man as the being-with-the-other, the being-in-encounter where there is mutual seeing, mutual speech and hearing, mutual assistance in the act of being, and mutual gladness.[9] Although all four of these characteristics are used to explicate the dialogical-dialectical relationship, and are therefore important, one of them — mutual speech and hearing — holds special significance for understanding the *logos*-structure of reality. In this section Barth describes the most subtle, complicated, and sophisticated relationships and functions which characterize human, as distinct from animal, life, and which exemplify covenantal form. Thus the most unique (the highest, the deepest) expression the human being knows, the process of conversation, becomes in Barth the analogy from ordinary experience for that which is beyond ordinary human understanding. Man uses analogies from his own personal and collective experience to think about God.

This analysis presupposes that man, through language, historically and collectively, constructs his understanding of the world and God and projects that understanding onto the ultimate environment — a presupposition set forth by Peter Berger and Thomas Luckmann in *The Social Construction of Reality*.[10] This analysis apparently contradicts Barth's understanding of scripture and revelation. However, it seems to me that it need not contradict his conclusions, but only unmask the processes by which language is formed and through which theological concepts are derived. Language about the divine or ultimate is based on analogies from natural and social life, e.g., the Kingdom of God from political life; God the Father from family patterns; etc. This is not a surprising observation, but rather acknowledges the historical finitude of language. Some theologies and philosophies derive their basic analogy from biology or physics — the organic, power, and mechanistic metaphors — or from politics and social relationships — contract and interaction metaphors. What is being said here is that the Bible and the Judaeo-Christian community, primarily, and Barth in his reflection upon them, have chosen, lived, thought, and written out of the covenantal metaphor. This analogy, in general, is derived from a particular form of relationship and interaction characteristic of political, social, and family interactions (rather than interactions occuring in physics or biology). From this analytical perspective, what Barth has done is to observe that Biblical thought has employed the human analogy of covenant, the most complex example of which is speech and hearing, as its primary metaphor for comprehending the relationship of God and man, and man and man. Demystifying this process does not, from my perspective, negate the possibility that there is an ultimate Reality to be known. It merely suggests that, given the options among alternative metaphors for theological understanding, there arises a need to choose among them.[11]

The stress on the importance of speech and hearing raises a further question: Does Barth's thought lead to indifference to culture, or does it acknowledge the creation of culture to be the special task of man? His critique of culture was twofold: it had inordinately influenced the basic assumptions of theology, and it too easily became a substitute for God, an idol. But if, as I contend, he stresses the speaking and hearing dimensions of the human being as a dialogical self, then he has lifted up for emphasis precisely those functions of persons which create culture.[12]

It seemed at first that Barth affirmed a "Christ-against-culture" stance or, at most, "Christ-and-culture in paradox."[13] If the previous argument is valid, he in fact affirmed the "Christ-as-transformer-of-culture" position. He was concerned that theology not be dominated by culture or culture-determined theologies. However, it now appears that the root metaphor he recovered, and its expression or revelation in Jesus Christ, affirms the nature of man as a dialogical-dialectical creature whose peculiar gift is the use of language and, thereby, the free construction of culture. There is a norm for and purpose to cultural formation, of course, but it too is dialogical-dialectical: the fullest expression of the double-covenant as revealed in Jesus Christ.

In summary, this section attempts to counter the tendency of some of Barth's critics and adherents to narrowly understand his discussion of the Word of God in terms of Scripture and Jesus Christ, and thus find him separating the church and scripture from the world and culture. In understanding Jesus Christ, the Word, the *logos* made flesh, as the conjoining of two analogous covenants, and in stressing speaking and hearing, Barth opens the private language of the church to a relationship with culture. Acceptance of covenantal relationship and action, embodied and enacted in Jesus Christ, better describes the crucial aspects of our human nature, while at the same time establishes norms and purposes for human existence. In conclusion, Bible study and preaching are important, but only if they do not curve back upon themselves. They also must be led to tred the *logos* catwalk Barth gives us to more fully relate the gospel to culture.

The Issue of the Individualism and Freedom of Man

On this issue Barth is under attack from opposite directions. We have already seen how Arnold Come has questioned Barth's explication of man's independence and freedom, saying that he seems "... to reduce man as created by God to an empty and impotent vessel into which God later pours his grace...."[14,15]

Now let us look at a criticism from the other side. Wayne Proudfoot subsumes Barth's understanding of man, ontology, and ethics under "The self as Will or Agent: The Individualistic Type."[16] His argument develops as follows: Existentialists, such as Buber and Bultmann, place the locus of encounter between God and person, and person and person, in the existential decision which is understood primarily as the dyadic encounter between wills.

> The doctrine of God in the individualistic type emphasizes the model of the agent and the attribute of freedom. Farrer directs the reader toward the apprehension of God through the analogy of the unity of the self in its willing. This view of God as primarily will or agent is present in the work of Karl Barth. Barth's discussion of knowing as participation was mentioned in connection with the monistic type [the first type], *but his doctrine of God and parts of his doctrine of the creature focus on the will and human freedom*....[17]
>
> The basic picture of the world offered by this conception is one of an aggregate of individuals. Each individual is conceived as a point of force or energy. The focus of this conception is on individuals interacting and colliding.[18]

In response, I argue that both of these interpretations of Barth are inadequate, and basically for the same reason: they fail to understand how dialogical-dialectical thought and ontology function in his work. <u>For Barth, man is linked to both God and man, but that linkage is understood through a dialogical-dialectical mode of relationship which results in separation of God and man as well as unity between them.</u> Each pole of the dialogic-dialectic — separation and unity — is augmented and nurtured by the other pole.

To argue that in Barth the human being is viewed as primarily will or agent ignores much of what has been reported in this Introduction. First, in his understanding of whole man, Barth sets forth man as body and soul, awareness and desire, willing and thinking, all in dialectical interaction. Thinking *and* willing, not just willing take the lead; they cannot properly be separated from one another, nor from awareness and desire. Second, man, as understood from the perspective of humanity, is related essentially to other persons. Man is social by nature. Within the dyadic interaction the "I" emerges, but that "I" is interdependent on the relationship of seeing and being seen, speaking and listening, aiding and needing aid. The autonomous individuals "of freely interacting and colliding wills" is not even close to Barth's description of humanity. Third, God is agency and will, freedom and love in action; however, if will is abstracted from the *logos* covenantal ontology, as Proudfoot has done, we are presented with only part of what Barth says. Covenantal reality includes actions and relationships, the *for* and the *with*, in the peculiar dialogical-dialectical manner of interaction. Concepts such as wisdom, name, logos, love, reconciliation of all persons, reason,[19] refer to this dimension. In reaction to Protestant and Catholic dogmatic rationalism, Barth does not stress the cognitive aspects of God's nature (omniscience, for example). At the same time, he does not reduce all his understanding of God and man and their relationship to will "conceived as a point of force or energy." There is structure as well as energy, action, or will.[20]

Further, it is important to develop the full implications of dialectical-dialogical thought. Barth's description of humanity (III. C. in this Introduction) and the subject of this publication, sets forth dynamic concepts which allow us to observe and describe the social processes of becoming a person, or individual (use of this term is dependent upon understanding the context). <u>Individuality results from the processes of interaction between persons, and cannot be understood apart from these others. A community, understood as formed by and of multiple dyadic relationships, is the context into which we are born.</u> The child becomes a person as parents, siblings, relatives, and friends interact with him or her. A child may depend too much on the community (be absorbed), or become separated from the community (be isolated); in both instances, however, the structure of his essential humanity, its dialogical character, has not been destroyed, but rather ignored or rejected, according to Barth. <u>The healthy development of the person occurs when there is a dialogical-dialectical "balance" between union and separation, community and individualism.</u> The critical factor is a dynamic process wherein personhood results from relationship with others—from exchanges and interactions of sight, speech, and aid. <u>Individuality is dependent on community.</u> In the process the strength is given by the others—through love, forgiveness, care—to become oneself. The other, by these special kinds of relationship which Barth is at great pains to describe, is the agent of individual personhood, and the person continues, in some sense, to be linked with the other. Of course, the determining quality that allows this process to function adequately is its linkage with God.

In summary, Arnold Come and Wayne Proudfoot, in their perceptions of Barth's concept of man (either as lacking or over-emphasizing individuality and freedom) reveal an inadequate reading of *The Church Dogmatics* and do not comprehend the ontology and logic of Barth's effort. <u>Barth's thought is the explication of a covenantal ontology, and that understood relationally and logically in a dialogical-dialectical context. Barth argues that such an interpretation need not and should not be dependent upon the philosophical systems currently or historically available; rather it derives from an understanding of the revelation which comes through the Old and New Testaments, and most</u>

definitively through Jesus Christ.[21] If this is true, it is not surprising that Barth finds such a metaphor illuminating the personal and social realities in which he participated.

Barth's Political Posture

There have been at least three objections to the relationship of theology and politics in Karl Barth's thought.[22] First, in stressing transcendence and eschatology, Barth is said to have neglected the practical and political. His theology offered little in guiding people in the nuanced choices involved in the immanent realm. The proclamation of the Word of God tended to negate man and his life in the world and led to political complacency. Second, he neglected the task of empirical analysis of the facts of human experience, especially in the area of economics. Third, although he did move from his theological reflection to political decisions, he did so in a non-systematic and hence arbitrary way. According to Reinhold Niebuhr, Charles West, and Emil Brunner, he did not reject communism and Nazism with equal vehemence; he did not condemn Russia's suppression of the Hungarian revolt, while he had been a key leader in the opposition to Hitler. According to Niebuhr, Barth's resistance to Nazism was ". . . dictated by personal experiences with tyranny and not by the frame of his theology. . . ."[23] Therefore, they claim his decisions were basically psychological, not theological. In summary, Barth is charged with being so wrapped up with the transcendent and abstract realm that he neglected the concrete world. Hence, he encouraged political complacency and made decisions personally on a psychological and, hence, arbitrary basis. It cannot be denied that there is sufficient material in the Barth corpus to lend credence to some of this attack. At a deeper level, however, as pointed out by George Hunsinger and others, this understanding fundamentally distorts what Barth was about.

Before responding to the three specific accusations, some general observations need to be made. Throughout Barth's lifetime, he not only was concerned with practical, concrete political life, but he also became and remained a Social Democrat. More significantly, each change in his theological perspective occurred because of, or at the least was intimately related to, a cultural and political crisis. In other words, his perception of the cultural and political consequences of theological beliefs and concepts — whether liberal, orthodox or variations of his own theology — affected the way he did theology. Barth's theology was done in genuine dialogue with praxis.

During his first pastorate in Geneva, he had encountered the profound misery of the working class, and by 1911, as a pastor at Safenweil, ". . . he had already developed profound socialist sympathies."[24] "What is important here is that a latent tension between

Barth's liberal theology and his socialist praxis began to mount."[25] In 1915 he became a member of the Social Democratic Party.[26] Also in 1915, he was appalled that ninety-three German intellectuals, among whom were some of his theological mentors, would publicly support the war policy of Wilhelm II. For Barth this signalled nothing less than the poverty of 19th-century liberal theology.

Just because I set such emphasis Sunday after Sunday upon the last things, it was no longer possible for me personally to remain suspended in the clouds above the present evil world, but rather, it had to be demonstrated here and now that faith in the Greatest does not exclude, but rather includes within it, work and suffering in the realm of the imperfect.[27]

He became for a period radical in his politics. "The political implications of God's kingdom are as radical as the theology from which they are drawn."[28] He said that the Christian must let ". . . the healing unrest that is set in his heart by God deepen, grow stronger, and augment the generally rising flood of the divine which will one day itself break through the dams."[29] Nevertheless, he maintained a critical stance and thought that political goals can receive no *direct* religious sanction.

Disillusionment with the embodiment of the socialist revolution in Russia forced him to reconsider the relationship between theology and socialism. In response, he resolved to root out the last vestige of *religious* socialism from his theology. "The socialist crisis had indicated a more fundamental theological crisis demanding a dialectical approach to both 'theory' and 'praxis'!"[30] The second edition of *Der Romerbrief* (1921) was the result of this rethinking. For the next ten years (1921-31) he suspended much of his intellectual concern with political praxis. Nevertheless, while more sobered, he did not abandon his socialist commitment. "In 1926 he could still speak of 'the justice and necessity' of the socialist struggle while castigating theology and [the] church for not having supported the legitimacy of the socialist cause. In 1928 he not only voted for the socialist party in the May elections . . . but afterward considered it important to communicate his decision to his colleagues."[31] Even during this period he related theology and political praxis. "What was at stake in these decisions [political] for Barth was the meaning of Christian hope. Ever since his encounters with the socialist movement and with Blumhardt, Barth had become convinced that Christian hope must remain true to earth — or else it would cease to be Christian hope. . . . This radical realism [of the socialist workers' movement — of head, heart, and stomach] was closer to the Christian hope for 'the resurrection of the flesh' than was liberal theology's abstract, inward idealism."[32] During this period Barth was working primarily on understanding the concept of God, but even this, or particularly this, was not irrelevant to political praxis.

For "Only a proper concept of God which was not reducible to religious experience could sustain the radical realism of resurrection hope and so remain true to the earth."[33]

Another turning point, the publishing of *Anselm: Fides Quaerens Intellectum* (1931), was also supported by his circulating a petition among his colleagues declaring personal and material solidarity with Gunter Dehn, a professor subjected to harassment by German nationalists and Nazi students. Only four other signatures could be obtained. This ". . . marked Barth's personal recovery of praxis and his entry to what would become the resistance of the church to Hitler."[34] From then on there was no question of the active engagement of his theological thought and political praxis. But from then on such engagement took another form. His thought became analogical not dialectical, positive not negative, and rational not irrational. This was the beginning of Barth's mature theology which became the *Church Dogmatics*.

In what follows, I want to respond to each of the three charges made most frequently in criticism of Barth's view of the relationship of theology and politics.

The Emphasis on Transcendence Led to Political Complacency.

"Every major development of his theology took place in a political context. . . . In each case it was a political crisis which compelled Barth to rethink the conceptual basis of his theology. In each case . . . he was largely seeking a better basis for his social action—one subject to unconditional norms rather than the capriciousness of the times."[35] Barth was not one who was isolated from the world. He was deeply involved. His thought moved from praxis to theology as well as from theology to praxis. He took the theoretical, especially the conceptions of biblical thought, seriously because he saw its determining consequences for praxis.

There was a conceptual link between Barth's theology and politics. Four aspects stand out: 1) He stressed the sovereignty of God. This de-absolutized any man-made system or structure, eventually including socialism itself. 2) He understood God to be the ground of the transformation of all things, of the entire world, and not simply of the interior life. 3) He saw clearly that God's love, revealed in Jesus Christ, was communal in scope rather than simply personal. 4) The Bible had convinced him that God's love and freedom was biased toward the poor, the marginal, the oppressed and dispossessed. It is difficult to sustain an argument that his theology leads to political complacency.

The Neglect of Empirical Analysis.

Further, it is difficult to sustain an argument that Barth was unacquainted with political and social-scientific literature. He remarked at the end of his career, "Don't forget to say that I have always been interested in politics and consider that it belongs to the life of the theologian. My whole cellar is full of political literature. I read it all the time. I am also an ardent reader of the newspaper."[36]

However, such a plea on his part is not sufficient to counter the critics' argument that he neglected empirical analysis. One can be well read in politics and economics but never become immersed in the empirical analysis which informs the best of political and social science.[37] I am not aware that he read much of this kind of "factual" information. His critics argue that being inattentive to such data led him to make gross and, therefore, inadequate judgments regarding political and economic options, from which greater acquaintance with the factual data and the "social laws" of the "real world" would have saved him. On the other hand, this neglect (if indeed he was neglectful) was not fatal. Seeing the forests and not the trees, he was able to observe the fundamental consequences of an economic and political system, and judge it by norms emerging from the revelation in Jesus Christ.[38] In addition, Barth was concerned with what determined the definition of "fact," with the construing or interpretation of the facts. Facts for him were important, but of prior importance was the recognition of the framework, the particular theory, used to define and order them. Barth understood that there is no neutral social science. The "facts" generated by social science in the Western world, and also the problems selected for study, often fit the interests of the capitalist system.

For whatever reason, he was less concerned with empirical analysis. This reduced his ability to see the rich texture of the social world and thus narrowed the variety of options available for political actions/choices. However, it is my opinion that his approach had greater potential for empirical analysis than he either developed or realized.

Barth's Moves from Theology to Politics Were Arbitrary; They Were Based on Psychology.

In preparation for a response to this charge, I will simplify (attempting not to distort) and recast Barth's discussion of capitalism and socialism in terms of alternative root metaphors. His stance might be described as follows:

1) Barth understood the gospel and Jesus Christ in terms of the covenantal metaphor.

2) He understood capitalism to be based on mechanistic and power metaphors which contradict the covenant, e.g., capitalism maximized the principle of self-interest vs. the common good; it was obsessed with the quantitative and calculative rather than with the qualitative; it was primarily concerned with one sector of existence (the economic) and failed to acknowledge the interrelationship of economics, politics, culture, etc.; it was exploitative and alienating in essence, rather than reconciling and humanizing.

3) On the other hand, he understood socialism, at least in theory, to be based on a mixture of organic, power, and covenantal metaphors which overlapped in significant ways, e.g., the gospel and socialism were concerned with the poor and the oppressed; they were both wholistic — the economic, political, and cultural were understood as interrelated and had to be studied in that way; the essential principle of socialism and the gospel was concern with others, with all persons, not self-interest; socialism was concerned with the qualitative, the new man and the new community, as well as with the quantitative.[39]

Although Barth was increasingly disenchanted with the particular embodiments of socialism, he, nevertheless, continued to see in it greater affinity with the gospel than capitalism contained.

Thus Barth's refusal to reject communism with the same vehemence as he had Nazism was not arbitrary or psychological. For him the affinities between socialism and the gospel were greater than between capitalism and the gospel. In addition, he considered Western anti-communism to be as grave a danger to the world as Eastern totalitarianism. At least communism did not presume to sanctify its actions with the gospel. One can argue the soundness of this judgment, but it is difficult to accuse Barth of being arbitrary or psychological.

In summary, the charge that Barth was complacent about the political world, or arbitrary in relating theology to politics, is clearly misconceived. That he was not sufficiently concerned with and informed about empirical analysis has a basis, but even this judgment needs clarifying. A ". . . lifelong political interest . . . led Barth to devote much of his career to relating theology and politics. A viable relationship, in his view, must be one of mutual clarification in which neither discipline is reduced to the terms of the other. Only if the two are not confused — with each retaining its own integrity — can either have anything to say. Theology must not be politicized, nor politics theologized. Theology can make its contribution to politics only by remaining theology, and vice versa."[40]

Three misconceptions of Barth's theology — a view of his understanding of the Word of God as narrow; a double misperception of his understanding of freedom as self-determination and individualism; and a misunderstanding of the way he related theology and politics — have mystified his interpreters and denied many a genuine choice for or against his reading of Christian theology. Barth was a man profoundly concerned with culture, with persons and community, and with politics. Barriers to an appreciation for this concern result in part from his preoccupation with establishing a clear understanding of the function of theology and the concept of God. However, for Barth, such a clarification was not an end in itself, for a major, if subordinate, criterion for the development of his theology was its implications and consequences for persons and society.

Another block to understanding Barth, according to my hypothesis, is that he operated out of the distinctive root metaphor of covenant, which is often only dimly seen and more often reduced to other metaphors, especially the contract or organic. His critique of philosophy and the social and physical sciences as criteria for theology and praxis reflect the recovery of this paradigm. Scripture embodies a distinctive *logos*, not present in current philosophical and scientific enterprises. One could expect significant misunderstanding of his positions by those committed to philosophies and theologies based on other paradigms. Given the changes in Barth's own theological and intellectual pilgrimage, it would be unlikely that *The Church Dogmatics* would have the imprimature of eternity. But, perhaps he has rediscovered and named a unique root metaphor and carefully developed its implications for theology and praxis.

Notes

1. Karl Barth, *Church Dogmatics*, I/1, p. 127.
2. Ibid., p. 130.
3. Ibid., p. 134.
4. Ibid., p. 178.
5. Ibid., p. 179.
6. One way to understand a particular theology is to discern the paradigm or metaphor basic to it. Root metaphors use a natural or social reality as analogous to theological "systems." I use a typology based on six root metaphors: mechanistic, power, organic (traditional and Whiteheadian), contract, symbolic interactionist, and covenantal. On the one hand, such typologies may grossly oversimplify the complexity and subtlety of a system of thought; on the other, they can clarify fundamental differences between families of thinkers. Further refinement is added when a metaphor is analyzed into its component parts, or dimensions. (See Stephen C. Pepper, *World Hypotheses* [University of California Press: Berkeley, 1966]; Ian Barbour, *Myths, Models, and Metaphors* [Harper & Row: New York, 1974]; and Stuart D. McLean, "The Contribution of 'Center of Value Theory,' 'Root Metaphor Analysis,' and 'Reference Group Theory,' to the Study of Religion," unpublished monograph.)
7. This is not a reference to the kind of dialectical thought characteristic in Barth's writing between the second edition of *Romerbrief* (1921) and *Anselm* (1931).
8. Although it is grounded in God's grace alone.
9. *Church Dogmatics* III/2, pp. 250-285.
10. Anchor Books: New York, 1967. This is obviously the statement of an argument with a long history and includes the thought of Freud, Feurbach, and Marx.
11. The question then becomes whether one choses Jesus Christ or, rather, understands oneself as chosen by him as the historical reality which most adequately comprehends the relationship of God and man, and man and man.

12. If one understands the concept culture, as used by the social sciences, as the total product of the processes of human activity, then language, social institutions, as well as material products, are involved (H. Richard Niebuhr, *Christ and Culture* [Harpers: New York, 1951]). Language is the crucial component in the construction of the patterns, orders, and meanings of our common life. It is used to shape and reshape every aspect of nature and place it in a context of meaning (including material products and social institutions). The patterns, forms, meanings—particularly the meanings—are created by the dialogical human beings as they use language.

13. H. Richard Niebuhr, *Christ and Culture* (New York: Harpers, 1951).

14. Arnold Come, *An Introduction to Barth's "Dogmatics" for Preachers* (Philadelphia: Westminster Press, 1963), p. 152.

15. Summary of response to Come: Man, in Barth's view, must be seen not only under the aegis of redemption, but also under creation and providence (even here Jesus Christ is the revelation of man—real man, humanity, and whole man). Providence is the sphere of God's free activity, but not of His direct and immediate activity. He maintains the creature by means of the creation and the context of creation (III/3, p. 65). While man is maintained by God in this sense, as whole man, he has thought, will, desire, and awareness in which freedom as self-determination is logically delineated and affirmed. Barth's discussion of will and thought, as related to time, specifically points to how man is given the capacity to function independently. This discussion is placed in the context of the person-to-person interaction (humanity), within which these aspects of man are developed.

16. Wayne Proudfoot, *God and the Self: Three Types of Philosophy of Religion* (Lewisburg: Bucknell University Press, and London: Associated University Presses, 1976), p. 96.

17. Ibid. Italics mine.

18. Ibid., p. 95.

19. A word Barth frequently uses in his discussion of Anselm. It refers to the character of the logos of God, the logos of persons, and the logos relationship between them. His later theology, post-1931, makes a deliberate attempt to overcome the bias toward the stress on will and agency of his earlier theology.

20. In root metaphor terms, Proudfoot analyzes Barth in terms of a power metaphor, in contrast to my analysis of the covenantal metaphor.

21. Barth is not beyond employing aspects of a variety of philosophies in an eclectic way; indeed, he must. But adherence to and dependence upon one or another philosophical system skews the truth of the biblical message for him. He has concluded that there is indeed a distinctive ontology operative in scripture, an ontology of covenant which is unique and salvatory for all persons. Whether or not this latter claim is accepted, Barth is to be credited with clearly discerning a distinctive metaphor whose presence has been obscured by our penchant for being dependent upon philosophical models alien to it.

22. The essence of this argument is found in George Hunsinger's chapter, "Toward a Radical Barth," in *Karl Barth and Radical Politics*, ed. and trans. George Hunsinger (Philadelphia: Westminster Press, 1976), pp. 181-227.

Criticisms of Barth

23. Reinhold Niebuhr, *Essays in Applied Christianity*, selected and edited by D. B. Robertson (New York: Meridian Books, Inc., 1959), p. 184.
24. *Karl Barth and Radical Politics*, ed. Hunsinger, p. 194.
25. Ibid., p. 194.
26. Ibid., p. 202.
27. Barth and Thurneysen, *Revolution and Theology in the Making: Barth-Thurneysen Correspondence, 1914-15*, trans. James D. Smart (Richmond, Va.: John Knox Press, 1964), p. 28.
28. *Karl Barth and Radical Politics*, ed. Hunsinger, p. 207.
29. Karl Barth, *Der Römerbrief* (First Edition, 1919), p. 390, as quoted in *Karl Barth and Radical Politics*, p. 208.
30. *Karl Barth and Radical Politics*, ed. Hunsinger, p. 212.
31. Ibid., p. 217.
32. Ibid., pp. 217-18.
33. Ibid., p. 218.
34. Ibid., p. 219.
35. Ibid., p. 224.
36. John Deschner, "Karl Barth as Political Activist," *Union Seminary Quarterly Review* 28 (Fall 1972): 55.
37. Social science is the process of gathering and ordering data into facts by strict rules of scientific procedure.
38. "One of the important events in the formation and consolidation of the 'Confessing Church' was a Reformed Synod held at the beginning of 1934 [4 January in Barmen]. . . . The focal point of the synod was the discussion of a 'Declaration on the Right Understanding of the Reformation Confessions in the German Evangelical Church Today', composed by Barth. . . . The synod adopted this Declaration without alteration, and the General Assembly of the Reformed Alliance for Germany, meeting at the same place, also adopted it on 5 January." (Eberhard Busch, *Karl Barth: His Life from Letters and Autobiographical Texts* [Philadelphia: Fortress Press, 1976], p. 236.) The Barmen Confession was the crucial document for the resistance movement in the Confessing Church in Nazi Germany.
39. Although I believe the above analysis, at least in rough outline, is a fair presentation of the way Barth thought, it could also be argued, from Barth's general perspective, that social reality does not yield to pure types of social and economic theory. Rather it is best described by an eclectic approach, e.g., that certain aspects of socialist theory accurately describe certain economic processes (e.g., imperialism) and that certain elements of capitalism or the market economy accurately describe other processes (e.g., supply and demand when there are many economic actors). Thus, these "laws" could be effectively utilized so long as the overall direction of the society was guided by concepts based on covenant.

Even strong defenders of the market economy, such as Wilhelm Röpke, *The Humane Economy* (Indianapolis: Liberty Fund, 1971), argue that capitalism by itself, set free from a religious context, is destructive — that classical Christianity is the necessary context for keeping capitalism humane. In root metaphor language, he sees the market economy (mechanistic metaphor) as destructive by itself; but, subordinated to or integrated within Classical Christianity (organic metaphor), its excesses are curbed and its benefits realized.

40. *Karl Barth and Radical Politics*, ed. Hunsinger, p. 181.

CHAPTER V

CONCLUSION

My argument has been that Karl Barth's major contribution to contemporary theology is the rediscovery of a unique metaphor which too often has been misunderstood through contract or organic categories. In *The Church Dogmatics*, III/2, Barth describes its applicability to the God-man relationship (real man), the person-to-person relationship (humanity), and to soul and body (whole persons). The subject of this republication explores the dynamic relationship of person with person, being-in-encounter, and indicates how Barth's theology/anthropology is related to cultural and social issues.

The caricatures of Barth would lead us to believe that he was complacent or unconcerned about man's life in culture and society. As we have seen, these illusions are easily dispelled by his personal life and commitments. However, regarding the structure and thrust of his theology, the question has continued to engage critics' pens and passions. If my thesis has merit, it should be clear by now that Barth developed a biblically-based theology which took God's transcendence seriously, and at the same time whose structure, dynamic, and thrust was intimately related to culture, politics, and social science itself. On the other hand, he was concerned that theology perform its proper function and not be confused with politics, culture, or social science. The proper understanding of God for him was not an abstract and esoteric end in itself, but was linked to praxis so that the consequences of God's relationship and action in Jesus Christ could be related not only to persons, but also to the total life of culture in which persons participate and by which they are affected.

MAN IN HIS DETERMINATION AS THE COVENANT-PARTNER OF GOD

That real man is determined by God for life with God has its inviolable correspondence in the fact that his creaturely being is a being in encounter—between I and Thou, man and woman. It is human in this encounter, and in this humanity it is a likeness of the being of its Creator and a being in hope in Him.

1. JESUS, MAN FOR OTHER MEN

Real man lives with God as His covenant-partner. For God has created him to participate in the history in which God is at work with him and he with God; to be His partner in this common history of the covenant. He created him as His covenant-partner. Thus real man does not live a godless life—without God. A godless explanation of man, which overlooks the fact that he belongs to God, is from the very outset one which cannot explain real man, man himself. Indeed, it cannot even speak of him. It gropes past him into the void. It grasps only the sin in which he breaks the covenant with God and denies and obscures his true reality. Nor can it really explain or speak of his sin. For to do so it would obviously have to see him first in the light of the fact that he belongs to God, in his determination by the God who created him, and in the grace against which he sins. Real man does not act godlessly, but in the history of the covenant in which he is God's partner by God's election and calling. He thanks God for His grace by knowing Him as God, by obeying Him, by calling on Him as God, by enjoying freedom from Him and to Him. He is responsible before God, i.e., He gives to the Word of God the corresponding answer. That this is the case, that the man determined by God for life with God is real man, is decided by the existence of the man Jesus. Apart from anything else, this is the standard of what his reality is and what it is not. It reveals originally and definitively why God has created man. The man Jesus is man for God. As the Son of God He is this in a unique way. But as He is for God, the reality of each and every other man is decided. God has created man for Himself. And so real man is for God and not the reverse. He is the covenant-partner of God. He is determined by God for life with God. This is the distinctive feature of his being in the cosmos.

But this real man is actually in the cosmos. He is on earth and under heaven, a cosmic being. He belongs to God, but he is still a creature and not God. The one thing does not contradict the other, but explains it. If we are to understand man as the creature of God, we must see first and supremely why God has created him. We must thus regard him from above, from God. We must try to see him as God's covenant-partner, and therein as real man. This is what we have done in the preceding section. But if we are to understand him as God's covenant-partner—which is our present task—we must return to the fact that God has created him and how He has done so, regarding him as a cosmic being, as this particular cosmic being. It is in this distinction from God, in his humanity, that he is ordained to be God's covenant-partner. In this continuation of theological anthropology we now address ourselves to all the problems which might be summed up under the title " The Humanity of Man." Our presupposition is that he is the being determined by God for life with God and existing in the history of the covenant which God has established with him. Only in this way—and we shall not allow ourselves to be jostled off the path which we have found—is he real man, in this being which consists in a specific history. But we must now see and understand this real man as a being distinct from God, as the creature of God, and to that extent as a being here below. It is as he is not divine but cosmic, and therefore from God's standpoint below (with the earth on which and the heaven under which he is), that he is determined by God for life with God. The creation of God, and therefore His positing of a reality distinct from Himself, is the external basis and possibility of the covenant. And the covenant itself is the internal basis and possibility of creation, and therefore of the existence of a reality distinct from God. We must now ask concerning man, the covenant-partner of God, from the cosmic standpoint, in his life here below, in distinction from God, and to that extent in his humanity. If we do not do this, we shall certainly have seen and understood the content of his being, but not the form inseparable from the content.

The question which will occupy us in this section is the necessary transitional question which borders and links the two essential ways of viewing him. Between the determination of man as God's covenant-partner on the one side, and his cosmic and creaturely being on the other, there is obviously an inner relationship, since we have to do with one and the same subject. His humanity can hardly be something which stands in alien remoteness from the fact that in this humanity he is the being which exists in this covenant-history. The man who, seen from above, from God, is the covenant-partner of God and real man as such, can hardly fail to be recognised in what he is below, in his distinction from God. He cannot be radically and totally hidden from himself in this distinction, as though he were a different being altogether. His divine determination and his creaturely form, his humanity, are certainly two very different things, as Creator and creature, God and man, are different. But they cannot contradict

1. Jesus, Man for other Men

each other. They cannot fall apart and confront each other in neutrality, exclusion or even hostility.

To be sure, there may be an actual antithesis. The covenant-partner of God can break the covenant. Real man can deny and obscure his reality. This ability for which there is no reason, the mad and incomprehensible possibility of sin, is a sorry fact. And since man is able to sin, and actually does so, he betrays himself into a destructive contradiction in which he is as it were torn apart. On the one hand there is his reality as God's covenant-partner which he has denied and obscured. And on the other, as something quite different and not recognisably connected with this reality, there is his creaturely form, the humanity which runs amok when it is denied and obscured in this way, and plunges like a meteor into the abyss, into empty space.

In relation to this dreadful possibility and reality even Holy Scripture speaks of two men, a first who is of the earth, earthy, and a second who is the Lord from heaven (1 Cor. 15^{47}). The very fact that the one who is really first has become the second, and the one who is really second the first, is an indication of the actual confusion to which there is reference in this passage. There is a similar indication in 2 Cor. 4^{16}, where in reference to a monstrous contradiction we are told that the outward man perishes, but the inward man is renewed from day to day. And when Col. 3$^{9f.}$ tells us that we are to put off the old man and put on the new, we have to remember that what is here called the old is really the new which has illegitimately obtruded itself and which we ought never to have put on, whereas the new is really true and proper man, and to that extent the old and original man which could be put off only in the reckless folly of sin. The confusion indicated in all these apostolic sayings is attested indeed by the very fact that they have to speak of two distinct men in hostile confrontation. It is to be noted, however, that only with relative infrequency does the Bible speak of man in this antithesis.

The good creation of God which now concerns us knows nothing of a radical or absolute dualism in this respect. We cannot blame God the Creator for what sinful man has made of himself. We do despite to Him if in relation to the human creatureliness of His covenant-partner we begin with the actual antithesis, making the contradiction in which he exists a basic principle, and thus overlooking or contesting the fact that he exists originally and properly in an inner connexion and correspondence between his divine determination and his creaturely form, between his being as the covenant-partner of God and his being as man. The fact that of all cosmic beings he belongs so particularly to God necessarily affects him particularly as the cosmic being he is. As the creative operation by which he is brought into being is a special one, so he himself as the one actualised by this work is a special creature, standing in connexion and correspondence with his divinely given determination. If God gives him this determination, whatever else he may be he is obviously one who is determined by it, a being to which this determination is not strange but proper. His humanity cannot, therefore, be alien and opposed to this determination, but the question of a correspondence and similarity between these two sides of his being necessarily arises. Our present question is how far his humanity as his creaturely form corresponds and is similar to his divine determination, his being as the covenant-partner of God.

Presupposing that it does in fact correspond to it, we may say that it does so indissolubly and indestructibly. To be sure, the correspondence and similarity may be covered over and made unrecognisable by the sin of man. It may well be that in consequence of the sin controlling human life we no longer see them at all in ourselves or others or human society, or do so in confused pictures which can be perceived and explained only with the greatest difficulty. It may well be that what we can actually see is so doubtful and equivocal that we despair of finding any solution for the problems involved. This is indeed the case to the extent that man is actually a sinner. We have to reckon with the fact that the similarity is indeed covered over and made unrecognisable. At this point, therefore, we undoubtedly have to do with a mystery of faith which can be disclosed only as we refer to God's revelation. On the other hand, if our creaturely form, humanity, has this similarity to our divine determination, the correspondence and similarity cannot possibly be taken away from it or destroyed. The power of sin is great, but not illimitable. It can efface or devastate many things, but not the being of man as such. It cannot reverse the divine operation, and therefore the divine work, that which is effected by God. Sin is not creative. It cannot replace the creature of God by a different reality. It cannot, therefore, annul the covenant. It cannot lead man to more than a fearful and fatal compromising of his reality, his determination. And so his humanity can be betrayed into the extreme danger of inhumanity. It can become a picture which merely mocks him. But man can as little destroy or alter himself as create himself. If there is a basic form of humanity in which it corresponds and is similar to the divine determination of man, in this correspondence and similarity we have something constant and persistent, an inviolable particularity of his creaturely form which cannot be effaced or lost or changed or made unrecognisable even in sinful man. And the task of theological anthropology is rightly to point to this inviolable and constant factor, so that it is seen as such. Theological anthropology as a doctrine of man as the creature of God has to do with constants of this kind. The being of man as the soul of his body is another unassailable and constant factor of this kind, as is also his being in time. With these anthropological mysteries of faith we shall have to deal in the further course of our exposition. But we must first consider the supreme constant to be found in the mystery of the correspondence and similarity between the determination of man and his humanity.

1. Jesus, Man for other Men

The practical significance of this question must not be missed. If the humanity of man genuinely corresponds and is similar to his divine determination, this means that the mystery of the being and nature of man does not hover indefinitely over human creatureliness. It touches and even embraces man below as well. In the form of this correspondence and similarity it dwells in him too. Even in his distinction from God, even in his pure humanity, or, as we might say, in his human nature, man cannot be man without being directed to and prepared for the fulfilment of his determination, his being in the grace of God, by his correspondence and similarity to this determination for the covenant with God. Even here below he does not exist in neutrality, but with a view to the decision and history in which he is real. Consciously or unconsciously, he is the sign here below of what he really is as seen from above, from God. And so he is wholly created with a view to God. It is not, of course, that he is intrinsically recognisable as this sign. Even in respect of this natural correspondence and similarity of human nature there is no natural knowledge of God. Even in this matter we are concealed from ourselves, and need the Word of God to know ourselves. But in this respect too, in our humanity as such, there is something in ourselves to know. In virtue of this correspondence and similarity, our humanity too has a real part in the mystery of faith.

But what is the right way to this mystery? Everything depends upon our finding the right way at this critical point in our investigation, and therefore in this transitional question. And here, as in theology generally, the right way cannot be one which is selected at random, however illuminating. The arbitrarily selected way would be one of natural knowledge inevitably leading into an impasse. We must be shown the right way. And the way which we are shown can only be the one way. We must continue to base our anthropology on Christology. We must ask concerning the humanity of the man Jesus, and only on this basis extend our inquiry to the form and nature of humanity generally.

That Jesus, who is true man, is also true God, and real man only in this unity (the unity of the Son with the Father), does not destroy the difference between divinity and humanity even in Him. And if in respect of this unity we have to speak of a divinity, i.e., a divine determination of his humanity too, it is not lacking in genuine humanity. There is a divinity of the man Jesus. It consists in the fact that God exists immediately and directly in and with Him, this creature. It consists in the fact that He is the divine Saviour in person, that the glory of God triumphs in Him, that He alone and exclusively is man as the living Word of God, that He is in the activity of the grace of God. It consists, in short, in the fact that He is man for God. But there is a humanity of the man Jesus as well as a divinity. That He is one with God, Himself God, does not mean that Godhead has taken the place of His manhood, that His manhood is as it were swallowed up or extinguished by Godhead, that His human form is a mere appearance, as the Roman Catholic doctrine of transubstantiation maintains of the host supposedly changed into the body of Christ. That he is true God and also in full differentiation true man is the mystery of Jesus Christ. But if He is true man, He has the true creaturely form of a man, and there is thus a humanity of the man Jesus. Therefore, as we turn to the problem of humanity, we do not need to look for any other basis of anthropology than the christological. On the contrary, we have to realise that the existence of the man Jesus is quite instructive enough in this aspect of the question of man in general.

This time we can state the result of our investigation at the very outset. If the divinity of the man Jesus is to be described comprehensively in the statement that He is man for God, His humanity can and must be described no less succinctly in the proposition that He is man for man, for other men, His fellows. We are now considering Jesus here below, within the cosmos. Here He is the Son of God. Here He is distinguished as a man by His divinity. But here He is human, Himself a cosmic being, one creature among others. And what distinguishes Him as a cosmic being, as a creature, as a true and natural man, is that in His existence He is referred to man, to other men, His fellows, and this not merely partially, incidentally or subsequently, but originally, exclusively and totally. When we think of the humanity of Jesus, humanity is to be described unequivocally as fellow-humanity. In the light of the man Jesus, man is the cosmic being which exists absolutely for its fellows.

We must first return to some earlier statements. The man Jesus is, as there is enacted a definite history in which God resolves and acts and He Himself, this man, fulfils a definite office, accomplishing the work of salvation. He does this in the place of God and for His glory. He does it as the One who is sent for this purpose. The Word and grace of God are exclusively at work in Him and by Him. He does it for God. This is again His divinity. But the humanity in which He does that for which He is sent is that He is there in the same totality for man, for other men. In no sense, therefore, is He there for Himself first and then for man, nor for a cause first—for the control and penetration of nature by culture, or the progressive triumph of spirit over matter, or the higher development of man or the cosmos. For all this, for any interest either in His own person or intrinsically possible ideals of this kind, we can find no support whatever in the humanity of Jesus. What interests Him, and does so exclusively, is man, other men as such, who need Him and are referred to Him for help and deliverance. Other men are the object of the saving work in the accomplishment of which He Himself exists. It is for their sake that He takes the place of God in the cosmos. Their deliver-

1. Jesus, Man for other Men

ance is the defence of the divine glory for which He comes. It is to them that the Word and grace of God apply, and therefore His mission, which is not laid upon Him, or added to His human reality, but to which He exclusively owes His human reality as He breathes and lives —the will of God which it is His meat to do. From the very first, in the fact that He is a man, Jesus is not without His fellow-men, but to them and with them and for them. He is sent and ordained by God to be their Deliverer. Nothing else ? No, really nothing else. For whatever else the humanity of Jesus may be, can be reduced to this denominator and find here its key and explanation. To His divinity there corresponds exactly this form of His humanity—His being as it is directed to His fellows.

We again recall the clear-cut saying in Lk. 2^{11} : " Unto you (men) is born this day in the city of David (the reference is to the son of Mary) a Saviour (i.e., your Deliverer)." He is the Son of Man of Daniel 7, who establishes the right of God on earth and under heaven by helping to his right the man who is vainly interested in himself and all kinds of causes—sinful and therefore lost man. He protects the creation of God from threatened destruction. He gives it (secretly and finally openly) its new form free from every threat. And He does this by liberating man from the threat of the devil and his own sin and the death which is its ineluctable consequence. This is His divine office. And in this office alone, as the New Testament sees it, He is also human and therefore a cosmic being. This being the case, we can readily understand why the New Testament can find no room for a portrayal or even an indication of the private life of the man Jesus. Naturally, it does not deny that He has this. It speaks clearly enough of His birth, of His hunger and thirst, of His family relationships, His temptation, prayer and suffering and death. But it discloses His private life only by showing how it is caught up in His ministry to His fellows which is the concrete form of His service of God. Hence the private life of Jesus can never be an autonomous theme in the New Testament. This is true even of His private life with God. The Johannine discourses contain extensive expositions of the relationship of the Father to the Son and the Son to the Father, but they do not attribute any independent aim to this relationship. In the strict sense, they do not stand alone, but tirelessly aim to show that the man Jesus is for others, near and distant, disciples, Israel and the world, and to show what He is for them, for man. What He is in His relationship as the Son to the Father is not something which He is and has for Himself. He does not experience or enjoy it as a private religious person. He is it as a public person. He manifests it in His relationship to His disciples and through their mediation to the whole world of men. It thus acquires at once the form of a specific action in relation to men and on their behalf. Hence Phil. $2^{6f.}$: " Who, being in the form of God, thought it not a prey to be equal with God : but made himself of no reputation, and took upon him the form of a servant." Or again, 2 Cor. 8^9 : " Though he was rich, yet for your sakes he became poor, that ye through his poverty might be rich." Or again, Heb. 12^2 : " Who for the joy that was set before him endured the cross, despising the shame." Or again, Heb. 2^{14} : " Forasmuch then as the children (of Abraham) are partakers of flesh and blood, he also himself likewise took part of the same ; that through the power of death he might destroy him that had the power of death, that is, the devil ; and deliver them who through fear of death were all their lifetime subject to bondage." Or again, Heb. $2^{17f.}$: " Wherefore in all things it behoved him to be made like unto his brethren, that he might be a merciful and faithful high priest in things pertaining to God. . . . For in that he himself hath suffered being tempted, he is able to succour them that are tempted." Or again, Heb. 4^{15}: " For we have not an high priest which cannot be touched (συμπαθῆσαι) with the feeling of our infirmities ; but was in all points tempted like as we are." Or again, the whole sequence of the life of Jesus as recounted by Peter in his address at Cæsarea in Acts 10^{38}, in which we are told that Jesus of Nazareth was anointed with the Holy Ghost and with power, and went about as a Benefactor (εὐεργετῶν), " healing all that were oppressed of the devil." According to the New Testament, this sympathy, help, deliverance and mercy, this active solidarity with the state and fate of man, is the concrete correlative of His divinity, of His anointing with the Spirit and power, of His equality with God, of His wealth. It is genuinely the correlative of His divinity, so that the latter cannot have any place in the picture of His humanity, as, for example, in the form of His " religious life," but, on the presupposition of His divinity, His humanity consists wholly and exhaustively in the fact that He is for man, in the fulfilment of His saving work. Similarly, His prophetic message and miracles, His life and death, stand under the sign of this relationship. He is wholly the Good Samaritan of Lk. 10$^{29f.}$ who had compassion on the man who fell among thieves and thus showed Himself a neighbour to him. And if the parable concludes with the words : " Go, and do thou likewise," this is equivalent to : " Follow thou me," and in this way a crushing answer is given to the question of the scribe : " And who is my neighbour ? " He will find his neighbour if he follows the man Jesus. Our first and general thesis can be summed up in the formula of the second article of the creed of Nicæa-Constantinople : *qui propter nos homines et salutem nostram descendit de coelis et incarnatus est*. The fact that the Son of God became identical with the man Jesus took place *propter nos*, for the sake of His fellow-men, and *propter salutem nostram*, that He might be their Good Samaritan.

In clarification, however, we must dig more deeply and say that in the being of the man Jesus for His fellows we have to do with something ontological. To be sure, the fact that He is a merciful Neighbour and Saviour is indicated and expressed in His words and acts and attitudes, indeed in the whole history of which He is the free Subject. But it is not the case that as this free Subject—for His is the divine freedom—He might have been something very different from the Neighbour and Saviour of His fellows, with a total or partial interest in Himself or a cause. That His divinity has its correlative in this form of His humanity, that it is " human " in this specific sense, i.e., in address to other men, is not arbitrary or accidental. Jesus would not be Jesus at all if we could say anything else concerning Him. He is originally and properly the Word of God to men, and therefore His orientation to others and reciprocal relationship with them are not accidental, external or subsequent, but primary, internal and necessary. It is on the basis of this eternal order that He shows Himself to be the Neighbour and Saviour of men in time.

He was the Head of His community before the existence or creation of all things in Him (Col. 1$^{17f.}$). For God " hath chosen us in him before the foundation of the world " (Eph. 1^4). " Whom he (God) did foreknow, he also did predestinate to be conformed to the image of his Son, that he might be the firstborn among many brethren " (Rom. 8^{29}). He was this first-begotten even when He came into the world (Heb. 1^6). And so an indefinite number of men are " given " Him, to use an expression which frequently recurs in the Fourth

Gospel. They belong to the Father, and He has given them to Jesus (Jn. 17⁶). He will not let them perish (Jn. 6³⁹, 18⁹), nor can any pluck them out of His hand (10²⁹), but they hear His Word (17⁸) and He will be glorified in them (17¹⁰). What has taken place and takes place between Him and them is only as it were the execution of an order which is valid and in force without either His or their co-operation, but both for Him and them. And the same is true of what will take place between Him and them. " I ascend unto my Father, and your Father ; and to my God, and your God " (Jn. 20¹⁷), namely, " to prepare a place for you," and then to return " and receive you unto myself ; that where I am, there ye may be also " (Jn. 14²ᶠ·). And yet that which is resolved concerning Himself and these men is undoubtedly willed by Jesus too : " Father, I will that they also, whom thou hast given me, be with me where I am " (Jn. 17²⁴, cf. 12²⁶).

It is of a piece with this that the solidarity with which Jesus binds Himself to His fellows is wholly real. There is not in Him a kind of deep, inner, secret recess in which He is alone in Himself or with God, existing in stoical calm or mystic rapture apart from His fellows, untouched by their state or fate. He has no such place of rest. He is immediately and directly affected by the existence of His fellows. His relationship to His neighbours and sympathy with them are original and proper to Him and therefore belong to His innermost being. They are not a new duty and virtue which can begin and end, but He Himself is human, and it is for this reason that He acts as He does.

We recall at this point the remarkable verb σπλαγχνίζεσθαι, which in the New Testament is used only of Jesus Himself and three closely related figures in the parables. The word denotes a movement in the " bowels " (in the sense of the innermost or basic parts). " To have mercy," or " to have pity," or " to have compassion," are only approximate translations as this movement is ascribed to the magnanimous king in relation to the hopeless debtor in Mt. 18²⁷, or the Samaritan on the way from Jericho to Jerusalem in Lk. 10³³, or the father of the prodigal son in Lk. 15²⁰, but especially as ascribed to Jesus Himself in face of the leper (Mk. 1⁴¹), the two blind men at Jericho (Mt. 20³⁴), the dead man at Nain and his mother (Lk. 7¹³), the hungry crowd in the wilderness (Mk. 8² and *par.*) and especially the spiritual need of the Galilean masses : " because they fainted, and were scattered abroad, as sheep having no shepherd " (Mt. 9³⁶). The term obviously defies adequate translation. What it means is that the suffering and sin and abandonment and peril of these men not merely went to the heart of Jesus but right into His heart, into Himself, so that their whole plight was now His own, and as such He saw and suffered it far more keenly than they did. ἐσπλαγχνίσθη means that He took their misery upon Himself, taking it away from them and making it His own. There is certainly no suggestion of a passive mood or attitude or the mere feeling of a spectator, as the word " sympathy " might imply. This is made perfectly plain by Mk. 9²² where the father of the epileptic boy says : " If thou canst do anything, βοήθησον ἡμῖν σπλαγχνισθεὶς ἐφ' ἡμᾶς." It is not in vain, but with the immediate consequence of practical assistance, that Jesus undergoes this inner movement and makes the cause of this man His own. He knows at once what to do. And the other stories in which the expression occurs speak similarly of effective help, and the parables of resolute decisions. The verb obviously refers to the action of Jesus, but it tells us that this has an inward source and is the movement of the whole man Jesus.

And this leads us to the further point that if the humanity of Jesus is originally and totally and genuinely fellow-humanity this means that He is man for other men in the most comprehensive and radical sense. He does not merely help His fellows from without, standing alongside, making a contribution and then withdrawing again and leaving them to themselves until further help is perhaps required. This would not be the saving work in the fulfilment of which He has His life. Nor would it serve the glory and right of God, nor help to their right the fellows for whom He is there. For it would not alter their state and fate as sinners fallen victim to death. It would not deal with the root of their misery. The menacing of the cosmos by chaos and the assault on man by the devil are far too serious and basic to be met by external aid, however powerful. And so the being of Jesus for His fellows really means much more. It means that He interposes Himself for them, that He gives Himself to them, that He puts Himself in their place, that He makes their state and fate His own cause, so that it is no longer theirs but His, conducted by Him in His own name and on His own responsibility. And in this respect we have to remember that so long as the cause of men was in their own hands it was a lost cause. Their judgment was just and destruction inevitable, so that anyone taking their place had necessarily to fall under this judgment and suffer this destruction. In His interposition for them the man Jesus had thus to sacrifice Himself in this cause of others. It was not merely a matter of His turning to them with some great gift, but of His giving Himself, His life, for them. It was a matter of dying for them. And if the cause of His fellows was really to be saved and carried through to success, if they were really to be helped, an unparalleled new beginning was demanded, a genuine creation out of nothing, so that the One taking their place had to have the will and the power not merely to improve and alleviate their old life but to help them to a basically new one. Interposing Himself for them, the man Jesus had thus to conquer in this alien cause. He could not merely relieve His fellows of their sin and bear for them its punishment, as though it were enough to set them in this neutral state and wipe the slate clean. He had also to give them the freedom not to sin any more but to be obedient where they had previously been disobedient. To be their Deliverer He had thus to rise again for them to a new life. This is the saving work by which the devilish onslaught on man is repulsed, the menacing of cosmos by chaos overcome and the divine creation inaugurated in a new form in which the glory and right of God are no longer bounded and can no longer be called in question by any adversary. The humanity of Jesus implies that in the execution of His mission as the incarnate Son of God He is for men in this comprehensive and radical sense. It implies that all other men can confidently keep to the fact that this sacrifice was offered once and for all for them, that this victory was won once and

1. Jesus, Man for other Men

for all for them, that the man Jesus died and rose again once and for all for them.

A sum of the whole message of the New Testament may very well be found in the question of Romans 8³¹ : " If God be for us, who can be against us ? " This is quite in harmony with the introductory preaching of Jesus according to the Synoptists (Mk. 1¹⁵ and *par.*) : " The kingdom of God is at hand," i.e., God has acted to establish His right among men and therefore to help men to theirs. But it is to be noted that the reality indicated has the concrete form of the man Jesus. He, as the Son of God, the Messiah, the Son of Man, is the indicated Deliverer. " God for us " in the New Testament is not the general proclamation of the love of God and His readiness to help. For it means that Jesus is for us. The immediate continuation in Rom. 8³² is that He " spared not his own Son, but delivered him up for us all," and so " how shall he not with him also freely give us all things ? " The preposition ὑπέρ c. Gen. (less frequently περί and διά, and only once, in Mk. 10⁴⁵ and *par.*, ἀντί) denotes this concrete form of the central declaration of the New Testament. Its meaning " for " signifies for the advantage or in the favour or interests of someone. It can also signify for the sake of a definite cause or goal. It can finally signify in the place or as the representative of someone. In the innumerable passages in the New Testament in which it is said of Jesus Christ that He acted ὑπέρ, the genitive points directly or indirectly to persons. In the majority of cases it is " for us " or " for you," i.e., the men of the community which recognises and confesses Jesus Christ, for His own in this immediate sense. In Eph. 5²⁵ it says expressly for the ἐκκλησία, in Jn. 10¹¹ for the sheep (of the Good Shepherd), in Jn. 15¹³ for His friends, and in Jn. 17¹⁹ for His disciples : " For their sakes I sanctify myself." Only once in the New Testament, as demanded by the context, is it " for me " (Gal. 2²⁰). In these cases the first and third meanings intercross. Jesus acts on behalf of these men, and in their place. The second meaning (of action for a cause or goal) arises where it is explicitly said " for our sins " (Gal. 1⁴, 1 Cor. 15³, 1 Pet. 3¹⁸, 1 Jn. 2²). In these cases what is signified is that He acts because the men referred to are sinners who must be helped, and therefore to expiate and remove their sins as the ground of the impending judgment. Gal. 1⁴ makes the express addition : " That he might deliver us from the present evil aeon, according to the will of God and our Father." And there are some passages where the circle of those to whom this applies still seems to be open outwards. Even in Mk. 10⁴⁵ and *par.* the reference is to the many for whom Jesus will give His life as a ransom, and Calvin himself did not dare to give to this πολλοί the meaning of a restricted number of men. In Jn. 11⁵¹f· we have the remarkable saying that Jesus was to die for the people " and not for that nation only, but also that he should gather together in one the children of God that were scattered abroad." The same extension is to be found even more plainly in 1 Jn. 2² : " He is the propitiation for our sins : and not for ours only, but also περὶ ὅλου τοῦ κόσμου." And so in 2 Cor. 5¹⁴⁻¹⁵ there is the twofold ὑπὲρ πάντων ἀπέθανεν ; in 1 Tim. 2⁶ we are told that " he gave himself a ransom ὑπὲρ πάντων " ; in Heb. 2⁹ we read " that he by the grace of God should taste death ὑπὲρ παντός " ; and most powerfully of all Jn. 6⁵¹ tells us that " the bread that I will give is my flesh, which I will give ὑπὲρ τῆς τοῦ κόσμου ζωῆς "—a saying which finds an exact parallel in the well-known verse Jn. 3¹⁶, where we read that " God so loved the world, that he gave his only begotten Son." What Jesus is " for us " or " for you " in the narrower circle of the disciples and the community He is obviously, through the ministry of this narrower circle, " for all " or " for the world " in the wider or widest circle. And in the majority of the relevant passages this action of Jesus for others (His disciples, His community, the many, all, the world) is His death and passion. This is the primary reference of the more general expressions which speak of His self-offering for men. But we must see the work in its totality. If it is the one side that He " was delivered for our offences," there is also the other that He " was raised again for our justification " (Rom. 4^{25}). It must not be forgotten that as the New Testament sees it the man Jesus who was given up to death is identical with the Lord now living and reigning in the community, and that this Lord again is the One whose universally visible return is for the community the sum of their future and of that of the world. He has overcome death in suffering it. He has risen again from the dead. And it is in this totality that He is " for men." He removes the sting of sin by taking it to Himself, by being made sin (according to the harsh expression of 2 Cor. 5^{21}), by dying for men as though their cause were His. But this delivering-up in our place, in which the traitor Judas is the strange instrument of the will of God, is something which He endures in the omnipotence of the Son of God, executing the divine commission and offering an acceptable sacrifice to God. It is not merely that He suffers Himself to be offered, but He Himself makes the offering, and triumphs in so doing. What is accomplished by Him is the destruction of human sin and the death which is its consequence. And it is done effectively and positively. In His resurrection He reveals Himself as the One He is—the genuine, true and righteous man, the real man, who kept the covenant which all others broke. He kept it in His self-offering, in His death for their sin. The divine and the human fulfilment of the covenant are one and the same in the act of obedience on the part of Jesus, in this final crisis of His saving work. He did this too, and He did it for men, in their favour, for the sake of their cause, and in their place. It was " an offering and a sacrifice to God for a sweetsmelling savour " (εἰς ὀσμὴν εὐωδίας, Eph. 5^2) which He offered " for " us. That is to say, He made us possible and acceptable and pleasing to God, representing us in such a way that we are right with Him. Continuing in the passage in Rom. 8 with which we began, we can thus read that there can be no complaint against the elect of God because God justified them, and no condemnation because Jesus Christ died and is risen again, being now at the right hand of the Father and making intercession for us (ὅς καὶ ἐντυγχάνει ὑπὲρ ἡμῶν, Rom. 8$^{33f.}$). But it is the Epistle to the Hebrews which reveals most frequently the positive significance of ὑπέρ. Jesus as πρόδρομος ὑπὲρ ἡμῶν has passed through the veil into the sanctuary (6^{20}). He has appeared ὑπὲρ ἡμῶν, in the presence of God (9^{24}). He ever lives εἰς τὸ ἐντυγχάνειν ὑπὲρ αὐτῶν (7^{25}). It is also to be noted that according to Paul's account the " for " has a place in the blessing of the bread at the institution of the Lord's Supper : τοῦτό μού ἐστιν τὸ σῶμα τὸ ὑπὲρ ὑμῶν (1 Cor. 11^{24}), and it is similarly used in the blessing of the cup according to the Synoptists : τοῦτό μού ἐστιν τὸ αἷμά μου τῆς διαθήκης τὸ ἐκχυννόμενον ὑπὲρ πολλῶν (Mk. 14^{24} and par.). But if the body and blood ὑπὲρ ὑμῶν or ὑπὲρ πολλῶν undoubtedly refer back to the life of Jesus offered in His death, the decisive event in the Supper is not this recollection as such, but present participation in the fruit of this sacrifice. The offering of My body and blood has for you the effect that as you eat this bread My life is given to you as yours, and that as you drink of this cup you may live with joy and not with sorrow, as innocent and not condemned. As I have given my life for you, it belongs to you. You may live and not die. You may rejoice and not mourn. Do this (" in remembrance of me ") as you eat this bread and drink this cup. Proclaim in this way the Lord's death till He come (1 Cor. 11^{26}), i.e., until His presence, already experienced here and now with this eating and drinking, is revealed to all eyes.

This is the humanity of the man Jesus—the concrete form of His humanity. And the following implications are to be noted.

There is implied first that Jesus has to let His being, Himself, be prescribed and dictated and determined by an alien human being (that of His more near and distant fellows), and by the need and infinite peril of this being. He is not of Himself. He does not live in an original humanity in which He can be far more glorious perhaps in virtue of His divine determination. No, the glory of His humanity is simply to be so fully claimed and clamped by His fellows, by their state and fate, by their lowliness and misery ; to have no other cause but that of the fatal Adam whom He now allows to be really the first, giving him the precedence, ranging Himself wholly with him for his salvation as the second Adam. If there is indeed a powerful I of Jesus, it is only from this Thou, from fallen Adam, from the race which springs from him, from Israel and the sequence of its generations, from a succession of rebels, from a history which is the history of its unfaithfulness. He is pleased to have His life only from His apostles, His community, those whom He called His own and who constantly forsook and forsake Him. He is pleased to be called by them to His own life, to be given the meaning of His life by them. He is pleased to be nothing but the One who is supremely compromised by all these, the Representative and Bearer of all the alien guilt and punishment transferred from them to Him.

There is also implied that His being is wholly with a view to this alien being ; that He is active only in the fact that He makes its deliverance His exclusive task. He moves towards the Thou from which He comes. Disposed by it, He disposes Himself wholly and utterly towards it, in utter disregard of the possibility that another task and activity might better correspond to His divine determination and be more worthy of it. After all, what are these fellow-men ? What are to Him all these representatives of the human race, the more pious and noble and the less ? Why should He not choose and adopt an original work, completely ignoring these pitiable figures in its execution ? Well, He does not do so. He finds it worth His while to live and work for His fellows and their salvation. He does not hold aloof from them. He does not refuse to be like them and with them and in that comprehensive sense for them. He gives Himself freely to them. He has only one goal : to maintain the cause of these men in death and the conquest of death ; to offer up His life for them that they may live and be happy. He therefore serves them, without prospect of reward or repayment, without expecting to receive anything from them which He cannot have far better and more richly without them. He therefore interposes Himself for Adam, for the race, for Israel, for His disciples and community.

" Whosoever of you will be the chiefest, shall be servant of all " (Mk. 10[44]). The man Jesus is the chiefest. He " came not to be ministered unto, but to minister " (v. 45). This is attested by what He said at the institution of the Lord's Supper in the Synoptists and what He did in the foot-washing in John. And He makes no demand upon His own in this respect which He has not first inimitably demonstrated with the act of His own life, thus giving it the character of a demand which can be understood only as the proclamation and offer of the grace of God manifested in Him.

We could hardly see the man Jesus as attested in the New Testament if we closed our eyes to the twofold fact that His being is both from and to His fellows, so that He is with them, and in this way man in His distinctive sovereignty. If we see Him alone, we do not see Him at all. If we see Him, we see with and around Him in ever-widening circles His disciples, the people, His enemies and the countless millions who have not yet heard His name. We see Him as theirs, determined by them and for them, belonging to each and every one of them. It is thus that He is Master, Messiah, King and Lord. "Selfless" is hardly the word to describe this humanity. Jesus is not "selfless." For in this way He is supremely Himself. The theme of the New Testament witness is a kind of incomparable picture of human life and character. What emerges in it is a supreme I wholly determined by and to the Thou. With this twofold definition Jesus is human.

And there is obviously no distance, alienation or neutrality, let alone opposition, between this human definition and the divine. His humanity is not, of course, His divinity. In His divinity He is from and to God. In His humanity He is from and to the cosmos. And God is not the cosmos, nor the cosmos God. But His humanity is in the closest correspondence with His divinity. It mirrors and reflects it. Conversely, His divinity has its correspondence and image in the humanity in which it is mirrored. At this point, therefore, there is similarity. Each is to be recognised in the other. Thus even the life of the man Jesus stands under a twofold determination. But there is harmony between the two. As he is for God, so He is for man; and as He is for man, so He is for God. There is here a *tertium comparationis* which includes His being for God as well as His being for man, since the will of God is the basis and man the object of the work in which this man is engaged.

For a true understanding, we can and must think of what is popularly called the two-fold law of love—for God and the neighbour (Mk. 12$^{29-31}$ and *par.*). It is no accident that it was Jesus who summed up the Law and the prophets in this particular way. He was speaking primarily and decisively of the law of His own twofold yet not opposed but harmonious orientation. He declared Himself, and therefore the grace of God manifested in Him, to be the sum of the Law. The two commandments do not stand in absolute confrontation. It is clear that Jesus did not regard love for God and love for the neighbour as separate but conjoined. Yet they are not identical. In Mt. 22^{38} the command to love God is expressly called the first and great commandment, and the command to love the neighbour is placed alongside it as the second. God is not the neighbour, nor the neighbour God. Hence love for God cannot be simply and directly love for the neighbour. Yet the command to love the neighbour is not merely an appended, subordinate and derivative command. If it is the second, it is also described as like unto the first in Mt. 22^{39}. A true exposition can only speak of a genuinely twofold, i.e., a distinct but connected sphere and sense of

1. *Jesus, Man for other Men*

the one love required of man. It has reference to God, but also to the neighbour. It has the one dimension, but also the other. It finds in the Creator the One who points it to this creature, fellow-man. And it finds in this creature, fellow-man, the one who points it to the Creator. Receiving and taking seriously both these references in their different ways, it is both love for God and love for the neighbour. Thus the structure of the humanity of Jesus Himself is revealed in this twofold command. It repeats the unity of His divinity and humanity as this is achieved without admixture or change, and yet also without separation or limitation.

We must now take a further step, for it is not only by way of His utter obedience to God, but because and in the course of it, that He so fully serves His fellows. The saving work in which He serves His fellows is not a matter of His own choice or caprice but the task which He is given by God. Its execution has nothing to do, therefore, either with the fulfilment of a duty or the exercise of a virtue. For He exists and lives in His saving work. He would not be the One He is if He lived in the execution of another work or in any sense for Himself or a cause alien to this work. He cannot be at all, and therefore for God, without being for men. Hence it is the glory of the One who has commissioned and sent Him, of God, which is revealed and proclaimed in the fact that He is for men. In this there is disclosed the choice and will of God Himself. God first and not the man Jesus is for men. It is He, God, who from all eternity has established the covenant of grace between Himself and man, and has pitied and received Him, pitying and receiving this particularly threatened and needy creature within the threatened cosmos of His creatures and for its deliverance and preservation. The whole witness and revelation of the man Jesus in time, the whole point of His life and existence, is that within the cosmos there should be declared as good news and operative as saving power the fact that God Himself is for man and is his Covenant-partner. God interposes Himself for him, sharing his plight and making Himself responsible for his life and joy and glory. God Himself is his Deliverer. He wills a free man in a free cosmos—freed from the threat to which man has culpably exposed himself and which he is powerless to avert. The God who willed and resolved this, and acted in this way in His incarnate Son, is the basis of the saving work of the man Jesus which has man—His fellow-men exactly as they are—as its object. It is not by accident, then, that Jesus is for man as He is for God. Between His divinity and His humanity there is an inner material connexion as well as a formal parallelism. He could not be for God if He were not on that account for man. The correspondence and similarity between His divinity and humanity is not merely a fact, therefore, but has a material basis. The man Jesus is necessarily for His fellows as He is for God. For God first, as the One who gives Him His commission, as the Father of this Son, is for man. This excludes any possibility of the man Jesus not being for man as He is for God.

Titus 3⁴ gives us the clear-cut description of the incarnation : ὅτε δὲ ἡ χρηστότης καὶ ἡ φιλανθρωπία ἐπεφάνη τοῦ σωτῆρος ἡμῶν θεοῦ. It is to be noted that in company with " kindness " (and in explanation of it) " love " seems here to be almost a quality of God Himself. It is almost integral to His very nature and essence to be our Saviour, ὁ σωτὴρ ἡμῶν θεός. We must be careful to understand this properly. God is not a creature, nor is He necessarily bound to any creature. It is His free decision and act to be " God our Saviour " and the Friend of man. But in this decision and act, in this self-determination to be our Saviour and Friend, we have an eternal presupposition of His creative work and therefore of all creatures. The One who came with the incarnation of His Word could not be other than He was. In His majesty and freedom God willed from all eternity to be for men " God our Saviour." The covenant fulfilled in time is a covenant resolved and established in God Himself before all time. There was no time when God was not the Covenant-partner of man. What appeared, therefore, in the epiphany of the man Jesus was not an accidental manner or disposition of this man, a moral disposition of this creature, but the χρηστότης of the Creator, which is identical with His φιλανθρωπία. This is the inner necessity with which Jesus is at one and the same time both for God and for man.

And now we must take a last and supreme step. There is freedom in God, but no caprice. And the fact that from all eternity God pitied and received man, the grounding of the fellow-humanity of Jesus in the eternal covenant executed in time in His being for man, rests on the freedom of God in which there is nothing arbitrary or accidental but in which God is true to Himself. God for man, participating in and making Himself responsible for him, securing for him fellowship with Himself and therefore His saving help—this whole mystery of the man Jesus is rooted in the mystery of God Himself, which is no mere fact or riddle, but full of meaning and wisdom. And as the mystery of the man Jesus is disclosed to us, we cannot say of the even higher mystery of God Himself that it is simply hidden from us and its meaning and wisdom are unattainable. If " God for man " is the eternal covenant revealed and effective in time in the humanity of Jesus, in this decision of the Creator for the creature there arises a relationship which is not alien to the Creator, to God as God, but we might almost say appropriate and natural to Him. God repeats in this relationship *ad extra* a relationship proper to Himself in His inner divine essence. Entering into this relationship, He makes a copy of Himself. Even in His inner divine being there is relationship. To be sure, God is One in Himself. But He is not alone. There is in Him a co-existence, co-inherence and reciprocity. God in Himself is not just simple, but in the simplicity of His essence He is threefold— the Father, the Son and the Holy Ghost. He posits Himself, is posited by Himself, and confirms Himself in both respects, as His own origin and also as His own goal. He is in Himself the One who loves eternally, the One who is eternally loved, and eternal love ; and in this triunity He is the original and source of every I and Thou, of the I which is eternally from and to the Thou and therefore supremely I. And it is this relationship in the inner divine being which is repeated and

1. *Jesus, Man for other Men*

reflected in God's eternal covenant with man as revealed and operative in time in the humanity of Jesus.

We now stand before the true and original correspondence and similarity of which we have to take note in this respect. We have seen that there is a factual, a materially necessary, and supremely, as the origin of the factual and materially necessary, an inner divine correspondence and similarity between the being of the man Jesus for God and His being for His fellows. This correspondence and similarity consists in the fact that the man Jesus in His being for man repeats and reflects the inner being or essence of God and this confirms His being for God. We obviously have to do here with the final and decisive basis indicated when we spoke of the ontological character, the reality and the radical nature of the being of Jesus for His fellow-men. It is from this context that these derive their truth and power. The humanity of Jesus is not merely the repetition and reflection of His divinity, or of God's controlling will; it is the repetition and reflection of God Himself, no more and no less. It is the image of God, the *imago Dei*.

The " image "—we must not forget the limitation implicit in this term. If the humanity of Jesus is the image of God, this means that it is only indirectly and not directly identical with God. It belongs intrinsically to the creaturely world, to the cosmos. Hence it does not belong to the inner sphere of the essence, but to the outer sphere of the work of God. It does not present God in Himself and in His relation to Himself, but in His relation to the reality distinct from Himself. In it we have to do with God and man rather than God and God. There is a real difference in this respect. We cannot, therefore, expect more than correspondence and similarity. We cannot maintain identity. Between God and God, the Father and the Son and the Son and the Father, there is unity of essence, the perfect satisfaction of self-grounded reality, and a blessedness eternally self-originated and self-renewed. But there can be no question of this between God and man, and it cannot therefore find expression in the humanity of Jesus, in His fellow-humanity as the image of God. In this case we have a complete disparity between the two aspects. There is total sovereignty and grace on the part of God, but total dependence and need on that of man. Life and blessedness may be had by man wholly in God and only in fellowship with Him, in whom they are to be sought and found. On God's side, therefore, we have a Saviour and Deliverer. And He does not enter into alliance with a second God in His eternal covenant with man as revealed in Jesus Christ. Nor does man become a second God when He takes part in this covenant and is delivered by this Deliverer. The one who enters into this covenant is always the creature, man, who would be absolutely threatened without this help and lost if thrown back upon his own resources. It is in the humanity, the saving work of Jesus Christ that the connexion between

God and man is brought before us. It is in this alone that it takes place and is realised. Hence there is disparity between the relationship of God and man and the prior relationship of the Father to the Son and the Son to the Father, of God to Himself.

But for all the disparity—and this is the positive sense of the term " image "—there is a correspondence and similarity between the two relationships. This is not a correspondence and similarity of being, an *analogia entis*. The being of God cannot be compared with that of man. But it is not a question of this twofold being. It is a question of the relationship within the being of God on the one side and between the being of God and that of man on the other. Between these two relationships as such—and it is in this sense that the second is the image of the first—there is correspondence and similarity. There is an *analogia relationis*. The correspondence and similarity of the two relationships consists in the fact that the freedom in which God posits Himself as the Father, is posited by Himself as the Son and confirms Himself as the Holy Ghost, is the same freedom as that in which He is the Creator of man, in which man may be His creature, and in which the Creator-creature relationship is established by the Creator. We can also put it in this way. The correspondence and similarity of the two relationships consists in the fact that the eternal love in which God as the Father loves the Son, and as the Son loves the Father, and in which God as the Father is loved by the Son and as the Son by the Father, is also the love which is addressed by God to man. The humanity of Jesus, His fellow-humanity, His being for man as the direct correlative of His being for God, indicates, attests and reveals this correspondence and similarity. It is not orientated and constituted as it is in a purely factual and perhaps accidental parallelism, or on the basis of a caparicious divine resolve, but it follows the essence, the inner being of God. It is this inner being which takes this form *ad extra* in the humanity of Jesus, and in this form, for all the disparity of sphere and object, remains true to itself and therefore reflects itself. Hence the factuality, the material necessity of the being of the man Jesus for His fellows, does not really rest on the mystery of an accident or caprice, but on the mystery of the purpose and meaning of God, who can maintain and demonstrate His essence even in His work, and in His relation to this work.

For this final step in our exposition we may refer to a narrow but sharply defined and therefore distinct line in St. John's Gospel. In this Gospel, and most strikingly in chapter 17, it emerges in a number of distinctive expressions which form a special group in the Gospel to the extent that they all indicate that the relationship of Jesus to the disciples is not original, but an exact copy of the relationship in which He stands to the Father and the Father to Him.

This first and original relationship is unmistakeably characterised in these passages, and distinguished from the second, by the fact that it is not within the creaturely world but outside it, before and above the whole history which is played out in the cosmos, and therefore in God Himself. According to Jn. 17[5]

1. Jesus, Man for other Men

there is a glory from which Jesus already comes as man, "which I had with thee before the world was." "I have glorified him," is said by the voice from heaven in 12^{28}, and in 1^1 He is the Word which was in the beginning with God. He is not, then, "of the world" ($17^{14, 16}$). The Father loved him (15^9, $17^{23, 26}$). But this aorist does not carry a historical reference to what was, but to what is as it was, to what continues as it began in that pre-temporal beginning. Hence Jesus is in the Father (10^{38}, $14^{10, 20}$, 17^{21}), the Father is in Him (10^{38}, 14^{10}, $17^{21, 23}$), and He and the Father ("we") are one (10^{30}, $17^{11, 22}$). And so He is sent by the Father into the world ($17^{3, 8, 18}$, etc.). This is the original, the relationship within the divine being, the inner divine co-existence, co-inherence and reciprocity.

And in full correspondence and similarity there is the relationship between God and man represented within the creaturely world, as a history played out in the cosmos, in the man Jesus, in His fellow-humanity, in His relationship to His disciples. We remember that the men concerned, in the first instance His disciples, belong properly to the Father, and that it is He who first loved them (14^{21}, 16^{27}, 17^{23}). But they are given by Him to the Son, and therefore to Jesus. Why? The basic answer is given by the word from heaven in 12^{28}: "I have both glorified him, and will glorify him again." The point is that the glory proper to Jesus in His relationship as Son to the Father is repeated and reflected on this new level and in this new relationship. "And now, O Father, glorify me . . . with the glory which I had with thee before the world was." "I pray . . . for them which thou hast given me . . . and I am glorified in them." In accordance with the fact that the Son is not of the world, the same can be said of the disciples ($17^{14, 16}$). In accordance with the fact that the Father is in Him, He is in them (17^{23}). In accordance with the fact that He is in the Father, they are in Him, Jesus (14^{20}). In accordance with the fact that He and the Father are one, they are to be one ($17^{11, 22}$), and "no man is able to pluck them out of his hand" (10^{29}). Finally, in accordance with the fact that the Father has sent Him into the world, He sends them (17^{18}). And if we now read: "Neither pray I for these alone, but for them also which shall believe on me through their word; that they all may be one; as thou, Father, art in me, and I in thee, that they also may be one in us: that the world may believe that thou hast sent me" (17^{20-21}), we are obviously reminded even in this context of the bursting of the inner circle of the community outwards in favour of all men, of the whole world. He who is already glorified by the Father in His relationship to Him is again glorified in them, in His relationship to men. Thus the divine original creates for itself a copy in the creaturely world. The Father and the Son are reflected in the man Jesus. There could be no plainer reference to the *analogia relationis* and therefore the *imago Dei* in the most central, i.e., the christological sense of the term.

Our starting-point was the question of the inner relationship between the determination of man as the covenant-partner of God on the one side and his creaturely and cosmic nature, his humanity, on the other; of the relationship which is not affected even by the sin of man, and therefore persists even in sinful man. We asked how far man's humanity may in all circumstances be a sign of his divine determination. We asked concerning the mystery of faith of the reference to the grace of God grounded in human nature as such. We have given a first answer to this question in relation to the man Jesus. The answer is that the inner relationship in this man is a relationship of clear agreement because His humanity, in correspondence and similarity with His determination for God and therefore with God Himself, as God's image, consists in the fact that, as He is for God, He is also for man, for His fellows. This gives us a valid basis on which to take up our true question—the anthropological question, directed to all men generally, of this relationship, of the sign given to man in His humanity, of the mystery of faith of the reference to the grace of God in human nature itself.

2. THE BASIC FORM OF HUMANITY

We now turn from the man Jesus to other men—to man in general. Christology is not anthropology. We cannot expect, therefore, to find directly in others the humanity of Jesus, and therefore His fellow-humanity, His being for man, and therefore that final and supreme determination, the image of God. Jesus is man for His fellows, and therefore the image of God, in a way which others cannot even approach, just as they cannot be for God in the sense that He is. He alone is the Son of God, and therefore His humanity alone can be described as the being of an I which is wholly from and to the fellow-human Thou, and therefore a genuine I. In this respect we do not even have to take into account the fact that all other men are sinners and have turned aside from God. This means, of course, that their humanity (in more or less complete antithesis to this description) actually develops from their contradiction of the Thou to fresh opposition, and cannot therefore be a genuine I. But let us assume that there is in every man at least a serious even if hopeless striving in the other direction. The difference between Jesus and ourselves is still indissoluble. It is quite fundamental. For of no other man can we say that from the very outset and in virtue of his existence he is for others. Of no other man can we say that he is the Word of God to men, and therefore that he is directly and inwardly affected by them, or sent, commissioned and empowered to be and act in their place and as their representative, interposing and giving himself for all others, making their life possible and actual in and with his own, and thus being for them, their guarantor, in this radical and universal sense. There can be no repetition of this in anthropology. We are the victims of idealistic illusions if we deck out the humanity of man generally with features exclusive to that of the man Jesus. Man generally may mean and give a great deal to His fellows, but he cannot be their Deliverer or Saviour, not even in a single instance. On the contrary, he is the being on whose behalf the man Jesus is that which is peculiar to Him.

On the other hand, when we ask concerning humanity in general, the fact of the distinctive humanity of Jesus clearly points us in a certain direction and warns us no less clearly against its opposite.

If the humanity of Jesus consists in the fact that He is for other men, this means that for all the disparity between Him and us He affirms these others as beings which are not merely unlike Him in His creaturely existence and therefore His humanity, but also like Him in some basic form. Where one being is for others, there is necessarily a common sphere or form of existence in which the " for " can be possible and effective. If other men were beings whose humanity stood under an absolutely different and even contradictory determination from that of Jesus, it would be idle and confusing to call both Jesus and these others " men." For in the two cases the term would refer to quite different beings which would be better denoted by different terms. It would also be difficult to see how the " man " Jesus could be for and from and to other " men," how He could be inwardly affected by their being, how He could be called and sent to be their Saviour and commissioned and empowered to accomplish their deliverance, how He could interpose Himself with His human life for these other beings, acting and suffering and conquering in their place and as their Representative. The whole distinction of His humanity would thus fall to the ground as quite impossible.

On the other hand, it would also be hard to see how these others could become what Christians are called in Rom. 14^{15} and 1 Cor. 8^{11}: the beings or brothers for whom Christ died; those who are helped by the death of Christ, for whose human existence His death can mean deliverance. The creaturely nature of these beings cannot be alien or opposed to that of Christ, for all the disparity.

Where the saving work of the man Jesus is possible and effective in others, where there is this fellowship between Him and others, we have to ask concerning a co-ordination between Himself and others which is not just established by this fellowship but presupposed in the fact that it is made possible and actual. We have thus to ask concerning a basic form of the humanity of other men, of man in general, in which there is given and revealed the presupposition of the fact that the man Jesus can be for them. Is it true that the character of the humanity of the man Jesus as fellow-humanity is not an accident but is grounded in the will of God? Is it true that in this character of His humanity Jesus is the image of God? We have seen that this question is to be answered in the affirmative, and on what grounds. But is it not also true that this God is the Creator not merely of the man Jesus but of all men, so that in the form, and especially in the basic form, of the humanity of all men we have to see the creaturely essence which they are given by God? On these basic assumptions, a theological anthropology is forced to recognise that the question of that presupposition is not merely legitimate but necessary.

We cannot, therefore, stop at the christological assertion that the man Jesus is for others. We have also to ask in respect of others how far as men they are beings which can be represented by the man

Jesus in His suffering and conquering. We have to ask what it is that makes them possible for the covenant which is revealed and operative for them, which God has concluded with them, in this being of Jesus. We have to ask what it is that makes them capable of entering into covenant with God as the creatures of God.

Self-evidently, we do not ask concerning a worth or merit on the basis of which man has a claim to be the covenant-partner of God and to have the man Jesus act on his behalf. There is no claim of this kind; no claim of the creature against the Creator. It is the inconceivable grace of God that He takes him to Himself, that in the fellow-humanity of Jesus the free choice of the divine will is revealed and exercised as love for man. But since it is revealed and exercised in this way, since this God who is inconceivably gracious to him is the Creator of man, of every man, then the creatureliness of man, his human nature, his humanity, cannot be alien to this grace of God (no matter how inconceivable its address to it) but must necessarily confront it as it were with a certain familiarity.

We must be clear what we mean even when we speak of being capable of entering into covenant. We do not ask concerning an ability on the part of man to take up the relationship to God in covenant with Him, to be His covenant-partner. His creaturely essence has no power to do this. He can do it only as God makes him His partner, as He calls him to take up this relationship, as he exists as the one who is summoned to do so. It is again the inconceivable grace of God that He concludes this covenant with man, that He calls him to it, and sets him in a position to respond. But since He does this—He who is also man's Creator—this is only to say again that man's creaturely essence cannot be alien or opposed to this grace of God, but must confront it with a certain familiarity. If for the restoration and defence of His glory in the cosmos the grace of God has claimed the man Jesus, this shows at least that human creatureliness is not regarded as unsuitable or unserviceable, but as adapted to be employed to this end. We do not ask, then, concerning a capacity to enter into covenant which man himself has to actualise, but concerning that which makes him as the work of His Creator possible, serviceable, adapted and well-pleasing as His covenant-partner before all other creatures, and to that extent capable of entering into covenant.

Here, too, we can and must ask concerning a certain correspondence and similarity. If God had given to man a nature neutral and opposed to His grace and love and therefore to the fellow-humanity of Jesus, alien and antithetical from the very outset to covenant-partnership with Himself, how would He have made him the being marked off for this partnership? A second creation would have been needed to make this partnership possible and actual. And this second creation, in contrast to the new creation attested in Scripture, would have to be regarded as a contradiction of the first, materially altering and even

2. The Basic Form of Humanity

replacing it. If we are to avoid this conclusion, there has to be a common factor, and therefore a correspondence and similarity, between the determination of man for this covenant-partnership and his creatureliness, between the humanity of Jesus and that of man generally.

Again, we cannot stop at the mere assertion that the man Jesus is the image of God. But in relation to other men we have to ask how far as men they are beings with which Jesus can be ranged as the image of God. If God has in this One, and only in this One, His own image in the cosmos ; if it is the inner essence of God which has its creaturely correspondence and similarity in His fellow-humanity, in His being for men, how can this be denied to those for whom He intervenes, to whom God has turned so seriously and totally in this One ? If this One is their Saviour and Deliverer—He whose humanity is to take their place and give His life for them—and if as such He is the creaturely image of God Himself, how can they be creatures which completely lack this image, which do not at least prefigure and indicate it, when they are creatures of the same God and determined as such for covenant-partnership with Him ? We emphasise again that there can be no question of their being simply and directly that which Jesus alone is. They are not simply and directly the covenant-partners of God as His creatures ; they are destined to become this. And this means concretely that they are destined to participate in the benefits of the fellow-humanity of that One, to be delivered by Him. In their creatureliness they have need of the fact, and they are promised, that He, the One who is the image of God, is for them. What they themselves are in their relationship to God depends on this determination. Its reality, therefore, is not in themselves, but in Him, that One. But this determination, this reality, is genuinely present and is to be taken seriously in Him. From the very first, even in their creatureliness, they stand in the light which is shed by Him. But if they are in His light, they cannot be dark in themselves, but bright with His light. We thus ask concerning their brightness in His light. To that extent we ask concerning the image of God in which every part as such has a share ; concerning the correspondence and similarity with the essence of God peculiar to humanity as such. If it were not wholly proper to it, how could it be compatible with the essence of God to give Himself to solidarity with man as He has done in making the covenant with Himself the meaning and purpose of its creation and therefore the determination of its humanity, in Himself becoming man in Jesus Christ ? For all the disparity, there is here presupposed a common factor, a parity, not merely between Jesus and other men, but, because between Jesus and other men, between God and man generally.

When we ask : What is humanity, human creatureliness ? we must first ask : What is its basic form ? In other words, to what extent does human essence correspond to the determination of man to be the covenant-partner of God ? Our criterion in answering this question is the humanity of the man Jesus. If, for all the distance, there is between His humanity and ours a common factor, a similarity for all the dissimilarity, now that we turn to ourselves, to man generally, we must first make a great distinction and differentiation in respect of the human essence presupposed in our question. We cannot start with the assumption that there is a known and accepted picture of man and humanity before which we can pause and from the contours of which we can read off that which corresponds and is similar in man to the humanity of Jesus, and therefore supremely his participation in the image of God actualised in the humanity of Jesus. In theological anthropology there can be no question of giving a theological meaning to a given text (in this case a picture of man assumed to be generally known and accepted). This procedure would merely arouse the justifiable suspicion that the text itself (the known and accepted picture of man) is the constant and certain factor, whereas the theological interpretation is variable and uncertain like any other. No, in theological anthropology what man is, is decided by the primary text, i.e., by the humanity of the man Jesus. And the application of this criterion means that a whole sphere of supposed humanity is ruled out as non-human from the very first, and cannot be considered, because that which in it is regarded and alleged to be human stands in a contradiction to the humanity of Jesus which denies the essential similarity between Him and us and therefore excludes the possibility of the human creature as a covenant-partner of God, thus destroying the unity of creation and covenant. It is against any line of anthropological investigation and exposition which results in this denial, exclusion and destruction that we are warned *a limine* by our christological basis, even though we may seem to have very good reasons for accepting the picture of man proposed. We do not have to regard as human, as the essence of man which God created good, that which measured by this criterion is non-human, i.e., not yet or no longer human. On the contrary, in the application of this criterion we are free to excise from the proposed picture of man all those features which are incompatible with the similarity which we presuppose for all the dissimilarity between the man Jesus and us other men. That which is incompatible with this similarity is *ipso facto* non-human.

The excision with which we must begin will be as follows. It is not yet or no longer seen what humanity is when there is ascribed to man an existence which is abstract, i.e., abstracted from the coexistence of his fellows. No enriching, deepening or heightening of the concept of humanity in other directions, even religious, can excuse, make good or compensate this basic defect. If we see man in and for himself, and therefore without his fellows, we do not see him at all. If we see him in opposition or even neutrality towards his fellows, we

2. The Basic Form of Humanity

do not see him at all. If we think that his humanity is only subsequently and secondarily determined, as an incidental enrichment, by the fact that he is not alone, we do not see him at all. If we do not realise and take into account from the very outset, from the first glance and word, the fact that he has a neighbour, we do not see him at all. At this point we have no option either to be tolerant or intolerant. We can only exclude. If a picture of man does not satisfy this demand, it has nothing whatever to do with the human essence in question, and it cannot be brought under discussion. We ask concerning the brightness of man in the light of the man Jesus, in the light of the fact that the man Jesus is for him, and therefore can be for him, because between the man Jesus and this other man there is similarity as well as dissimilarity. A man without his fellows, or radically neutral or opposed to his fellows, or under the impression that the co-existence of his fellows has only secondary significance, is a being which *ipso facto* is fundamentally alien to the man Jesus and cannot have Him as Deliverer and Saviour. To be sure, He is the Deliverer and Saviour of sinful man, and therefore of the man who denies His fellow-humanity, acting as though he had no God and no neighbour, and therefore showing himself to be supremely non-human. But this does not mean that this sinner has ceased to be a man, or that we are allowed or even obliged to interpret His inhumanity as his humanity or the work of sin as the good creation of God. Even the sinful man who denies his humanity and in a blatant or more refined way turns his back on his fellows stands in the light of the humanity of Jesus. He acts contrary to his humanity, and he cannot be excused the guilt which he incurs by projecting a picture of man according to which his inhumanity—his isolation from his fellows, or neutrality or opposition in relation to them, or the casualness of their significance for him—belongs to his humanity as a possibility of the nature which he has been given by his Creator. No, even as he denies it, his creaturely nature stands in the light of the humanity of Jesus, and it is bright in this light, accusing him of sinning in his inhumanity not only against God and his neighbour but also primarily and finally against himself, and yet not ceasing to bind him to his Saviour and Deliverer. To sin is to wander from a path which does not cease to be the definite and exclusive path of man even though he leaves it. The fact that man sins does not mean that God ceases to be God and therefore man man. In this context, too, we must say that man does not accomplish a new creation by sinning. He cannot achieve any essential alteration of the human nature which he has been given. He can only shame this nature and himself. He can only bring himself into supreme peril. But the fact that he has in the man Jesus his Saviour and Deliverer is the pledge that he has not ceased to be a man, a being ordered in relation to this Jesus. The fact that the Good Shepherd has acted on behalf of His lost sheep shows that He does not give it up for lost but still numbers it with His flock and deals with it as His own and not an alien possession. This is what makes the idea of a man without his fellows, in any form, quite intolerable. This is what rules it out from the very first. Theological anthropology cannot enter the sphere where this man without his fellows is considered as a serious possibility. It knows man well enough as the man of sin, but not as the man who actualises his creaturely nature in his sin, whom God has created for this actualisation. It cannot blame God for what man has made of himself. And it cannot exculpate man from the permanent reproach of the transgression with which he denies the truth, the truth of his Creator and his own truth. We take sin lightly if we spare sinful man this reproach, giving him the evasion that as a sinner he has forfeited and lost his humanity, or that God has created him in a humanity in which he can choose either to be man or not, and in which inhumanity is more probable than humanity. Every supposed humanity which is not radically and from the very first fellow-humanity is inhumanity. At this point a distinction must be made *a limine*, and humanity must be protected against its decisive and definitive destruction. If we take away fellow-man from the picture of man, and describe the latter as a being which is alien, opposed or casual in relation to him, we have not merely given an inadequate or partially false representation of man, but described a different being altogether. There is nothing else for it. In this respect theological anthropology must be quite pitiless in its opposition to every attempt to seek real man outside the history of his responsibility to God. The very reality of man in his responsibility before God necessarily gives us the negative rule for an understanding of the basic form of his humanity—that in no circumstances may it be sought in that abstraction, in a humanity without the fellow-man.

At this point two marginal observations may be made on the general theological situation, especially at the present time.

1. The last war, with all that led up to it and all its possible consequences, has posed afresh the problem of humanity from the particular angle of the question of the rights, dignity and sanctity of the fellow-man. Humanity stands at the crossroads. In its future development as humanity, will it be for man or against him ? Behind the political, social and economic possibilities there stands always with the same urgency, if in different forms, the necessity of this decision. The lot may be cast one way or the other according to the various anthropological views more or less consciously adopted. And it may well be that an anthropology and ethics of compromise is no longer adequate because the dynamic of a resolute humanity without the fellow-man may perhaps steal a march on all mediating positions and finally dominate the field with fatal consequences. Those who cannot approve this development are seriously asked to-day whether they are capable of producing from their own anthropology and ethics an equally and even more dynamic championship of the fellow-man. And the further question then becomes insistent, as it is already, whether any anthropology or ethics is able to do this apart from the Christian. A wholehearted adoption of this position is possible only where the hostility, neutrality and antithesis between man and man is radically overcome, i.e., in the pre-

2. The Basic Form of Humanity

supposed concept of humanity, and known and rejected as inhumanity. Where this is not the case, there can be only half-way teachings, and it is doubtful whether even a delaying action can be successful against the assault of a humanity without the fellow-man. The exclusiveness which dares—because it must—to repudiate this humanity as inhumanity *a limine* and without discussion is not possible, as far as one can see, except on the basis of a Christian and theological anthropology and ethics.

2. But all that glitters is not gold, and we cannot accept as genuine Christian and theological anthropology everything that claims to be such. Where the claim is justified there will necessarily be ruthlessness at this point, i.e., in the rejection of all humanity without or against the fellow-man. And this raises the question of its criterion and its consistent application. If it has a christological basis, then, as we have seen, it has a criterion which will prove to be divisive from the very first, at the very first sight of the object. A humanity without the fellow-man will necessarily be abandoned as inhuman at the very first step. Humanity for man will remain as the only possibility. But in modern theology it is not the rule to base anthropology on Christology and therefore to use this criterion from the very outset. The question arises whether the same radicalness and ruthlessness are really possible on the other paths which are more customary. Perhaps they only lead again to mediating and therefore indefensible positions. Perhaps this type of Christian and theological anthropology cannot offer any effective resistance to the onslaught of a humanity without the fellow-man. And in the light of its lack of radicalness and ruthlessness the question then arises whether it can really claim to be a Christian and theological anthropology at all.

We have to rule out the possibility of a humanity without the fellow-man. Hence we must not discuss it. But it will be worth our while to consider briefly what we are ruling out, what conception of man we are passing by without discussion. We may begin by admitting that it is not self-evident that it should be ruled out in this way, and thus passed by without discussion. In doing this, we follow the higher right of theological necessity. But on behalf of the rejected humanity which is either without or against the fellow-man, or pays him only casual attention, it may be argued that it is not only infinitely more appealing but even self-evident on a non-theological view. If we bracket the Christian judgment, does not the word "man" immediately and at bottom definitively conjure up a being which is basically and properly for itself, so that although it may be vaguely recognised in others it can and is seen immediately and directly only in the self? According to this constantly victorious conception humanity consists in the fact that I am, that I am for myself, and neither from nor to others. In certain circumstances this "I am" can have a powerful radius. And it is not to be subjected to a moralistic judgment and condemnation as limitation or self-seeking. For after all, it will somewhere embrace others as well. The only trouble is that basically and properly it is without them or against them or only secondarily and occasionally with them and for them. "I am"—this is the forceful assertion which we are all engaged in making and of which we are convinced that none can surpass it in urgency or importance; the assertion of the self in which we can neither be replaced by any nor restrained by any. " I am " means that I satisfy myself even in the sense that I have to do justice to myself, that I am pressingly claimed by myself. " I am " means that I stand under the irresistible urge to maintain myself, but also to make something of myself, to develop myself, to try out myself, to exercise and prove myself. " I am " means further, however, that in every development and activity outwards I must and will at all costs maintain and assert myself, not dissipating and losing myself, but concentrating even as I expand, and getting even as I give. It means that I must and will acquire and have personality. But the radius is even wider than this. " I am " means that I may and must live ; that I may and must live out my life in the material and spiritual cosmos, enjoying, working, playing, fashioning, possessing, achieving and exercising power ; that I may and must in my own place and within my own limits— and who is to say where these are to be drawn ?—have my share in the goods of the earth, in the fulness of human knowledge and capacity, in the further development of human technique and art and organisation. These are powerful projections of the " I am " outwards into space and time and its truth and poetry, or rather its poetry and truth, its myth and history. And to these projections there certainly belongs the fashioning of a relationship to what is called " heaven " in the Bible and " God," " the gods," or " the divine " elsewhere ; the construction of a positive or negative, believing or sceptical, original or conventional position with reference to the ultimate limits and mystery of life, the incomprehensible which will finally confront all our comprehension. And inevitably in this onward progress of the " I am " the encounter with fellow-men will have its own specific and determinative part ; the burning questions whether this or that person is important or indifferent to me, whether he attracts or repels me, whether he helps and serves or obstructs and harms me, whether he is superior to me or I can master him and am thus superior to him. To these projections there also belong the dealings with him, with all the selection and rejection, the conflict, peace and renewal of conflict, the constant hide-and-seek, the domination and dependence, the morality and immorality which these dealings inevitably involve and without which life would certainly be much easier and simpler but also much poorer and duller. The only thing is that here too we have a projection of the " I am " outwards. Even the many forms of our fellows are ultimately elements in our own myth or history, not found but invented and decked out by us, and merely speaking the words which we put on their lips. There are merely more or less serviceable or unserviceable figures in our own play, drawn into ourselves to the extent that we have in some way transformed them into something that belongs to us. In their genuine otherness and particularity they are without like the rest of the cosmos. Originally and properly within I am still alone by myself : in my freedom in relation to the

2. The Basic Form of Humanity

whole cosmos; with my poetry and truth; with the question of my needs and desires and loves and hates; with my known and sometimes unknown likes and dislikes; with my capacities and propensities; as my own doctor, as the sovereign architect, director, general and dictator of the whole, of my own earth and heaven, my cosmos, God and fellow-men; as the incomparable inventor and sustainer of myself; in first and final solitude. Within this total conception there is naturally an infinite range of colours and contours, of nuances and emphases, to the final and apparently self-exclusive extremes. It is a unity only in general. In detail the variations are so great as to make the common features almost unrecognisable. It never repeats itself. It constantly takes on new forms not only in the different ages and cultures, not only in the distinction of individuals, but also within their own specific development, in youth and maturity and age, in the changing stations and circumstances of life. But we should not be misled. The " I am " may often be less powerfully at work as the basis and beginning of all things. We may not always see that in everything else we really have projections of this I. Our fellows in their otherness and particularity may often be more forcefully and obstinately and pertinently at work than our depiction suggests. Yet the overwhelming unity of the whole remains—of an attempted humanity in which the fellow-man has no constitutive function. And, if for a moment we suspend our Christian judgment, we at once recognise that it is the most obvious thing in the world to answer the question of humanity with perhaps a more profound and purified and convincing modification of this view. We have to realise what it means that theological anthropology cannot grasp this most obvious of all possibilities, but must reject it *a limine*.

By way of illustration we may refer to Friedrich Nietzsche. We do this for two reasons. He developed this conception of humanity with unequalled logic and perspicacity. And in his refusal to evade its deepest root and supreme consequence, in his enthusiastic acceptance of them, he resolutely and passionately and necessarily rejected, not a caricature of the Christian conception of humanity, but in the form of a caricature the conception itself. He shows us how necessary it is that we for our part must less violently but no less resolutely reject the conception of humanity of which he is a classical exponent.

In 1888 Nietzsche wrote his *Ecce homo*, which was published in 1908. This is an autobiography, of the same genre as Augustine's and Rousseau's *Confessions*, but with no admission of mistakes, and constituting an unequivocal final testimony for the future interpretation of the author. Shortly after writing it, Nietzsche was declared to be afflicted with an incurable mental sickness. It was understandable that Franz Overbeck, one of his closest friends, should at first prevent its publication. But he was not justified on material grounds, for whether Nietzsche was already ill or not when he wrote this book there can be no doubt that in it he rightly perceived and summed up the final intentions of his purposes and work as they had marked him from the very first.

On the first page of *Ecce homo* we read in heavy type the statement: " Hear me, for I am he; do not at any price mistake me " (Krönersche-Klassiker-Ausgabe, p. 307). And even more menacingly on the final page, again in heavy type: "Am I understood?—Dionysius against the Crucified..." (p. 433). The first saying is a bizarre but genuine form of the first and final proposition of humanity without the fellow-man. Nietzsche liked to see it represented in the form of the ancient Greek god Dionysius. The second is the repudiation of Christianity self-evident on the basis of this humanity.

"Hear me, for I am he; do not at any price mistake me." We shall first try to see what this means. Goethe too, whom Nietzsche usually although not always mentioned respectfully as a precursor, wanted to be regarded and estimated as "he," with a certain solemnity and joyous reverence making himself and his way and culture and work the theme of special consideration and explanation, and having an obvious consciousness of himself. But Nietzsche was basically and properly self-consciousness and nothing more. His angrily uncertain: "Do not at any price mistake me" and later his eager: "Am I understood?" would have been quite unthinkable on the lips of Goethe. Goethe was on the same path as Nietzsche, an exponent of the same "I am," but he knew when to stop, and said certain ultimate things about this beginning and end either not at all or very seldom and with great caution. He knew how often and not unjustly he was praised for keeping to the golden mean. He could do so, and necessarily, because his self-consciousness was continually filled with the most attentive and deeply interested world-consciousness. The quiet fulfilment of almost uninterrupted work in the world outside gives to his picture, and his occasional self-portraits, the character of a cheerful sanity in which he could not be tempted by any anxiety lest he should be confused with others, because he was far too worldly wise even to make this a matter of debate. But Nietzsche was the prophet of that humanity without the fellow-man. He did not merely reveal its secret; he blabbed it out. He was in a non-classical form what Goethe was in a classical. Apollo did not content him; it had to be Dionysius. Was he no longer sure of himself, as Goethe so obviously was? He once described himself as a victim of decadence, an example of the decline of the human type which he thought to be perfect and sometimes found to be represented and actualised in certain respects in Goethe. Did he perhaps really speak the final word of this humanity? At any rate, he had to cry out something which was in Goethe, and to which he occasionally gave expression, but which he wisely preferred to keep to himself—the fact that in a last and deepest isolation he and he alone was the eye and measure and master and even the essence of all things. What Goethe quietly lived out Nietzsche had to speak out continually with the nervous violence of ill-health.

Basically, when he was not engaged in polemics but spoke positively, Nietzsche never spoke except about himself. If we study him, it constantly strikes us how little he deals with material and objective problems. What he himself was not, if it did not repel him and he it, interested him only as a paradigm and symbol, or, to use his own expression, a projection of himself. And even when he repelled, and was repelled, it was only because the object concerned either could not be used as a paradigm of himself (like Christianity), or could no longer be put to this service (like the later Wagner). Nietzsche was originally a Greek philologist, but he no longer needed Greek philology when he had discovered Dionysius as "the one root of all Greek art," as the "philosophising god," and this Dionysius was none other than himself, Friedrich Nietzsche. For a while he devoted himself with fiery energy to natural science under the banner of evolution, but when probably in this sphere he had discovered the "will to power" as the supreme and proper form of human existence—and this, of course, as an unmistakeable but impressive symbol of his own will—the subject did not present him with any further interest or problems. He wrote concerning "Schopenhauer as Educator," but the instructive Schopenhauer was admittedly he himself. And he magnified Wagner so long as he could find and represent in him himself and his own paganism—which was no longer possible after the

2. The Basic Form of Humanity 103

personal injury done him by Wagner's *Parsifal*, in which he discerned a pilgrimage to Canossa. " Delight in things, it is said, but what is really meant is delight in oneself through the medium of things " (*Menschliches, allzu Menschliches*, p. 366)—this is something which Goethe could never have admitted. Nietzsche did not merely admit it; he openly championed it as a maxim. In fact, he never really had any other. And so Zarathustra too—and there was little need for the pride with which Nietzsche expressly assures us of the fact—is none other than he himself, and this time the true Nietzsche. Nietzsche admits that by his ophthalmic affliction he had been redeemed from " the book " and had not read for many years—" the greatest benefit which I have ever experienced " (*Ecce homo*, p. 384). For to read as the scholar reads is not to think but simply to answer to an attraction, to react. " I call it criminal that at the crack of dawn, in all the youth and freshness of his powers, the scholar—a decadent—should read a book " (p. 349). There is apparently only one exception : " As I see it, it is one of the most singular distinctions that anyone can evince to take up a book of my own :—I myself will guarantee that he will take off his shoes, not to speak of boots. . . . When Doctor Heinrich von Stein once honestly complained that he could not understand a word of my Zarathustra, I told him that this was quite usual. To have understood, i.e., experienced six sentences of it is to be lifted on to a higher mortal plane than ' modern ' men can reach " (p. 355). Nietzsche was of the opinion that with his Zarathustra he had given humanity a greater gift than any so far given (p. 309). He declared that in comparison with it the rest of human activity was poor and limited ; that a Goethe or a Shakespeare could not last a single moment in this atmosphere of tremendous passion and exaltation ; that face to face with Zarathustra Dante was merely a believer and not one who creates truth, a masterful spirit, a destiny ; that the authors of the *Veda* were priests and unworthy to unloose the shoes of a Zarathustra. And this is only the least to be said concerning it, giving no conception of the distance, the " azure isolation " of the work. " The spirits and qualities of all great souls put together could not produce a single speech of Zarathustra " (p. 400 f.). Naturally this sounds disordered. But it is the position which Nietzsche indicated, and to the representation of which he dedicated his life's work. And what is this position but the " I am " of humanity without the fellow-man, except that this time it is adopted without condition or restraint, in all its nakedness ? I am—in " azure isolation." Nietzsche often thought that he lived in indescribable wealth in this isolation, and these were the moments when he could beseechingly and yet also angrily point to the fact that he had infinite things to give, that infinite things were to be received from him. But then he had to contradict himself, for how could he give wealth and life and joy in this isolation ? On the contrary, " when I have given myself for a moment to my Zarathustra, I walk up and down the room for half an hour, unable to master an unbearable spasm of sobbing " (p. 432).

> " The desert grows : woe to those who fight it,
> Stone grates on stone, the desert gulps and swallows,
> And dreadful death looks gleaming brown
> And cowers—life is a cowering . . .
> Forget not man, hired out to pleasure,
> Thou art the stone, the desert, thou art death " (p. 447).

And how is Zarathustra to be anything for others or give anything to them ? If there were others, he would not be Zarathustra. " First give thyself, O Zarathustra " (p. 471). But he cannot do this even if he desired now that it has been and is his necessity and triumph to be " 6,000 feet beyond man and time " (p. 391). " The whole fact of man lies at a dreadful distance below him " (p. 309).

> " Alone !
> And who would dare
> To be a guest,
> Thy guest ? . . ." (p. 449).

To whom is he, the superman, the absolute " I am," to give himself ? And if there is someone, will he thank him for this or any gift ?

> " Who can love thee,
> The unattainable ?
> Thy blessing makes all dry
> And poor in love
> —a thirsty land . . ." (p. 470).

To this very day Nietzsche has been much admired and honoured and loved. But he had no use for the fact ; he could not love in return. Nothing is more striking than that he had no use at all for women. " They all love me," he could say, but without any satisfaction. He can only ignore them or heap upon them scorn and his choicest invective. And in his very rejection of them he regards himself as " the first psychologist of the eternal-feminine " (p. 363). Yet in addition he cannot repay or be faithful to even the best and most sincere of his male friends. " At an absurdly early age, when I was only seven, I knew that no human word would reach me, but has this ever caused me any obvious concern ? " (p. 353). " An extreme candour towards me is for me a necessary condition of existence ; I cannot live in conditions of insincerity. . . . This means that my intercourse with men constitutes no little problem of patience ; my humanity does not consist in fellow-feeling with men, but in restraint from fellow-feeling. . . . My humanity is a continual self-conquest." It is also to be noted, of course, that Nietzsche described the contempt for man, misanthropy, as his greatest danger, and one from which he thought that he had finally redeemed himself. But how ? By fleeing to a height " where there are no companions to sit at the well " and drink with him.

> " On the tree of the future we build our nest ;
> Eagles will bring us solitary ones food in their beaks.
> Not food which the unclean may eat,
> For they would think they were eating fire,
> And burn their mouths.
>
> We have no homesteads here for the unclean,
> To their bodies and spirits our fortune
> Would be an icy cavity,
> And we shall live over them like strong winds,
> Neighbours of the eagles and the snow and the sun,
> Like strong winds " (p. 329 f.).

In this way Zarathustra is lord even of misanthropy. But how ? " Man is for him something unshaped, material, an ugly stone which needs the sculptor." His only impulse towards man is that of the hammer to the stone.

> " Oh, ye men, in the stone there sleeps a picture,
> The picture of all pictures !
> Oh that it must sleep in the hardest and ugliest stone !
> My hammer rages furiously against its prison,
> And pieces fly from the stone,
> But what care I ! " (p. 406 f.).

Has he ever been obviously concerned that man is either unattainable or attain-

2. The Basic Form of Humanity

able only in such a way as to cause a repugnance from which he must seek that lofty refuge with the eagles and strong winds ? And yet Zarathustra does frequently seem to be very greatly troubled by this inaccessibility. It is intrinsic to the superman, to Dionysius, to Zarathustra to be almost torn asunder by sorrow at having to be the superman, Dionysius, Zarathustra.

> " The world—a door
> To a thousand deserts silent and cold !
> Who has lost
> What thou lost, can find no rest.
>
> Thou standest pale
> Condemned to winter wandering
> Like smoke
> Always seeking the cold heavens.
>
> Fly, bird, rasping
> Thy song like a wilderness-bird !—
> Conceal, thou fool,
> Thy bleeding heart in ice and disdain !
>
> The crows cry
> In whirring flight to the city.
> —Soon it will snow
> And woe then to him who has no home ! "
> (*Fröhl. Wiss.*, p. 392 f.).

The only thing is that he soon rises up again like the eagle, scorning himself for his weakness, and finding joy and exultation and self-glory in the very thing which pains him :

> " Yea, I know whence I derive !
> Insatiable as the flame,
> I burn and consume myself.
> All I touch is light,
> And what I leave a cinder.
> I am indeed a flame ! "
> (*Fröhl. Wiss.*, p. 30).

Which prevails—the complaint or the rejoicing ? " I know my fate. The memory of something dreadful will be linked with my name, of an unparalleled crisis, of the most profound clash of conscience, of a decision conjured up against everything that has so far been believed and demanded and held sacred. I am no man ; I am dynamite " (*Ecce homo*, p. 422). Is this complaint or rejoicing, or both ? In the same breath Nietzsche can call himself both the incomparable bearer of good news and the " destroyer *par excellence.*" " I am easily the most terrible man there has ever been, but this does not mean that I am not also the greatest benefactor." He promises that only because of him are there renewed hopes. And yet he prophesies : " There will be wars such as never were on earth. Only after me will there be high politics on earth " (p. 412, 423 f.). According to view or inclination, we can be deaf to his true message, rejecting or believing either the one or the other, the *evangelion* or *dysangelion*, but his real place is beyond good and evil, not merely like that of a Hercules choosing between the two, but genuinely as the place of the superman, who conjoins good and evil and evil and good in himself, and is thus, like Voltaire, " a *grandseigneur* of the spirit " (p. 380), " the first true man " (p. 423). It is thus that Nietzsche is he, and declares the fact, proclaiming himself and refusing to be mistaken. " I am the first immoralist " (p. 377, 386, 424). Immoral does not mean non-moral. There is no point in making him a bogeyman in this sense. His immoralism consists in the fact that he has the question of morality behind him, that like God he is without " tables," that he " invents " his own categorical imperative (*Der Antichrist*, p. 216), that he is his own table. With the conclusion of the *Götzendämmerung* in the same year, 1888, there followed indeed a " seventh day ; the stroll of a God along the Po " (*Ecce homo*, p. 413). The one who strolls in this way along the Po is the great " he " whom Nietzsche proclaims and whom he will not have mistaken for any other.

A clever man of our own day has called Nietzsche " the greatest horse-coper of any age." It cannot be questioned that we have here a genuine short circuit, a genuine deception and self-deception. But I should hesitate to accept that severe judgment because it would apply to too many things and people whose last intentions are merely represented with less restraint and we might almost say with greater honesty by Nietzsche. Goethe, Hegel, Kant and Leibniz would come under the same condemnation, and not just a specifically German spirit, but the spirit of all European humanity as fashioned and developed since the 16th century. Outside Germany it has become customary to-day to represent and castigate Nietzsche as one of those who must bear responsibility, and even primary responsibility, for preparing and making possible National Socialism. There is something in this. But it must not be forgotten that Nietzsche directed his most scathing terms against the German nationalism of his age, the age of Bismarck, so that any contribution he made to its development was highly indirect. More positively, dismissing Germany as the " plain " of European culture, he liked to remember that he was half-Polish by descent, and valued no literature or culture more highly than the French. And was he not the man who at the very height of the age of Bismarck expressed the view that it would be worth looking for a time to Switzerland to escape the opportunist outlook prevailing in Germany ? And, like so many others, he praised Italy, and historically the Italian Renaissance, as his true home, perversely maintaining that he found his superman most adequately portrayed in its most notorious representative, Cæsar Borgia. But the Italian Renaissance was the mother and model not merely of Italian but of all European humanity in the modern age. And so Nietzsche-Zarathustra emphatically wished to be understood as a European, as the best and only and final European. If his representation of humanity is " horse-coping," the same is true at root—a hidden and suppressed, but very real root—of a number of others as well. And if Nietzsche prepared the ground for National Socialism, the same may be said with equal justification of other manifestations and expressions of the European spirit during the last centuries. It is thus a very serious and responsible undertaking genuinely to oppose the humanity which he represented. The same consideration holds good in respect of his mental ill-health. If it was only as one who was mentally ill that he was capable of this representation, or conversely, if he became mentally disordered in the course of it, the question who was really deranged amongst them may be seriously asked in relation to many who were perhaps healthy in mind, or seemed to be so, only because they did not or would not see that to be a consistent champion and representative of this humanity is necessarily to be or to become mentally sick. The current affirmation and accusation are so serious that there is every reason to hesitate before making them.

We now turn to the other saying : " Am I understood—Dionysius against the Crucified."

At a first glance, it does not seem as if the book will finally lead to this antithesis, or that Nietzsche all the time wishes it to be taken in the sense of this antithesis. Prior to the last five pages of the *Ecce homo* we are not directly prepared for it even by the occasional flashes which anticipate this conclusion. Its pregnancy and violence do not seem to stand in any real relationship to the polemic of the book or of the life-work of Nietzsche summed up in it. Nietzsche

2. The Basic Form of Humanity

was an indefatigable fighter. Proclaiming that existence on high, he could hardly be otherwise. He was always against what others were for. " I am the anti-donkey *par excellence*, and therefore a monster in world history." The continuation is, of course, as follows : " In Greek, and not only in Greek, I am the Antichrist." And under this title Nietzsche wrote a whole book in 1886. Yet we cannot conclude from the book that this was more than one of the many fronts on which he was active as " anti-donkey." Nietzsche attacked the philosophy, morals, art, science and civilisation of his own and most earlier times, and in none of these spheres did he fail to leave dead and wounded behind him. Often rather sketchily in detail, but always with a sure intuition for essentials, for true correspondence and opposition, he attempted with equal taste and ruthlessness in all these fields a " transvaluation of all values " in the light of the superman and his will to power. It was only natural, therefore, that he should also attack Christianity. But that as " anti-donkey " he should supremely and decisively be " Antichrist," that everything should finally become a formal crusade against the cross, is not immediately apparent, but has to be learned and noted from a reading of Nietzsche. Yet it must be learned and noted if we are to understand him. The strange culmination in the *Ecce homo* is no mere freak. For the book about Antichrist was not just one among many. Nietzsche did not fight on all fronts in all his books. And yet there is not a single one of them, so far as I can see, in which he did not have whole sections or notable individual statements devoted to Christianity and directed in more or less violent polemic against it. And the polemic gained in weight and severity with the passage of time. We might describe this conflict as a swelling base accompanying the others and finally overwhelming and taking them up into itself, until finally there is only the one theme : " Dionysius against the Crucified."

But a second point has also to be learned and noted. The Antichrist has a definite and concrete sense. If he opposes Dionysius to the Crucified, according to the last five pages of the *Ecce homo* this means that he opposes him, or rather himself, to what he calls Christian morality. Already in the sphere of morals as such it might have been said that this was not just one of Nietzsche's foes but like Christianity itself the great enemy which he always had in view when he fought the philosophy, art, science and civilisation of his time. From the very outset Nietzsche was concerned about ethics, and it was for this reason and in this sense that he was an " immoralist." And morality and Christianity finally coalesced for him in a single detestable form, so that wherever he encountered morality he thought that he could see and deplore and attack Christianity. The last five pages of the *Ecce homo* begin with the words : " But in a very different sense as well I have chosen the word immoralist as my banner, my badge of honour ; I am proud to have this word as a mark of distinction from humanity. For no one previously has experienced Christian morality as something beneath him. For this there was required a hardness, a perspective, a hitherto unheard-of psychological depth and radicalness. Christian morality has previously been the Circe of all thinkers—they stood in its service. Who before me has descended to the depths from which there gushes out the poison of this kind of ideal—of world-renunciation ? " (p. 428). And then he continues : " Am I understood ?—What separates and marks me off from the rest of humanity is that I have discovered Christian morality." Discovered it as that which has corrupted humanity ! " Not to have seen this before seems to me to be the greatest stain which humanity has on its conscience . . . an almost criminal counterfeiting *in psychologicis*. Blindness in face of Christianity is the crime *par excellence*, a crime against life itself. . . . Millennia and nations, first and last, philosophers and old wives—apart from five or six moments of history, and myself as the seventh—have all been equally guilty in this respect " (p. 429). And again : " Am I understood ? . . . The discovery of Christian morality is an event without parallel, a veritable catastrophe. Whoever sheds light on it is a *force majeure*, a destiny, breaking the history of humanity into two parts. One either lives before him or after him. . . . The lightning of truth shatters that which formerly stood completely secure. Let him who understands what is destroyed see to it whether he has anything still in his hands " (p. 432). Nietzsche means that which must now be destroyed (it is not yet destroyed) on the basis of this epoch-making discovery. He thus concludes with Voltaire : *Ecrasez l'infame*. And this is what leads him to his final word : " Am I understood ?—Dionysius against the Crucified."

It is not self-evident that Nietzsche's general offensive should finally be against Christianity in this sense and under this sign. Again, in the *Ecce homo* itself and the earlier writings there seems at first to be a certain discrepancy of polemical standpoint. The offence of modern man is primarily at the incredible fact of the past reaching from remote ages into the present in the form of Christianity. " When on a Sunday morning we hear the old bells sounding, we ask ourselves : Is it really possible ? This all has to do with a crucified Jew of two thousand years ago who said that he was the Son of God " (*M. allzu M.*, p. 126). The Greek in him is offended at the " non-Greek element in Christianity " (*ib.*, p. 127). The philologist is offended at the exegetical and historical methods of the apostle Paul : " All these holy epileptics and seers did not possess a thousandth particle of the integrity of self-criticism with which a modern philologist reads a text or tests the truth of a historical event. . . . In comparison with us, they are moral cretins " (*W. z. Macht*, p. 123). He is also incensed at the imprudence, impatience and crudity of modern Christian theologians which drive the philologist in him almost to frenzy (*Antichrist*, p. 280 ; *W. z. Macht*, p. 152). Again, the æsthete in him experiences " a kind of inexpressible aversion at contact with the New Testament " : little, bad-mannered bigots who quite uncalled-for try to speak about the deepest problems ; a quite undistinguished type of man with the swelling claim to have more and indeed all value ; something of *foeda superstitio ;* something from which we withdraw our hands in case of defilement (*ib.*, p. 141). " We would no more choose to be ' early Christians ' than Polish Jews. . . . They have a nasty smell. I have looked in vain even for one redeeming feature in the New Testament. It does not contain anything free or generous or open or sincere. Humanity has not even made its first beginning at this point " (*Antichrist*, p. 269). Arguments are also used which show that it was not for nothing that Nietzsche was the friend of F. Overbeck. The greatest witness against Christianity is the pitiable figure of the everyday Christian, whose complacency—he has no thought of seeking his salvation with fear and trembling—is a clear demonstration that the decisive assertions of Christianity are of no importance (*M. allzu M.*, p. 128). It is the Church, which is the very thing against which Jesus preached and taught His disciples to fight, embodying the triumph of that which is anti-Christian no less than the modern state and modern nationalism (*W. zur Macht*, p. 131, 145). It is to be noted that the fact that Nietzsche will have nothing to do with God is so self-evident that it plays no part at all in his arguments against Christianity. In the *Ecce homo* he said that he knew atheism neither as an experience nor as an event, but by instinct. " God is dead "—there is no need for heat or polemics. But is he quite so sure about this ? The Dionysius-dithyrambs of 1888 show that he must have had some misgivings on the point. An " unknown God " obtrudes his obviously dangerous being in the speeches of a curious opponent of Zarathustra, and he is not a complete stranger to Nietzsche himself, this hunter, thief, robber, bandit, this great enemy, this executioner-God etc., who tries to penetrate into his heart, his most secret thoughts (p. 457). But we need not pursue this aspect. Nietzsche's heart was not in contesting the existence of God, or in the other arguments to which we have referred. His central attack, into which he flung himself with all his force, was upon what he called Christian morality. All his other assaults upon Christianity derive their secret strength,

2. The Basic Form of Humanity

and are initiated and directed, from this point. Even in the *Antichrist* this motif has become the *cantus firmus*, suppressing all the others.

But what is the absolutely intolerable and unequivocally perverted element which Nietzsche thinks that he has discovered, and must fight to the death, in Christian morality, and in this as the secret essence of all morality? Why is it that he must finally act in this matter as if there were no other foe upon earth, and no more urgent task than to vanquish it? The answer is given by Nietzsche himself with a hundred variations and nuances the complicated pattern of which we cannot follow, but the content of which is perfectly clear. It is because Christianity is not really a faith, and is not really " bound to any of its shameless dogmas," and does not basically need either metaphysics, asceticism, or " Christian " natural science, but is at root a practice, and is always possible as such, and in the strict sense has its " God " in this practice (*Antichrist*, p. 249, *W. z. Macht.* p. 155), that Nietzsche encounters it as the last enemy on his own true field. For he himself is finally concerned about a definite practice; he is decisively an ethicist. And he encounters it as an enemy because it opposes to Zarathustra or Dionysius, the lonely, noble, strong, proud, natural, healthy, wise, outstanding, splendid man, the superman, a type which is the very reverse, and so far has managed to do this successfully with its blatant claim that the only true man is the man who is little, poor and sick, the man who is weak and not strong, who does not evoke admiration but sympathy, who is not solitary but gregarious—the mass-man. It goes so far as to speak of a crucified God, and therefore to identify God Himself with this human type, and consequently to demand of all men not merely sympathy with others but that they themselves should be those who excite sympathy and not admiration. " The neighbour is transfigured into a God . . . Jesus is the neighbour transposed into divinity, into a cause awakening emotion " (*W. z. Macht*, p. 142). " The absurd residuum of Christianity, its fables, concept-spinning and theology, do not concern us; they could be a thousand times more absurd, and we should not lift a finger against them. But this ideal we contest " (*ib.*, p. 154). Nietzsche contests it as the greatest misfortune of the human race thus far. For it was the practical victory of a religion and morality of slaves, of failures, of those who go under, of the colourless, the mistaken, the worthless, the under-world, the ghetto, the variegated mass of abjects and rejects, those who creep and crawl on the earth revolting against all that is lofty (*Antichrist*, p. 124, 229, 263, 278 f.). It was " typically Socialist teaching." " What I do not like at all about this Jesus of Nazareth and His apostle Paul is that they put so many things into the heads of little people, as though their modest virtues were of some value. The price was too high; for they have brought into disrepute the far more valuable qualities of virtue and manhood, opposing a bad conscience to the self-esteem of the excellent soul, and betraying even to self-destruction the noble, generous, bold, excessive inclinations of the strong " (*W. z. Macht*, p. 142 f.). And this pernicious ideal is Christianity both in kernel and in substance right up to the present day. It has been able to insinuate itself into the whole of Western culture, philosophy and morality to their great detriment, namely, at the price of the surrender of their Greek inheritance and their surreptitious and flagrant barbarisation. And apart from six or seven upright figures no one has ever even noticed the fact right up to the present time. " God has chosen what is weak and foolish and ignoble and despised in the eyes of the world, is how the formula ran, and *décadence* conquered *in hoc signo*. God on the cross—do we still not understand the terrible background significance of this symbol?—Everything that suffers, everything that hangs on the cross, is divine. We all hang on the cross and therefore we are all divine. . . . We alone are divine. . . . Christianity was a victory, and a more excellent way went down before it— Christianity is the greatest misfortune of the human race thus far " (*Antichrist* p. 279).

This was what Nietzsche discovered as Christian morality, and this was his attack against it: the attack in which all his onslaughts on Christianity finally have both their origin and issue; the attack which finally emerged in *Ecce homo* as the common denominator of his whole Dionysian offensive. What happened to the man that he had finally to burst out in this frenzied way and to give to his whole life-work the stamp of this outburst: Dionysius against the Crucified?

If we are to understand what took place, we must again draw some comparisons. Goethe, too, had no great time for Christianity. Nor did he merely repudiate the enthusiasm of his friend Lavater and similar contemporary manifestations of Christianity, but there lived and reverberated in him something of the Greek to whom the cross is foolishness, and we may even suspect that he was personally a far more obstinate pagan than Nietzsche. But his repudiation remained cool and good-tempered and mild. For what are the occasional slights which he allowed himself, as in his famous juxtaposition of the four annoyances, "tobacco-smoke, bugs, garlic and †"? As he was content to be Apollo or preferably Zeus, as he did not think of dramatising himself and his Hellenism in the form of Dionysius (he finally rejected this possibility in his Tasso, who is certainly no Dionysius), so he never even dreamed of compromising himself by explicitly and passionately opposing Christianity as Nietzsche did. And the same is true of the great philosophical Idealists of the time, of Kant, Fichte, Schelling and Hegel. If they could not make much of the Christianity of the New Testament, they were restrained and cautious and sparing in their criticisms, trying to interpret it as positively as possible within the framework of their systems, within the limits of their own understanding. They did not oppose to it any Zarathustra. Among them there was indeed a Herder and a Schleiermacher, with their strange but subjectively quite seriously meant attachment to Christianity and the Church. It is a little different with the heirs and disciples of this classical period. We undoubtedly have to say of a Feuerbach or a Strauss that—more akin to Nietzsche—they suffered all their lives from Christianity, and made it their main task to combat it. But on poor Strauss Nietzsche looked down as from a tower and laughed. He did not even remotely see himself as in the same class. And he was right. What was their critical philosophy and philosophy of religion to him, their biblical and dogmatic criticism, their contesting of Christianity in the name of modern reason and the modern view of things? Strauss certainly could not have introduced a Dionysius-Zarathustra (any more than Martin Werner in our own day), and certainly not the friend of nature, Feuerbach.

The new thing in Nietzsche was the fact that the development of humanity without the fellow-man, which secretly had been the humanity of the Olympian Goethe and other classical figures as well as the more mediocre, reached in him a much more advanced, explosive, dangerous and yet also vulnerable stage—possibly its last. The new thing in Nietzsche was the man of "azure isolation," six thousand feet above time and man; the man to whom a fellow-creature drinking at the same well is quite dreadful and insufferable; the man who is utterly inaccessible to others, having no friends and despising women; the man who is at home only with the eagles and strong winds; the man whose only possible environment is desert and wintry landscape; the man beyond good and evil, who can exist only as a consuming fire. And so the new thing in Nietzsche's relationship to Christianity necessarily consisted in the fact that this pressed and embarrassed him in a way which the others had not seen, or at most had only sensed. On this view Christianity seemed to be so incomparably dreadful and harassing, presenting such a Medusa aspect, that he immediately dropped all the other polemics which he needed to proclaim his Zarathustra in favour of the necessary battle against this newly discovered side of Christianity, and all the other attacks on it, whether in the form of the dignified rejection of Goethe, the speculative reinterpretation of the classical Idealists, or the rational

2. The Basic Form of Humanity

objections of their successors, necessarily seemed to him to be irrelevant, stupid and even—and especially—frivolous. These predecessors had not seen how serious the matter was or how much was at stake. They could not do so, because on the positive side they did not go far enough and were not consistent enough. At bottom, they really knew nothing of the " azure isolation " of the superman. They had been left far, far behind by Zarathustra. They still crept along the ground, having only an inkling of the proximity of the eagles and strong winds in which alone real man can breathe. How could they see the true danger in Christianity ? How could they fail either to reach a frivolous compromise with this enemy, or, if they knew and attacked it as such, to commit the serious error of leaving it intact where it was really dangerous ? Nietzsche, however, was consistent on this positive side. He trod the way of humanity without the fellow-man to the bitter end. And this enabled him, and him alone, to see the true danger at this point.

And the true danger in Christianity, which he alone saw at the climax of that tradition, and on account of which he had to attack it with unprecedented resolution and passion—and with all the greater resolution and passion because he was alone—was that Christianity—what he called Christian morality—confronts real man, the superman, this necessary, supreme and mature fruit of the whole development of true humanity, with a form of man which necessarily questions and disturbs and destroys and kills him at the very root. That is to say, it confronts him with the figure of suffering man. It demands that he should see this man, that he should accept his presence, that he should not be man without him but with him, that he must drink with him at the same source. Christianity places before the superman the Crucified, Jesus, as the Neighbour, and in the person of Jesus a whole host of others who are wholly and utterly ignoble and despised in the eyes of the world (of the world of Zarathustra, the true world of men), the hungry and thirsty and naked and sick and captive, a whole ocean of human meanness and painfulness. Nor does it merely place the Crucified and His host before his eyes. It does not merely will that he see Him and them. It wills that he should recognise in them his neighbours and himself. It aims to bring him down from his height, to put him in the ranks which begin with the Crucified, in the midst of His host. Dionysius-Zarathustra, it says, is not a God but a man, and therefore under the cross of the Crucified and one of His host. Nor can Dionysius-Zarathustra redeem himself, but the Crucified alone can be his Redeemer. Dionysius-Zarathustra is thus called to live for others and not himself. Here are his brothers and sisters who belong to him and to whom he belongs. In this Crucified, and therefore in fellowship with this mean and painful host of His people, he has thus to see his salvation, and his true humanity in the fact that he belongs to Him and therefore to them. This Crucified is God Himself, and therefore God Himself is only for those who belong to His host. They are then the elect of God. And Dionysius-Zarathustra can be an elect of God only if he belongs to them. Away, then, the six thousand feet, the azure, the isolation, the drinking from a lonely well ! Everything is back to disturb and destroy the isolation. The fellow-man has returned whom Zarathustra had escaped or to whom he merely wanted to be a hammer, and he has returned in a form which makes escape impossible (because it embodies something which even Zarathustra cannot escape) and which makes all hammering futile (because in this form of suffering man there is nothing really to hammer).

This was the new thing which Nietzsche saw in Christianity and which he had to combat because he found it so intolerable, wounding and dangerous. It was for this reason that in the last resort his " anti-donkey " meant Antichrist. And it was only perhaps a relic of the frivolity of which he accused others that sometimes he could act as if Christianity were mere donkey-dom and he could meet it with the corresponding attitudes and measures. We might well ask how it was that all their life long even Strauss and Feuerbach found it necessary to keep hammering away at what they declared to be so bankrupt a thing as Christianity, especially in a century when it no longer cut a very imposing figure outwardly, and the battle against it had long since ceased to be a heroic war of liberation. But we have certainly to ask why Nietzsche was guilty of the Donquixotry of acting in the age of Bismarck as if the Christian morality of 1 Cor. 1 constituted the great danger by which humanity necessarily found itself most severely imperilled at every turn. Yet the fact remains that Nietzsche, did take up arms against Christianity, and especially the Christianity of 1 Cor. 1, as if it were a serious threat and no mere folly. And he had to do so. We cannot explain this necessity in purely historical terms, which in this context means psychological and psycho-pathological. That Nietzsche became deranged in this attack, or that he was deranged to undertake it, merely throws light on the fact; it does not alter the necessity. The one who as the heir, disciple and prophet of the Renaissance and its progeny discovered the superman was quite unable—irrespective of historical and psychological circumstances—to overlook the fact that in Western culture, in face of every repudiation, reinterpretation or assault, persisting in spite of every evacuation, there existed at least in the form of the Greek New Testament such a thing as Christianity, so that from the pages of the New Testament he was inevitably confronted by that figure, and could only recognise in that figure the direct opposite of his own ideal and that of the tradition which culminated in him, and was forced to protest and fight against it with the resolution and passion which we find in Nietzsche, not as against asininity, but with the final resolution which is reserved for a mortal threat.

Naturally there is an element of caricature in his depiction. Those who try to fight the Gospel always make caricatures, and they are then forced to fight these caricatures. Nietzsche's caricature consists in his (not very original) historical derivation of Christianity from a revolt on the part of slaves or the proletariat, for which Paul and other mischievous priests provided a metaphysical foundation and super-structure, and which thus became an incubus on the unhappy West. We all grasp at such aids as are available. And the 19th century had tried to bolster up Christianity with historical interpretations of this kind. Nietzsche was undoubtedly conditioned by his age when he thought that he could regard Christianity as typical Socialist teaching and contest it as such; for there did not lack those who in his own time thought that they should praise and commend it as typical Socialist teaching, or at least find a positive place for it as a transitional stage. At this point Nietzsche was perhaps loyally and sincerely a little class-conditioned. According to the Marxist analysis, he belonged to the middle-class, although in a form worthy of Zarathustra. In this respect he was at one with D. F. Strauss, to whom the moderate Social Democratic teaching of the period was as a red rag to a bull. But this is not really essential. The caricature which he served up was itself an element in his resistance and attack. And of this attack we have to say that it was well aimed, that it centred on the point which was vital for Nietzsche as the most consistent champion and prophet of humanity without the fellow-man. It is another matter, and one that objectively considered is to the praise of Nietzsche, that he thus hurled himself against the strongest and not the weakest point in the opposing front. With his discovery of the Crucified and His host he discovered the Gospel itself in a form which was missed even by the majority of its champions, let alone its opponents, in the 19th century. And by having to attack it in this form, he has done us the good office of bringing before us the fact that we have to keep to this form as unconditionally as he rejected it, in self-evident antithesis not only to him, but to the whole tradition on behalf of which he made this final hopeless sally.

We now know against what orientation of research and representa-

2. The Basic Form of Humanity

tion of humanity we are warned *a limine* by the humanity of Jesus Christ, and having secured our rear we can look in the direction to which we are positively directed by this fact. The humanity of Jesus consists in His being for man. From the fact that this example is binding in humanity generally there follows the broad definition that humanity absolutely, the humanity of each and every man, consists in the determination of man's being as a being with others, or rather with the other man. It is not as he is for himself but with others, not in loneliness but in fellowship, that he is genuinely human, that he achieves true humanity, that he corresponds to his determination to be God's covenant-partner, that he is the being for which the man Jesus is, and therefore real man. If we overlook the fact of his being in fellowship, and see him for himself, constructing him in terms of an abstract " I am " in which others are not yet or no longer included, everything collapses, and in respect of the concept of the human we are betrayed into an obscurity in which it is no longer possible to make any real distinction between what may be called humanity and inhumanity. We must avoid this path. We must press straight on from the fact that the humanity of man consists in the determination of his being as a being with the other.

Before we move on from this point, we must try to clarify three of the terms employed in this definition.

1. We describe humanity as a determination of human being. Man is, as he is created by God for God, as this creature of God for covenant-partnership with God. But this being is a wholly definite being. It corresponds in its own way to its particular creation and to the meaning and goal of the particularity of its creation. The manner of its being is a likeness of its purpose and therefore of the fact that it is created by God for God. This parabolic determination of human being, this correspondence and similarity of its nature in relation to its being as such, is humanity.

2. We describe humanity as a being of man with others. With this cautious expression we distinguish humanity generally from the humanity of Jesus. There is also a being for others in the relation of man to man. But only the humanity of Jesus can be absolutely exhaustively and exclusively described as a being for man. There can be no question of a total being for others as the determination of any other men but Jesus. And to the humanity of other men there necessarily belongs reciprocity. Others are for them as they are for others. This reciprocity cannot arise in the humanity of Jesus with its irreversible " for." We are thus satisfied to describe the humanity generally with which we are now dealing as a being of the one with the other, and we shall have to show to what extent this includes a certain being of the one for the other.

3. We describe humanity as a being of the one man with the other. Fundamentally we speak on both sides in the singular and

not in the plural. We are not thinking here in terms of individualism. But the basic form of humanity, the determination of humanity, according to its creation, in the light of the humanity of Jesus—and it is of this that we speak—is a being of the one man with the other. And where one is with many, or many with one, or many with many, the humanity consists in the fact that in truth, in the basic form of this occurrence, one is always with another, and this basic form persists. Humanity is not in isolation, and it is in pluralities only when these are constituted by genuine duality, by the singular on both sides.

The singular, not alone but in this duality, is the presupposition without which there can never be humanity in the plural.

We may now move forward, and for the sake of clarity we shall begin with an analysis of the statement " I am," which we have so far understood only as the axiom of humanity without the fellow-man, but which will help us to a true understanding and exposition once we appreciate its true significance. The statement " I am " is ultimately a confession—and perhaps *the* confession—of the man Jesus ; He therefore permits and requires of us an interpretation on which, as at least a corresponding and similar if not an equal confession in the mouth of others, it has a human and not an inhuman form ; an interpretation which does not point us in the direction which we cannot take, but in the opposite and right direction, the being of one man with the other.

What is meant by " I ? " I pronounce the word, and in so doing, even if I only do so mentally or to myself, I make a distinction, but also a connexion. In thinking and speaking this word, I do not remain in isolation. I distinguish myself from another who is not I and yet also not It, not an object, but one who can receive and estimate and understand my declaration " I " because he can make a similar declaration to me. In making this distinction, I presuppose, accept and make, as far as I am able, a connexion with him as one who is like me. Addressing this object as I, I distinguish him not only from myself but from all other objects, from every It, placing myself on the same level or in the same sphere with him, acknowledging that I am not without him in my sphere, that this sphere is not just mine but also his. The mere fact that I say " I " means that I describe and distinguish the object to which I say it as something like myself ; in other words, that with my " I " I also address him as " Thou." By saying " I," I implicitly address and treat him as " Thou." Not, be it noted, as " He " or " She." So long and so far as he is only He or She, he is really It, an object like others, in a different sphere from mine, unlike myself ; and my distinction from him and connexion with him are not yet human. But in this case I do not speak to him ; I speak about him. And the word " I " is meaningful in relation to the one with whom I speak about him. It has no reference to himself. If I speak to him and not about him, he is neither It, He

2. The Basic Form of Humanity

nor She, but Thou. I then make the distinction and connexion in relation to him in the specific form of a demarcation in virtue of which my sphere is no longer my own but his, and he is like me. But there is more to it than this. For when I say " I " and therefore " Thou " to someone else, I empower and invite and summon him to say " Thou " to me in return. The declaration " I " in what I say is the declaration of my expectation that the other being to which I declare myself in this way will respond and treat and describe and distinguish me as something like himself. When he accepts my " I "—and in turning to him I count on it that he is able to do so—he cannot possibly regard me as an It or a mere He or She, but I am distinguished from all other objects for him as he is for me, and distinguished from and connected to me as I am from and to him. And it can only be a matter of fulfilment that he for his part should admit his recognition of this fact by pronouncing the word " Thou " and thus proclaim himself not merely as something like an I but actually as an I. Thus the word " Thou," although it is a very different word, is immanent to " I." It is not a word which is radically alien, but one which belongs to it. The word " I " with which I think and declare my humanity implies as such humanity with and not without the fellow-man. I cannot say " I," even to myself, without also saying " Thou," without making that distinction and connexion in relation to another. And only as I think and say " I " in this way, only as I make this specific distinction and connexion with this word, can I expect to be recognised and acknowledged by others as a " Thou," as something like an " I," and more than that as a real " I," and therefore to be confirmed in the human determination of my being, and regarded, treated and addressed as a human being.

On this basis, what is meant by " I am ? " It certainly means that I posit myself : myself as this being in the cosmos ; myself in all the freedom and necessity of my being ; myself in the totality of the movement of my distinctions and connexions in relation to what is for me the outside world ; myself in my desire and ability to project myself into this world. There can be no objection to this formal description of " I am." But what does all this mean if I cannot say " I " without also saying " Thou," and being a Thou for this " Thou," and only in this way receiving confirmation that I am ? What does " I am " mean on this presupposition ? Who and what am I myself as I confirm my being in this way ? What kind of a being is it in the freedom and necessity of which I posit myself, distinguishing and connecting myself, projecting myself outwards ? One thing at least is certain. A pure, absolute and self-sufficient I is an illusion, for as an I, even as I think and express this I, I am not alone or self-sufficient, but am distinguished from and connected with a Thou in which I find a being like my own, so that there is no place for an interpretation of the " I am " which means isolation and necessarily consists in a description of the sovereign self-positing of an empty subject by eruptions of its pure, absolute and self-sufficient abyss. The I is not pure, absolute or self-sufficient. But this means that it is not empty. It is not an abyss. And so the being of the I cannot consist in the eruption, history and myth of an abyss. On the contrary, as I am—the genuine I—I am in distinction and connexion to the other which in the fact that I am is Thou, my Thou, and for which I am a Thou in return, thus receiving confirmation of my own being, of the " I am." " I am " is not an empty but a filled reality. As I am, the other is like me. I am as I am in a relation. And this means that as I posit myself—I should not be myself if it were otherwise—I at once come up against the fact that there takes place a corresponding self-positing and being on the part of the one whom I must see and treat as Thou as I think and declare myself as I. With this self-positing and being of his he comes towards me, or rather the Thou comes (for that is what he is as I am I in relation to him), and comes in such a way that I cannot evade him, since he is like myself and therefore Thou as surely as I am I, and therefore my sphere is not mine alone but his as well. What I am and posit as myself, I am and posit in relation to his positing and being, in distinction from and connexion with this alien happening which is characterised by the fact that I can see and recognise and accept this alien being and positing as one which corresponds to my own. This alien being and positing does not belong, therefore, to the general mass of happenings in the external world. In face of it I cannot refer back to myself, asserting and developing myself from myself as from a neutral point quite apart from it. The being and positing of this Thou reaches and affects me, for it is not that of an It, but of the Thou without which I should not be I. In its decisive content as a work of the Thou it is not the outside world which I can leave to itself, avoid or control. The work of the Thou cannot be indifferent to me, nor can I evade or master it. I cannot do this because as I do my own work, as I am myself and posit myself, I am necessarily claimed by and occupied with the being and positing of the Thou. My own being and positing takes place in and with the fact that I am claimed by that of the other and occupied with it. That of the other sets limits to my own. It indicates its problems. It poses questions which must be answered. And there are answers for which it asks. I am in encounter with the other who is in the same way as I am. I am under the conditions imposed by this encounter. I am as either well or badly I fulfil the conditions imposed by this encounter. Even if I fulfil them badly, I am as measured by these conditions. I have no being apart from them. I cannot posit myself without coming up against the self-positing of the other. I have no line of retreat to a place where he does not come up against me with his self-positing. If I had, it could only be that of a return to the inhumanity of a being without the

2. The Basic Form of Humanity

being of the other, of the " I am " of an empty subject, of an I which cannot be more than an illusion. And here, too, we must consider the matter from the other side. As I myself am, and posit myself, I confront the other no less than he does me with his being and positing. He is my Thou, and therefore something like myself, in the sphere which is my own. My being and positing is for him more than the external world. Hence he cannot retreat before me into himself, and in this way exist without me. Since I am not an It, but an I and therefore a Thou, he is reached and affected by me no less than I am by him. He, too, is unable to leave aside or to evade or control my work. He, too, is claimed by and occupied with my being and positing. He, too, stands under the conditions which I create for him. I am his encounter as he is mine. In being myself, I cannot help being what I am for him. In this sense, too, there is no line of retreat to a place where I exist neutrally for him, where I do not affect him, where I do not owe him anything, where I with my being and positing do not have to take any account of his. The only line of retreat is again that of a retreat to inhumanity—to the inhumanity of a being without the Thou in relation to which I can be alone, to the " I am " of an empty subject which cannot find fulfilment or really be a human subject, but is always, or always becomes again, an illusion.

" I am "—the true and filled " I am "—may thus be paraphrased : " I am in encounter." Nor am I in encounter before or after, incidentally, secondarily or subsequently, while primarily and properly I am alone in an inner world in which I am not in this encounter, but alongside which there is an outer world in which amongst other things I certainly come up against being, against the being of the Thou, and have to reckon with it, but in such sort that this is not at all essential, since essentially I am always outside this encounter, and can always retreat into this world apart. No, at the very root of my being and from the very first I am in encounter with the being of the Thou, under his claim and with my own being constituting a claim upon him. And the humanity of human being is this total determination as being in encounter with the being of the Thou, as being with the fellow-man, as fellow-humanity. To this extent we must oppose humanity without the fellow-man. This is the reach of the likeness in unlikeness, of the correspondence and similarity between the man Jesus and us other men. The minimal definition of our humanity, of humanity generally, must be that it is the being of man in encounter, and in this sense the determination of man as a being with the other man. We cannot go back on this. We cannot be content with anything less or weaker. We cannot accept any compromise or admixture with the opposite conception which would have it that at bottom—in the far depths of that abyss of an empty subject—man can be a man without the fellow-man, an I without the Thou.

But we must be more precise. Being with means encounter.

Hence being with the other man means encounter with him. Hence humanity is the determination of our being as a being in encounter with the other man. We shall now try to understand the content of this encounter.

The basic formula to describe it must be as follows: " I am as Thou art." Naturally the word " as " does not imply that the " Thou art " is the cause, even the instrumental cause, or the true substance of the " I am." In this respect an excess of zeal in conflict with the idealistic concept of humanity has sometimes led to the emptying out of the baby with the bath-water. Man has been constructed wholly in the light of the fellow-man, and the " I am " has formally disappeared in the " Thou art." The word " as " does not tell us where human being is created—for this we can turn only to God the Creator —but how. It tells us that every " I am " is qualified, marked and determined by the " Thou art." Owing it to God the Creator that I am, I am only as Thou art ; as, created by the same God, Thou art with me. Neither the I am nor the Thou art loses its own meaning and force. I do not become Thou, nor Thou I, in this co-existence. On the contrary, as I and Thou are together, their being acquires the character, the human style, of always being I for the self and Thou for the other. As we are in this encounter we are thus distinguished. On both sides—we shall return to this—the being has its own validity, dignity and self-certainty. Nor is this human being static, but dynamic and active. It is not an *esse* but an *existere*. To say man is to say history. On a false understanding no less than a true we are forced to put the statement " I am " in the form of a little history, describing it as that self-positing. Similarly, the statement " Thou art " denotes a history. Therefore in our formula : " I am as Thou art," we do not describe the relationship between two static complexes of being, but between two which are dynamic, which move out from themselves, which exist, and which meet or encounter each other in their existence. The " I am " and the " Thou art " encounter each other as two histories. It is to be noted that they do not just do this subsequently, as though there were one history here and another there which at a certain point became a common history ; as though there were an " I am " here and a " Thou art " there which in the continuation of their two-sided movement came together and became a partnership. But in and with their creation, and therefore in and with the two-sided beginning of their movement and history, they are in encounter : I am as Thou art, and Thou art as I am. To say man is to say history, and this is to speak of the encounter between I and Thou. Thus the formula : " I am as Thou art," tells us that the encounter between I and Thou is not arbitrary or accidental, that it is not incidentally but essentially proper to the concept of man. It tells us noologically that this concept would at once be empty if the view basic to it were that of a pure subject and not of the subject in this encounter. And it tells us

2. The Basic Form of Humanity

ontologically that we have to do with real man only when his existence takes place in this encounter, only in the form of man with his fellow-man.

On this basis we shall now try to see what are the categories, the constant, decisive and necessary elements in this history or encounter, and to that extent what are the categories of the distinctively human. Great caution is needed at this point. Things which might be said about man without his fellow, qualities and characteristics of that empty subject, are out of place here, because they have no " categorical " significance in the description of humanity, i.e., they tell us nothing about being in encounter and therefore about that which is properly and essentially human. Thus the fact that I am born and die ; that I eat and drink and sleep ; that I develop and maintain myself ; that beyond this I assert myself in face of others, and even physically propagate my species ; that I enjoy and work and play and fashion and possess ; that I acquire and have and exercise powers ; that I take part in all the works of the race either accomplished or in process of accomplishment ; that in all this I satisfy religious needs and can realise religious possibilities ; and that in it all I fulfil my aptitudes as an understanding and thinking, willing and feeling being—all this as such is not my humanity. In it I can be either human or inhuman. In it I am only asked whether I am human or inhuman. In it all I must first answer the question whether I will affirm or deny my humanity. It is only the field on which human being either takes place or does not take place as history, as the encounter of I and Thou ; the field on which it is revealed or obscured that " I am as Thou art." That I exist on this field, and do so in a particular way, does not of itself mean that I am human. But as I exist on this field and in this way, in this restriction or development, poverty or wealth, impotence or intensity, it has to become true and actual that I am human and not inhuman in my existence. There is no reason why in the realisation of my vital, natural and intellectual aptitudes and potentialities, in my life-act as such, and my participation in scholarship and art, politics and economics, civilisation and culture, I should not actualise and reveal that " I am as Thou art." But it may well be that in and with all this I deny it. It may well be that in all this I am only man without my fellow-man, and therefore not really human at all. Nothing of all this is in itself and as such the glory of my humanity.

> For example, it is not the case that motherhood or work ennoble as such. It is also not the case that an accomplishment or achievement in any of these spheres ennobles as such. It can all be supremely inhuman. And there can be supreme humanity where it is all absent. Self-evidently, of course, it is equally untrue to try to seek nobility in the absence of distinction on this field, e.g., with a certain perverseness in sickness or poverty or insignificance or the lack of culture. It is rather the case that on this whole field both the positive and the negative only acquire a positive or negative meaning in respect of their

relationship to humanity—and have to acquire it in the fulfilment of that history.

The question of the humanity of human being is independent of everything which takes place or does not take place on this field. Or conversely, this whole field with all that takes place or does not take place on it is an empty page on which there has still to be written the answer to the question of the humanity of human being. And this answer is written with the enactment of the history, the realisation of the encounter, in which " I am as Thou art." Hence as the constant, decisive and necessary categories, marks and criteria of humanity we can take into account only the elements which characterise this encounter constantly in all the circumstances which may arise on this field, decisively in face of all circumstances, and necessarily in the midst of all possibilities ; the forms in which there takes place : " I am as Thou art."

Being in encounter is (1) a being in which one man looks the other in the eye. The human significance of the eye is that we see one another eye to eye. It is man who is seen in this way, not things, or the cosmos, but at the heart of things and the cosmos man, and man not after the manner of things or the cosmos, but in his distinction and particularity as man within the cosmos. It is man who is visible to man, and therefore as the other, as the one who is thus distinct from the one who sees him. This one cannot see himself, but he can and must see the other. That this should take place, that the other should be visible to and seen by him as man, is the human significance of the eye and all seeing. Seeing is inhuman if it does not include this seeing, if it is not first and supremely, primarily and conclusively, this seeing—the seeing of the fellow-man. But this is only the one half. When one man looks the other in the eye, it takes place automatically that he lets the other look him in the eye. And it is a necessary part of the human meaning of the eye that man himself should be visible to the other : not an outward form, a something which might be like the rest of the cosmos ; but man himself, the man who as such is particular and distinct within the cosmos. This one is visible in the seeing eye of the one for the other who comes to see him even as he is seen by him. To see the other thus means directly to let oneself be seen by him. If I do not do this, I do not see him. Conversely, as I do it, as I let him look me in the eye, I see him. The two together constitute the full human significance of the eye and its seeing. All seeing is inhuman in which the one who sees hides himself, refusing to be seen by the fellow-man whom he sees. The point is not unimportant that it is always two men, and therefore a real I and Thou, who look themselves in the eye and can thus see one another and be seen by one another. But we may now put the same thing rather more generally and say that being in encounter is a being in the openness of the one to the other with a view to and on behalf of the other.

2. The Basic Form of Humanity

" I am as Thou art " is basically fulfilled in the fact that I am not closed to thee but open. I am not Thou, and thy being is not mine nor mine thine. But I with all that I am encounter thee with all that Thou art, and similarly Thou dost encounter me, and if this is the encounter of two men and not the collision of two things it means that Thou and what Thou art are not closed to me, and that I for my part do not remain closed to thee and what Thou art. As I am and Thou art we are open to one another. I know thee as a man, as something like myself, and I make it possible for thee to know me in the same way. We give each other something in our duality, and this is that I and Thou are men. We give each other an insight into our being. And as we do this, I am not for myself, but for thee, and Thou for me, so that we have a share and interest in one another. This two-sided openness is the first element of humanity. Where it lacks, and to the extent that it lacks, humanity does not occur. To the extent that we withhold and conceal ourselves, and therefore do not move or move any more out of ourselves to know others and to let ourselves be known by them, our existence is inhuman, even though in all other respects we exist at the highest level of humanity. The isolation in which we try to persist, the lack of participation which we show in relation to others and thus thrust upon others in relation to ourselves, is inhumanity. The expression: " That is no concern of mine," or : " That is no concern of yours," is almost always wrong, because it almost always means that the being of this or that man is nothing to me and my being nothing to him ; that I will neither see him nor let myself be seen by him ; that my eyes are too good for him and I am too good for his eyes ; that my openness reaches its limit in him. But conversely, where openness obtains, humanity begins to occur. To the extent that we move out of ourselves, not refusing to know others or being afraid to be known by them, our existence is human, even though in all other respects we may exist at the very lowest level of humanity. (It is not necessarily the case, but seems to be a fact of experience, that where we think that in other respects we are nearer the depths than the heights of humanity we are generally much more open with and for one another, and to that extent, in spite of all appearances to the contrary, much more human than on the supposed heights.) The duality into which we enter when we encounter one another directly and not indirectly, revealed and not concealed as man with man ; the participation which we grant one another by the very fact that we see and do not not see one another, and let ourselves be seen and not unseen by one another, these are the first and indispensable steps in humanity, without which the later ones cannot be taken, and which cannot be replaced by the exercise of any human capacity or virtue, however highly rated this may rightly or wrongly be. It is a great and solemn and incomparable moment when two men look themselves in the eye and discover one another. This moment, this mutual look, is in some sense the root-formation of all humanity without which the rest is impossible. But it is to be noted again that in the strict sense it can take place only in duality, as I and Thou look one another in the eye. Where a man thinks he sees and knows a group, or a group a man, or one group another group, ambiguity always arises. After all, it might be only a matter of psychology and not the other man, of pedagogics and not the child, of sociological statistics and systematisation and not the individual, of the general and not the particular, which is the only thing that really counts in this respect. This is the dangerous—and usually more than dangerous—limit of all planning and philanthropy, but also of all doctrine and instruction, of all politics, and especially of all socialism. Whether on the one side or the other or both there is maintained or broken a closed and blind existence, thinking and speaking in the group, whether the one concrete man is invisible or visible to the other concrete man, is what decides whether there is humanity in all this or not.

Bureaucracy is the form in which man participates with his fellows when this first step into mutual openness is not taken, and not taken because duality is evaded for the sake of the simplicity of a general consideration and a general programme. Bureaucracy is the encounter of the blind with those whom they treat as blind. A bureau is a place where men are grouped in certain classes and treated, dismissed or doctored according to specified plans, principles and regulations. This may very well have the result that the men themselves, both those who act and those who are acted upon, are invisible to one another. A bureau does not have to be an office. Many a man unwittingly sits and acts all his life in a private bureau from which he considers how to treat and dismiss men according to his private plans, and in the process he may never see the real men and always be invisible to them. Certainly, there can and must be the bureau, both public and private. Bureaucracy does not hold sway in every bureau. But every bureau is situated hard by the frontier beyond which bureaucracy raises its head, and with it inhumanity, even on the presupposition of the most altruistic of intentions. It is not the man who works in a bureau, for to some extent we all have to do this, but the bureaucrat who is always inhuman. In this whole matter we may perhaps refer to the parable of the eye in Mt. 6$^{22f.}$: " The light of the body is the eye : if therefore thine eye be single ($ἁπλοῦς$), thy whole body shall be full of light. But if thine eye be evil ($πονηρός$), thy whole body shall be full of darkness." With this human picture of the good or bad eye the parable refers to the open or closed relationship of man to the imminent kingdom of God. " If therefore the light that is in thee be darkness, how great is that darkness ! " But it is no accident that this particular picture, that of the clear or clouded eye, is chosen to illustrate this relationship.

Being in encounter consists (2) in the fact that there is mutual speech and hearing. The matter sounds simple, and yet it again consists in a complex action : I and Thou must both speak and hear, and speak with one another and hear one another. No element must be lacking. This is the human significance of speech. At this point we are on a higher level than the first. It is a good thing to see and to be seen. But there is a good deal more to humanity than that.

2. The Basic Form of Humanity

The openness of encounter is excellent and indeed indispensable as a first step. But encounter is not exhausted in openness. Openness alone is no guarantee that I reach thee and Thou me, that there is thus a real encounter. Openness, seeing and being seen, is always a receptive and not a spontaneous happening. By mere seeing we either do not know one another at all or only imperfectly, for on the plane of mere seeing the one has no opportunity of putting himself before the other, i.e., of interpreting himself, of declaring who and what he is, what his person and being are according to his own understanding of himself. On the plane of mere seeing the one who sees has to form his own picture of the other, understanding the man himself and what he is and does from his own standpoint, and measuring and judging him by his own standards. The other has not contributed anything of his own to make himself knowable. To know him, he is thrown back entirely upon his own resources. And this limitation is a burden to the one who is seen as well. So long as he is known only by sight, he is compelled to exist for the one who sees him in the picture which he has formed of him. He is no more than what he seems to be in his eyes and according to his standards. He has not been able to do anything to give a different and perhaps better and more truthful representation. With his own self-interpretation he still stands impotently before the interpretation which the other has adopted from mere sight, wondering, no doubt, whether he has any real insight into him at all. And if in the encounter of I and Thou there is to be not merely mutual consideration but a mutual contact and intersection of being and activity, if there is to be a field of common life in which the I and Thou not only see themselves but continually have themselves and continually have to take each other into practical account, surely something more is demanded to secure the required intercourse than the pictures mutually formed and the arbitrary notions conceived on both sides? These pictures in which alone they exist for one another may well hamper instead of helping the intercourse, making it impossible rather than possible. So long as these pictures are normative, it may well be that both parties are only acted upon instead of acting. The extreme case is not excluded that seeing and being seen do not prevent the one or the other or both from entering into this intercourse as a man without his fellow-man, and thus being a genuine and perhaps quite immovable obstacle to true intercourse, leading inevitably to conflict instead of co-operation. What is needed at this point is speech—the human use of the mouth and ears. Humanity as encounter must become the event of speech. And speech means comprehensively reciprocal expression and its reciprocal reception, reciprocal address and its reciprocal reception. All these four elements are vital. Man speaks and hears a good deal. But the line on which he is human in speaking and hearing is a fine one, and there must not be the slightest deviation from it either on the one side or the other.

The I has thus to express itself to the Thou. A word spoken by me is my active self-declaration to the Thou, my spontaneous crossing of the necessary frontier of mere visibility in relation to the other. As I take to words, I testify that I am not leaving the interpretation of myself to the Thou, but am going to help him by at least adding my self-interpretation. As I speak, I set the other in a position to compare his own picture of me with my own, with my own conception of myself. I help him to answer the immediate question whether his picture of me is correct. That I express myself does not mean in the first instance—and from my standpoint it ought not to mean—that I aim to relieve, defend or justify myself against the wrong which I am done or might be done by the picture which the other has of me. My self-expression may later acquire this sense. But this cannot be its primary intention on my part. The real meaning of the fact that I express myself to the other is that I owe him this assistance. Thus my self-expression, if it is genuinely human, has nothing whatever to do with the fear of being misunderstood or the desire to give a better portrait of myself and vindicate myself before him. It is not for nothing that when this intention lurks behind self-expression it usually fails to attain its end. My word as self-declaration is human only when, in seizing the opportunity of making myself clear and understandable, I have before me the necessary concern of the other not only to see but also to understand me, to escape the uncertainty of the view which he has of me, and the embarrassment caused by this uncertainty. I can help him in this respect only as I tell him who I am, what I think of it, what my view is, with whom and what he has to do in me and my whole being according to the insight gained according to the best of my own knowledge and conscience. I can help him in this way with my word. Only when I speak with him with this purpose in view—not for my own sake but for his—do I express myself honestly and genuinely to him. Words are not genuine self-expression when in some respect I keep back myself, not representing or displaying myself. Words are not genuine self-expression when I represent myself in another guise than that in which I know myself to the best of my information and conscience. Nor are they genuine self-expression when they are perhaps a mask—*la parole est donnée à l'homme pour déguiser sa pensée*—by means of which I try to prevent the other from understanding me, and thus do not really intend to express myself at all. How can I take the Thou seriously as a Thou if I express myself to him but do not really intend to express myself at all? How can I then be in true encounter with him? How can my speech be human speech or my mouth a human mouth? To take the Thou seriously is to be concerned for the Thou in self-expression and self-declaration; to have regard in my self-representation for this other who necessarily has to do with me for good or ill; to do my best not to leave him to his own devices in the unavoidable task of

2. The Basic Form of Humanity

making something of me. Only on this presupposition will my self-expression in relation to him be true and not false.

But the I has also to receive the expression of the other. A word heard by me is the active self-declaration of the Thou to me. The other, too, aims to cross the frontier of mere visibility. He, too, does not leave me to the picture which I have formed of him. He, too, tries to represent himself, inviting me to compare my picture of him with what he himself has to contribute. He, too, aims to help me. For this reason and with this intention he speaks with me. To receive or accept him in this sense is to listen to him. I do not hear him if I assume that he is only concerned about himself, either to commend himself to me or to gain my interest, and that he makes himself conspicuous and understandable, forcing himself and his being upon me, only for this reason. When he speaks to me, I must not be affected by the fact that in innumerable instances in which men express themselves to me this might actually be the case or appear to be so. What matters now is the humanity of my hearing, and this is conditioned negatively by the fact that at least I do not hear this other with suspicion, and positively by the fact that I presuppose that he is trying to come to my help with his self-expression and self-declaration. In relation to him I am in the uncertainty and therefore the embarrassment of knowing him only by sight and therefore equivocally; of knowing him, and with whom or what I have to do in him, only from my own standpoint. This is where the word comes in. He is now trying to fill in or correct my conception of him by his own. He is trying to the best of his ability to help me over the difficulty in which I find myself, giving me by his word the opportunity to verify my view of him. My hearing is human, i.e., I have open ears for the other, only when I listen to him on this presupposition. Only then do I find a place for his self-declaration. If I do not accept the fact that my view is incomplete and needs to be supplemented and corrected, that it may indeed be wholly distorted; if I do not suffer from the embarrassment caused by the Thou so long as I have to interpret him from myself and his self-declaration is withheld; if I do not see and deplore the obvious lacuna at this point, there can be no place for the word of the Thou. However loudly it beats against my ear, I cannot hear; my ear is not in any sense a human ear, and I do not take seriously the Thou of the fellow-man unhesitatingly subordinated to myself. To take the Thou seriously and therefore to have a human ear is to move towards the self-declaration of the other and to welcome it as an event which for my own sake must take place between him and me. It is necessary for me that the other should represent and display himself to me no matter what this may involve or entail. I am not a true I and do not genuinely exist without him. I am only an empty subject if I do not escape that difficulty in relation to him. How can I help thanking him for the favour which he does me by expressing himself ? Whatever he may have in view, whatever he may want of me, however sincere or insincere he may be in what he does, the point at issue, the objective significance of the event of his self-expression to me, is that now at least this supreme favour is done me. Hearing on this presupposition is human hearing of the self-expression of the fellow-man.

But there is another side to the matter. The I is not merely concerned to express itself, but also to address the Thou. The word spoken by me is my impartation to the Thou. Self-declaration to the other cannot be an end in itself. What is the point of crossing that frontier of mere visibility, what inconvenience it may cause the other that I represent myself to him, how little it may genuinely concern him, if the point between us is not that in my self-expression I have something objective to offer and impart for his appropriation! Why do I necessarily try to make myself clear and explain myself to him ? We have given as our reason the fact that he cannot fulfil the task of knowing me by sight alone. But why does he have to know me at all ? He has to know me, we must now continue, because I am for him the sum of something objective which he needs as a subject but which is in the first instance unattainable, being concealed in me. We remember that I am not Thou, nor Thou I. Hence what the other comes to see in me is something new and strange and different. I am outside for him, an unknown being, near and yet remote. But when he sees and encounters me, I cannot remain strange. Being so near, I cannot continue to be remote. Since there has to be intercourse between us, I cannot be merely external, a self-enclosed object. In this form I am a vital need to him so long as no bridge is built or way found from him to me. His difficulty so long as he knows me only by sight is that he has no way to me ; that he cannot appropriate the new and strange and different thing in me, and therefore cannot have intercourse with me. For this reason he has to know me. And for this reason I have an obligation to make myself known. I have something to say to him, i.e., I have to entrust to him what would remain unknown so long as he knew me only by sight, the new and different thing in me. This is the meaning of the word of address from the one to the other. The word of address is necessary as a kind of penetration from the sphere of the one into the sphere of another being. As I address another, whether in the form of exposition, question, petition or demand, but always with the request to be heard, I ask that he should not remain in isolation but be there for me ; that he should not be concerned only with himself but with me too ; in other words, that he should hear. Address is coming to another with one's being, and knocking and asking to be admitted. As I address him, I allow myself to unsettle and disturb him by drawing attention to the fact that I am there too. In certain cases this may well be a thankless task. For we cannot take it for granted that he is

2. The Basic Form of Humanity

conscious of needing the objective thing which I can offer and impart; that he wants the new and strange and different thing which I am for him; that he thinks it a vital matter that there is no bridge or way between him and me and therefore he cannot have intercourse with me; that he is willing and ready to accept that penetration from my sphere to his, to be told something by me. On the contrary, it is far more likely that the conscious wish of the other will be that I should leave him in peace. But we must not allow this fact to obscure the real point at issue. It merely reminds us that in the genuine address of the I to the Thou we have to do with the imparting of something objective, with the disclosure of a particular side of the great matter of the life to be lived in common by the I and the Thou. The words with which I turn to the other, seeking him out and perhaps reaching him, are human when the new and strange and different thing with which I knock and demand entrance as I address him is directed at himself, when it penetrates to him as a vital element which constrains and is important and indispensable for him. It is thus a human address when in my claim to be heard by the other I have something decisive for himself to give him. Basically, however, there can be no doubt that one man needs another, and particularly in respect of that in which the other is unknown to him; that one man has something decisive to give another; that so long as one man does not know another this is a vital need which waits to be satisfied. And because this is the case, nothing can basically compromise the human duty and obligation of addressing the other. We cannot consider the matter merely from the standpoint of the personal need of the one. It is obvious that personal need, when it arises, may just as well constrain to silence as to speech, leading to isolation rather than to fellowship, and therefore not to the addressing of another. What have I to say and offer and impart with my words? How can I expect that the other will want to listen to me? Why I cannot be silent but am required to speak is that I necessarily abandon him and leave him to his own devices if I spare myself what is perhaps the thankless venture, and him the unwelcome penetration of his sphere, and withhold from him that which he definitely ought to know, but cannot know until I tell him. I cannot withhold it, because he encounters me as a man, and I should not take him seriously as a man if I did not seriously try to find the way from me to him. No matter what the results, I cannot refrain from knocking. The humanity of the encounter between I and Thou demands that I should not merely make a few tentative efforts in this direction, but do my utmost. Speaking on this presupposition, not for one's own sake but for that of the needy other, is human speaking.

But again the I has to receive the address of the Thou. The words of the Thou heard by me are his impartation to the I. The other has not represented himself to me merely that I should consider him from without. He has not expressed himself to me that he should remain for me a mere object. I have not heard him if the distance between him and me remains. As he speaks with me, his aim is to be known by me, i.e., to seek me out in his own new and strange and different being, and therefore to be seen and grasped from within. This time it is he who comes to me, trying to find a bridge, a way, an open door. It is he who wills to be in me. This is the purpose of his speaking, expounding, questioning and requesting, of his concern, of his claim and the requirement imposed by it. It may appear to me that he wants something from me. In spite of appearance, do I see what is really at stake ? It is really a matter of myself. I cannot be I without accepting this claim of the other, without letting him come to me, and therefore without hearing him. It is a matter of satisfying my vital need, in which I should necessarily sink if I remained alone, if the other and the objective thing with which he knocks on my door and seeks admission were to remain objective, if I did not make it my own. I am in encounter with him, and what is to become of me, how can I be in encounter with him, if he is merely external, an unknown object of consideration, remote even in his proximity ? The question may be raised whether I have any room for him ; whether I can make anything of him ; whether he will really be helped and served by my hearing him and allowing him to come to me. What can it mean for him if I allow this penetration into my sphere, as though he were definitely in good hands with me ? Surely the claim of the fellow-man, however modest, demands far too much for me ever to dream of meeting it. Far too much stands behind the words of others for me ever to hope, even with the best will in the world, to do them justice. Each fellow-man is a whole world, and the request which he makes of me is not merely that I should know this or that about him, but the man himself, and therefore this whole world. It is tempting—and might even seem to be an act of humility in face of too great a task—not to listen too much or too seriously to what is said by the other. Might it not be too presumptuous, and awaken false hopes, to open the door too wide and not just a little ? Is it not too much to demand that I should really and seriously know the man himself ? But the first question is not what we can achieve in this matter, or what it can mean for the other. The first question is what is to become of us if we do not listen to him, if we refuse to allow this penetration into our sphère either as a whole or in part. Whatever may happen to him, whether he is helped or not, or much or little, there he is and there I am : he in his new and strange and different form, so impenetrable and yet so near that I cannot escape him but have to see and have him, speaking to me and expecting to be admitted ; and I in my intolerable isolation (intolerable because it is threatened by his presence), in the seclusion in which I cannot maintain myself now that the encounter with him has taken place, hearing in

2. The Basic Form of Humanity

my ears the words with which he is trying to impart himself to me. Even for my own sake, to save myself like the unjust judge, what option have I but to listen to what the other has to say to me, and therefore to open up myself and receive what he has to give? So long as I do not stand under this compulsion, so long as I have not grasped that it is not just a matter of the other but of myself, so long as I can think that I can avoid hearing the other without harm to myself, I do not give a human hearing, even though humility may demand a thousand times that I hear only in part or not at all. Human hearing of the other takes place on the presupposition that I am affected myself if I do not hear him, and do so in all seriousness.

Drawing the various aspects together, we again emphasise that the human significance of speech, of the human mouth and human ear, depends absolutely upon the fact that man and his fellow speak to one another and listen to one another; that the expression and address between I and Thou are reciprocal. As we can look past people, we can also talk past them and hear past them. When this happens, it always means that we are not in encounter and therefore inhuman. But we talk and hear past them when there is no reciprocity. Two men can talk together openly, exhaustively and earnestly. But if their words serve only their own needs, it may well be that as they talk together each is only trying to assure and help himself, so that they do not reach one another or speak to mutual advantage, but merely talk past one another. How can it be otherwise, how can they find each other, when they are not sought by one another, but each is merely speaking for himself and not for the other? Two monologues do not constitute a dialogue. A dialogue, and therefore the humanity of the encounter of I and Thou, begins only when the spoken word becomes a means to seek and help the other in the difficulty which each entails for the other. On this presupposition the two do not merely speak together, in a commonly produced sound of words, but they genuinely talk with and to one another in human words. The converse is true in hearing. Two men may listen very openly and attentively and tensely to one another, but if there is not in both a genuine need to listen, if they merely listen but not honestly for their own sake, the words mutually spoken will not reach their goal, but their ears will be closed so that they hear past one another. This is inevitable. As hearers, we can find only what we seek. From this standpoint, a dialogue begins only when the hearers are concerned about themselves, about the removal of their own difficulty in respect of the other, so that the words of the other are received and welcomed as a help in this embarrassment. Without this presupposition, hearing is merely a common endurance of a commonly produced sound of words. Only on this presupposition is it mutual hearing, a hearing in which not only the words are human, but also the ears for which they are destined.

No specific proof is required to show that there is much practical justification for suspicion in relation to human words as such. Only words ! Nothing but words ! Empty words ! Words are " sound and fury." There is good cause for the disillusionment expressed in these phrases. Most of the words which we speak and hear obviously have nothing whatever to do with conversation between I and Thou, with the encounter of man and man, with the attempt to speak with one another and listen to one another, and therefore with humanity. Most of our words, spoken or heard, are an inhuman and barbaric affair because we will not speak or listen to one another. We speak them without wanting to seek or help. And we listen to them without letting ourselves be found or helped. This is the case not only in private conversation but in sermons, lectures and discussions, in books and articles. This is how we both hear and read. What we speak and write and hear and read is propaganda. And the result is that our words are emptied and devalued and become mere words. We live in a constant deflation of the word. Yet we have to realise that suspicion and disillusionment are not the way to improve things either here or anywhere. It is not the words that are really empty. It is men themselves when they speak and hear empty words. It is the I which is empty in relation to the Thou, one empty subject confronting another. What is not yet or no longer grasped is that neither I nor Thou can be human in isolation, but only in encounter, and that the word spoken and heard, which leads them both beyond a mere reciprocal view and notion, can be the means in the use of which they can both become human. As we speak with one another and listen to one another, we at least have the possibility for being in encounter, and thus stand on the threshold of humanity. So long as we can speak and hear, there is no compelling force to keep us without, no obstacle to the word spoken and heard finding its fulfilment in a proper use. With suspicion and disillusionment in relation to the word we basically turn our back on humanity. For this reason, although suspicion and disillusionment are no doubt justified in practice, we must not in any circumstances allow them house-room.

Being in encounter consists (3) in the fact that we render mutual assistance in the act of being. We now climb a step higher. There is a being for one another, however limited, even in the relationship of man and man in general. And human being is not human if it does not include this being for one another. As openness between the I and the Thou, their reciprocal visibility, is only a preparatory stage to their mutual expression and address, so the latter cannot be an end, but only the means to something higher, to fellowship in which the one is not only knowable by the other, but is there for him, at his disposal within the necessary limits. Perhaps being in encounter, humanity, is very restricted and broken at the lower levels ; perhaps so little is known in practice about saving openness and therefore real speaking and hearing between one man and another, because even at the lower levels it is a matter of the way to this higher. We see that it is this higher which claims us. We must see and be seen, speak and listen, because to be human we must be prepared to be there for the other, to be at his disposal. We thus hesitate. We are afraid. This is too much to ask. And because this is too much, everything that leads to it is too much : sincere seeing and letting oneself be seen ; sincere speech between man and man. There is indeed a necessary connexion at this point. If I and Thou really see each other and speak

2. The Basic Form of Humanity

with one another and listen to one another, inevitably they mutually summon each other to action. At this higher level it is a matter of the human significance of human activity. If our activity is to be human, this is not guaranteed merely by the fact that it is determined in form by human understanding and volition, art or technique. No degree of perfection which it may have in these respects can ensure that it is not an empty subject which is at work, the man who, because he is without his fellow-man, has not become human, who has not discovered the relationship of I and Thou and therefore himself, who has not become a real I. He may be engaged in the most forceful action both intensively and extensively, and yet he lacks everything for true humanity if he lacks the one thing—that he is not in encounter, and is not therefore human, and has no real part in humanity. Action in encounter is action in correspondence with the summons which the Thou issues to the I when it encounters it, and therefore (for everything is reciprocal in this matter) in correspondence with the summons which the I for its part issues to the Thou in this encounter. The humanity of my activity includes both the fact that I act as one who has received the call of the other and also the fact that I do so as one who has called and must continually call the other. The distinction between human activity and inhuman is not the same as that between altruistic and egoistic. Egoistic activity—for there is a healthy egoism—can be thoroughly human if, without denying itself as such, it is placed at the service of the summons issued by the Thou to the I. And altruistic activity—for there is an unhealthy altruism—can be supremely inhuman if it does not derive from the summons of the one to the other, but the one acts under the illusion that he does not need the other just as much as the other now seems to need him. Action, and therefore being in encounter, and therefore human action, carries with it the twofold correspondence that the other has summoned me and I him ; that he really needs me and I him ; that I act as one who is called but who also calls. This is the higher thing which is decisive beyond mere reciprocal sight and speech and hearing ; the fellowship to which these preliminary stages necessarily lead. It consists in the fact that the one is at the disposal of the other in his activity, and *vice versa*. It is this fellowship—and there is still, of course, a good deal more to be said concerning it—which leads the encounter of I and Thou to its goal and makes human being human. It is actualised concretely in the fact that we render mutual assistance in the act of our being. View and concept are necessarily limited. We cannot replace one another. I cannot be Thou, nor canst Thou live my life. I cannot accept thy responsibility, nor Thou mine. For I and Thou are not inter-changeable. I and Thou are ultimate creaturely reality in their distinction as well as their relationship. If the man Jesus, even though He is Himself, is for us in the strictest sense, living for us, accepting responsibility for us, in this respect, acting as the Son of God in the power of the Creator, He differs from us. This is His prerogative, and no other man can be compared with Him. Correspondence to His being and action consists in the more limited fact that we render mutual assistance. This correspondence is, of course, necessary. Measured by the man Jesus, humanity cannot be less than this for any of us. If our action is human, this means that it is an action in which we give and receive assistance. An action in which assistance is either withheld or rejected is inhuman. For either way it means isolation and persistence in isolation. Only the empty subject can be guilty of such isolation, refusing either to give assistance or to accept it. Only the action of the empty subject and not real man can be autarchic. The more autarchy there is, the more dangerously we skirt the frontier of inhumanity. The more humanity there is, the more the autarchy of our action is pierced. Assistance is actively standing by the other. It is standing so close by him that one's own action means help or support for his. It thus means not to leave him to his own being and action, but in and with one's own to take part in the question and anxiety and burden of his, accepting concern for his life, even though it must always be his and we cannot represent him. Assistance means to live with the other. As we see one another and speak and listen to one another, we call to one another for assistance. As man, as the creature of God, man needs this assistance, and can only call for it. And as man, as the creature of God, he is able and ordained to render assistance to his fellow-man and to receive it from him. God alone, and the man Jesus as the Son of God, has no need of assistance, and is thus able to render far more than assistance to man, namely, to represent him. For us, however, humanity consists in the fact that we need and are capable of mutual assistance. In the very fact that he lives, man calls to his fellow not to leave him alone or to his own devices. He knows well enough that he has to live his own life and bear responsibility for it. But he also knows that he cannot do this if his fellow does not spring to his side and give him his hand and actively stand by him. He cannot be for him in the strict sense. This is possible only for God. But he can be at his disposal. He can be so near to him that his being supports though it does not carry him; that he gives him comfort and encouragement though not victory and triumph; that he alleviates though he does not liberate. In the very fact that he lives, man calls for this help that only his fellow-man can give—the being which is in the same position, which can know him, which can enter into his situation and prescribe and offer the help required. No other being can come so near as to offer what is needed in the way of help. No other can know him so well, or see him as he is, or speak with him and listen to him. And so—in so far as he calls for assistance and not for that which God alone can give—he calls to his fellow-man. An action is human in which a man, even as he tries to help himself, also

2. The Basic Form of Humanity

summons the help of his fellow, reaching out for the support which he alone can give. His action might seem to be very noble but it is not human if he really thinks that he can be self-sufficient and refuses to ask for help. In this very likeness to God he becomes inhuman. In this apparent nobility he falls into the abyss. Nor is this because there is no one to help. This might sometimes be the case, and it only goes to show how much that help is needed. But primarily it is because he betrays and denies his own being with his pretended self-sufficiency. Turning his back on the helping Thou he cannot be an I. He is transformed and dissolved into an empty subject. And he is thus plunged into misery even though in spite of his perversion a hundred helping hands are stretched out to him on all sides. If we will not let ourselves be helped, others cannot help us however much they would like to do so. My humanity depends upon the fact that I am always aware, and my action is determined by the awareness, that I need the assistance of others as a fish needs water. It depends upon my not being content with what I can do for myself, but calling for the Thou to give me the benefit of his action as well.

The other aspect of the same situation follows a similar pattern. In the very fact that he lives a man is summoned by his fellow-man. The latter does not wish to be left alone or to his own devices in his action. I cannot represent him. I cannot make his life-task my own. He cannot expect this from me. He must not confuse me with God. And he will certainly have no reason to do so. I must try to help myself, and he will have to do the same. But as he tries to do so, he has the right to expect that I shall be there for him as well as myself, that I shall not ignore him but live with him, that my life will be a support for his, that it will mean comfort, encouragement and alleviation for him. This is what he requests. His whole action is always this call for my assistance. And as I act for my part, I always stand under this expectation ; this cry for help always reaches me. Perhaps I will not look him too straight in the eye, or let him look too straight into mine ; perhaps I will not speak too sincerely with him, or listen too sincerely to him, because to look straight and speak sincerely is at once—and the more sincerely the more compellingly—to accept this cry for help. I may do so willingly or unwillingly, well or badly, but the cry goes out and somehow reaches me. I am not a thing, nor is my fellow. But as a man I have a direct awareness that my fellow—in the same position as myself—stretches out his hand to me and seeks my support. I know that he too is not God and cannot therefore be self-sufficient. And I also know that what he expects of me—namely, a little support—does not exceed my powers, that this little assistance is not in any sense a divine but a very human work which may rightly be expected, that I am able to render it, and under an obligation to do so. I cannot evade my fellow who asks for it. I must stand by him and help him. I become inhuman if I resist this awareness or try to escape the limited but definite service I can render. The humanity of my action is again at stake, and therefore I myself. An action is human when a man who must help himself either well or badly also accepts the call for help issued by another and gives his need a place in the determination of his own action. My action is human when the outstretched hand of the other does not grope in the void but finds in mine the support which is asked. It is inhuman if I am content merely to help myself. It is to be noted that I do not plunge the other but myself into perdition, namely, inhumanity, if I refuse him my support and do not do the modest thing which I could do. If he has called and claimed me, he has done what he can for the humanity of his action. It is I who am affected if I withhold my help. As much as in him lies, he is in encounter. But I am not. I am without the Thou. And therefore I cannot be an I. I transform myself on this side into an empty subject. I am in misery. I am the void in which the other gropes. I am thus a futile being, however perfect may be the help which I give myself, thus satisfying my own needs. If we will not help others, there is no help even in the most perfect self-help. My humanity depends upon the fact that I am always aware, and my action is determined by the awareness, that I need to give my assistance to the Thou as a fish needs water. It depends upon my answering the call of the other, and acting on his behalf, even in and with what I do for myself.

> For an understanding of this third step, which is as it were the goal of all that we have so far said, it is to be noted that humanity is not an ideal nor its exercise a virtue. We do not speak of man imagined on the basis of a hypothesis, whose picture we have to fill out, and yet can always escape with the excuse that real man is very different. We are not guilty of idealisation when we say of man that he is created and ordained to receive help from his fellow-man and to give help to his fellow-man. We are speaking of real man. And we are speaking of him realistically, whereas all the descriptions of man in which the presupposition is normative of an empty subject isolated from the fellow-man can only be called idealistic in the wrong sense. For in them, in more or less consistent approximation to Zarathustra, the reference is to a man who does not and cannot exist, but can only be the vision of a maniac. The counterpart of the man Jesus ; the picture of man who, although he is not God, is adopted by God in the man Jesus ; the picture of the man whom God is for as He is for the man Jesus ; the picture of this man is the realistic picture of real man. No optimistic law or lofty aim is given us on this view, but the primitive factuality of our situation as it is—that man is not alone, but with his fellow-man, needing his help and pledged to help him. Is there anything extraordinary in this demand ? Is there any real demand at all ? Can there be any virtue merely in accepting our true situation ? The only extraordinary thing, the only demand, would be the madness and folly of leaving this situation, of ceasing to be human. To be human, and therefore to act accordingly, confessing both the need of assistance and the willingness to render it, is supremely natural and not unnatural. It is the most obvious thing to do, whereas the opposite is by far the most artificial. What is demanded is simply that man should not wander away but be himself in the best sense of the term, keeping to the determination which he has been given as a man. It is to be noted that

2. The Basic Form of Humanity

at the place and in the form in which Christian anthropology sees him man cannot make the favourite excuse that too much is expected of him, that he is given too high and holy a destiny. On the contrary, all that he has to do is simply to see himself in the situation in which he actually finds himself, keeping to this situation, and not trying to adapt himself to any other.

But being in encounter consists (4) in the fact that all the occurrence which we have so far described as the basic form of humanity stands under the sign that it is done on both sides with gladness. We gladly see and are seen; we gladly speak and listen; we gladly receive and offer assistance. This can be called the last and final step of humanity. Or, we might equally well say, this is the secret of the whole, and therefore of the three preceding stages. Our description of the three preceding stages still lacks a certain dimension without the underscoring of which we still fall short of the human as such. All that we have so far said about the relationship of I and Thou, and therefore the basic form of humanity, however realistic outwardly the picture of real man, might seem to be no more than the description of a fairly complicated mechanism, or, more organically, of a perfect flower unfortunately detached from its roots. I see the Thou and am pleased to be seen by him. I speak with him and hear as he speaks with me. I need him, and see that he needs me. But all this may take place and be understood and yet leave a great unseen lacuna which must be filled if there is to be true and serious humanity. It may all be merely an inhuman description of the human. It may all lack a decisive, all-animating and motivating dynamic, and therefore the real substance or soul of the human without which all the humanity of our being, however perfect externally, is only external, but internally and properly and essentially is inhuman. In conclusion, therefore, we shall try to incorporate this true and inward element into our picture of real man, of human man, expressly asking concerning the dynamic, the substance or soul of it all, and therefore the secret of humanity.

There must be no confusion. We ask concerning the secret of humanity as such. We presuppose that it is the humanity of the man whose determination is to be the covenant-partner of God. It is the great secret of man that he belongs to God, that God is for him, and for him in the person of the man Jesus. We do not now speak of this great mystery, but of the lesser yet not inconsiderable secret of his humanity, of his human nature, as this is fashioned in correspondence with his determination for covenant-partnership with God. It would not correspond to this determination if it did not contain within itself as such a secret. Because it corresponds to the determination of man, and therefore to the great secret, we must ask concerning its own lesser and in some sense immanent secret. There is no sense in trying to dispute this secret. We do not really honour the great secret of man, which consists in his relationship to God, by ignoring the fact that the man who enters into this relationship to God is fashioned by the same God in such a way that even in his creaturely mode of existence as such, and therefore in his humanity, he is not without mystery, but the bearer, executor and guardian of a secret which is not inconsiderable in its own place and manner.

We cannot solve the mystery as such. That is to say, we can only show that it is a secret by our attempt to describe it. But after all, has not all that we have said concerning humanity been more in the nature of indication than direct description ? Has not all that we have finally said concerning the human significance of the eye and mouth and ear and action pointed beyond itself to something decisive which is itself concealed, so that although we can point to it we cannot pinpoint it ? If, then, we turn to consider this decisive thing as such, this can only mean that we admit that in our whole description of humanity we can only denote and indicate its final derivation and true essence. With all that we can say we merely point to something inward and hidden which is the meaning and power of its describable exterior. We everywhere point to its secret. And we must now do this expressly, and therefore in the form of a particular discussion, and to that extent in relation to a final and supreme level of the concept of humanity.

The obvious lacuna in our description of humanity consists, however, in the fact that we have not explicitly affirmed that being in encounter, in which we have seen the basic form of humanity, is a being which is gladly actualised by man. I think that this unpretentious word " gladly," while it does not penetrate the secret before which we stand, does at least indicate it correctly as the *conditio sine qua non* of humanity.

The alternative to " gladly " is not " reluctantly " but " neutrally "—which means that I am free to choose between " gladly " and " reluctantly." Do I really have the choice of actualising being in the encounter between I and Thou either gladly or reluctantly ? Am I in some sense free to do justice either gladly or reluctantly to the human significance of eyes and mouth and ear and action, and therefore of my whole relationship to the Thou, of which we have been considering the positive content ? Can I in some way have both possibilities at my disposal, reserving them both for myself ? If we describe the humanity of man in terms such as these, even though we may have had a true perception of the earlier stages, and have portrayed them correctly, we have obviously not taken it seriously as a determination of the true being of man, of man himself. We are still (or again) looking past real man, who is not capable of this reservation and control.

For what would this neutrality between gladly and reluctantly really mean ? It would mean that the being of man in encounter is a real fact, the actual situation in which he finds himself and cannot outwardly escape without self-alienation. If he is to do justice to his situation, and therefore to himself, he has thus no option but to keep to the fact, with all that it involves, that the I is ordered in relation to the Thou and the Thou to the I, and that this order must be realised. He thus subjects himself to this order as to an ineluctable

2. The Basic Form of Humanity

law of nature. He actualises the reciprocal openness, the reciprocal self-expression and address, the reciprocal assistance, and therefore the whole concept of humanity to the best of his knowledge and conscience, well aware that he has no real option. But he does have one option, and may leave it open, namely, whether he does it all gladly or reluctantly. In his innermost being, or—to use the popular, and biblical, and very expressive phrase—in his heart, he remains at a point above the gladly or reluctantly, from which he can decide either for the one or the other; either for or against a spontaneous acceptance of this encounter; either for or against a willing participation in the Thou; either for or against an inner Yes as the motive of this participation. The law is thus binding, but only externally. Basically and properly it is not binding. He can affirm and fulfil it as a law which is not his own but an alien law, not established by himself but laid upon him and prescribed for him.

If we accept this view, at the last hour we take a decision which compromises all that we have said and apparently secured. For the unavoidable implication is that the mutual relationship of I and Thou is only an accidental *fact* of human existence, although inescapable and to be respected only as such, but that it does not finally effect the essence of man, man himself, since it is alien to his innermost being. In his essence, his innermost being, his heart, he is only what he is gladly. If we do not speak primarily of what he is gladly, we do not speak of his essence, of himself. If it is an open question whether he is human and engaged in the encounter of I and Thou gladly or reluctantly, this means no more and no less than that it does not belong to his essence as man to be human. He is it in fact, because he has no option in the unavoidable presence of his fellow-man. But in himself he might not be. At bottom, in the innermost recesses of his proper self, he is not. Humanity is alien to him. It is a kind of hat which he can put on and take off. It is not intrinsic to him. It is not the law which he prescribes for himself as a man. It is not the freedom in which he draws his first breath. His first and true freedom is the strange freedom of choice in which he can satisfy the law laid upon him from without either gladly or reluctantly. He breathes first in this freedom, not in the freedom to do justice to his humanity gladly. And this means that, even if he does justice to his humanity, and does it gladly, it is without root, without dynamic, without substance, without soul.

The secret of his humanity, however, is that in his being in the encounter of I and Thou we do not have to do with a determination which is accidental and later imposed from without, but with a self-determination which is free and intrinsic to his essence. He is not a man first, and then has his fellow-man alongside him, and is gladly or reluctantly human, i.e., in encounter with him. He is a man as he is human, and gladly in the sense that there can be no question of a "reluctantly." He is unequivocally and radically human. He follows the voice and impulse of his own heart when he is human, when he looks the other in the eye, when he speaks with him and listens to him, when he receives and offers assistance. There are no secret hiding-places or recesses, no dark forest-depths, where deep down he wills or can will anything else. He himself is human. He himself, in the sense described in those three stages, is not without but with his fellow-man. He would not be a man if he were without and not with his fellow-man. This is the great lacuna in our previous exposition which we must now fill to the best of our ability. This is the dimension which we must now especially and expressly indicate.

That man is not without his fellow-man is not an accident which overtakes him. It is no mere contingent fact. It is not a given factor with which he must arbitrarily wrestle and to which he must somehow adjust himself. From the very outset, as man, he is not without but with his fellow-man. Nor is he one essence with his fellow-man. He is with him in the sense that he is one being and his fellow-man another. We have always had occasion, and have so now, to remember that I am I and Thou Thou; that Thou art Thou and not I. In humanity it is not a question of the removal and dissolution but the confirmation and exercise of duality as such. At this point, as in the relationship with God, identity-mysticism is not the way to do justice to the facts. Man and fellow-man, I and Thou—this means mutual limitation. But in this relationship, which is not a relationship of things but the very different relationship of people, limitation means mutual determination. And this determination is inward as well as outward. It is not therefore added to his essence, to the man himself, as though it were originally and properly alien to him and he to it, and at some level of his being he were not determined by it. He is not free in relation to it, but as he is determined by it. He is himself in this determination. The externality of the different fellow-man who encounters me has this in common with the very different externality of the God distinct from me—that it is also inward to me; inward in the sense that this external thing, the other man, is inward and intrinsic to me even in his otherness. Man is not the fellow-man, but he is with him. I am not Thou, but I am with Thee. Humanity is the realisation of this " with." As two men look one another in the eye, and speak with one another and listen to one another, and render mutual assistance, they are together. But everything depends on whether they are not merely together under a law imposed from without, or merely accepting an unavoidable situation. To be sure, there is a law here—the law of the Creator imposed as such on the creature. And there is a situation in which man finds himself—created by the fact that he is not alone, but the fellow-man is present with him. But that law of God is given him as his own law, the law which he himself has set up, the law of his own freedom. Only as

2. The Basic Form of Humanity

such is its validity genuine according to the intention of its Giver. Valid in any other way, it would be obeyed by man, but only as an alien law imposed from without and not as his own law. It would not, therefore, be obeyed gladly. Man would know the other possibility of either not obeying it at all or doing so reluctantly because he himself wills or can will something very different. It would not, then, be valid or known at all. But if he does not really know it, this means that he does not know himself. He is not himself but lost outside himself. For he is himself as he stands under this law as the law of his own freedom. When he is obedient to it in this way, as to the law of his own freedom, he realises that " with "—with the fellow-man, with the Thou—by inner as well as outer necessity, and therefore gladly and spontaneously. Being together thus acquires the character of something absolutely spontaneous. The fellow-man is not merely imposed or thrust upon man, or the Thou upon the I, so that the encounter has almost the instinctive form of a " falling-out," i.e., of a secret or open reversal of encounter, or movement of retreat, in which a hasty greeting is exchanged and then the one seeks safety as quickly as possible from the other, withdrawing into himself for fear of violation and in the interest of self-assertion. On the contrary, the fellow-man belongs to man, the Thou to the I, and is therefore welcome, even in his otherness and particularity. I have waited for Thee. I sought Thee before Thou didst encounter me. I had Thee in view even before I knew Thee. The encounter with Thee is not, therefore, the encounter with something strange which disturbs me, but with a counterpart which I have lacked and without which I would be empty and futile. The situation between man and man is genuinely inescapable, and I do real justice to it, only if it is not subject to my caprice even in the sense that I am not free inwardly to accept or reject it, but can only accept it, knowing that it is only and exclusively in this situation that I am myself, and can act as such. Humanity is the realisation of this togetherness of man and man grounded in human freedom and necessary in this freedom.

We have to safeguard this statement against two misunderstandings. The first in this. Humanity in the highest sense cannot consist in the fact that the one loses himself in the other, surrendering or forgetting or neglecting his own life and task and responsibility, making himself a mere copy of the other, and the life and task and responsibility of the other a framework for his own life. Man is bound to his fellow-man, but he cannot belong to him, i.e., he cannot be his property. This is impossible because if he did he would not see and recognise in him what he is to him, namely, the other. In paying him what seems to be so great an honour, he would pay him too little. In asking what is apparently so complete a self-sacrifice, he would withhold himself. He would encroach too much upon him by changing the encounter with him into a union. He would force himself upon him, and thus become a burden commensurate neither with the dignity nor powers of the other. We cannot subject ourselves to a fellow-man without doing him the deepest injury. For what he can expect of me as another cannot be that I should cease to be his Thou, and therefore to stand before him in my distinction from him. What he gladly and in freedom desires of me is that I should be with him. But I escape him if I lose myself in him, ceasing to be for him a genuine counterpart. He intends and seeks me in my uniqueness and irreplaceability, as a being standing and moving on its own feet. He has no use for a mere adaptation to himself, existing only in dependence on him. I thus escape my fellow-man if I depend on him. He cannot accept this gladly. And the result will be that, unable to use me, he will repulse me, startled by this encounter which is no true encounter, and withdrawing into himself or even turning against me. Make no mistake, there is an excessive relationship to the fellow-man in which the very relationship in which humanity ought to be attained is supremely inhuman because it is not realised that it can arise and persist only in two-sided freedom, and not in the bondage of the one for the sake of the freedom of the other. To belong to another is man's bondage. If I am his property, I am no longer with him gladly. Our being together has become a constraint to which I myself am subject and which I seek to lay on the other. But in this togetherness of mutual constraint I can only at bottom despise myself and cause myself to be despised by the other, having first despised the other by encroaching too much upon him. Humanity is thus the realisation of this togetherness only when I do not lose but maintain myself in it, living my own life with the other, accepting my own task and responsibility, and thus keeping and not overrunning the proper distance between us.

The second misunderstanding is the direct opposite. Humanity in the highest sense cannot consist in the fact that the one only intends and seeks in the other himself, and thus uses the encounter with him to extend and enrich and deepen and confirm and secure his own being. Being in encounter is no more active subjection than passive. It has nothing whatever to do with a campaign of conquest as in cheap love-stories. If I want the other for myself, I do better to stay at home. For there can be no worse self-deception than to desire to be with the other in order to find myself in him. In so doing, do I not forget even my own uniqueness and irreplaceability? I cannot find myself in the other, nor is this what I can intend and seek and strive after gladly and in the necessity of my own freedom. If in the other I seek myself at a higher or deeper level, the Thou is for me merely my extended I. I do not respect it as a being which does not belong to me but must be true to itself and not violated. And in these circumstances I experience something which I can experience only reluctantly, namely, that I am really quite alone even with this

2. The Basic Form of Humanity

Thou which I have supposedly conquered and appropriated and made my own. Moreover, I have missed the opportunity of experiencing what I might have experienced gladly. In violating the freedom of the other, I have forfeited my own. I have despised him, and in so doing I have basically despised myself. The fellow-man is bound to me only in the sense that he does not belong to me. If I treat him as though he were my own property, he is no longer bound to me. And I need not then be surprised if the supposed and false coming together is really a falling-out, and the encounter between us sooner or later becomes a mutual attack or a mutual withdrawal. Because the relationship has an excessive form, it is wrong from the very first, and the attempt to realise it is bound to end in failure.

The way of humanity, and therefore the way to realise the togetherness of man grounded in human freedom and necessary in this freedom, does not lie between these two misunderstandings but above them. In a togetherness which is accepted gladly and in freedom man is neither a slave nor a tyrant, and the fellow-man is neither a slave nor tyrant, but both are companions, associates, comrades, fellows and helpmates. As such they are indispensable to one another. As such they intend and expect and seek one another. As such they cannot be without one another. As such they look one another in the eye, and speak and listen to one another, and render mutual assistance. All this is impossible if they meet as tyrant and slave. Between tyrant and slave there is no genuine encounter, and even genuine encounter ceases to be genuine to the extent that it is understood and actualised on the one side or the other as the encounter of tyrant and slave. Only in the atmosphere of freedom can it be genuine. Companions are free. So are associates. So are comrades. So are fellows. So are helpmates. Only what takes place between such as these is humanity.

What we indicate in this way is really the *secret* of humanity. For here we have to do with an element in the concept which, in contrast to those previously mentioned, cannot be described or at any rate grounded or deduced from elsewhere, but can only be affirmed as the living centre of the whole. At a pinch we can describe, and have tried to do so, how the encounter takes place between men who meet gladly and in freedom, how they open up themselves to one another, and speak with one another, and listen to one another, and help one another. But in so doing we presuppose as the living centre of the whole the decisive point that they meet gladly and in freedom, not as tyrants and slaves, but as companions, associates, comrades, fellows and helpmates. But how are we to describe this decisive thing? We can say of what takes place between men only something to the following effect—that there is a discovery, the mutual recognition that each is essential to the other. There is thus enacted the paradox that the one is unique and irreplaceable for the other. But this means that there is also an electing and election. Each can affirm the other as the being with which he wants to be and cannot be without. But this leads to mutual joy, each in the existence of the other and both in the fact that they can exist together. For in these circumstances even the co-existence is joy. The fact remains that common existence is still something posited and given, but this givenness is now clear and vital in an active willing of this fellowship, a willing which derives quite simply from the fact that each has received a gift which he necessarily desires to reciprocate to the best of his ability. And if it is asked in what this gift consists, the answer must be that the one has quite simply been given the other, and that what he for his part has to give is again himself. It is in this being given and giving that there consists the electing and election, the mutual acceptance, the common joy, and therefore the freedom of this encounter—the freedom in which there is no room for those misunderstandings, in which both can breathe as they let breathe, in which both keep their distance because they are so close, and are so close because they can keep their distance. But what else is the discovery but the discovery how great and unfathomable and inexpressible is the secret that this may be so. The fact that it may be so, the why and wherefore of it, is never understood. It is simply effected without disclosing itself. It is a pure fact, inward as well as outward. It is the truth of the situation, not only of an outward but also of an inward and mutually recognised or established situation. Thus all words fail at the decisive point. And they fail at the point where we have to describe how and why each man has his own creaturely existence, and is this particular man in fulfilment of it, and continually rediscovers himself as such. Even what is to be discovered at this point is a riddle to which there is no key apart from faith in God the Creator. Nor do we have here two points, two discoveries, two mysteries. For that which cannot be fathomed or expressed, but only established in the fulfilment of our existence, is the one secret of humanity. Man discovers the uniqueness and irreplaceability of the other man in his actuality as the companion, associate, comrade, fellow and helpmate which he is given, and in this way and this way alone, in all the necessity of the presence of this other, he discovers his own uniqueness and irreplaceability, and therefore his own being and actuality as a man. Or conversely, he discovers himself as this particular man existing for himself, and in this way and this way alone, in all the necessity of his own existence, he discovers the other man as the being which is with him and to which he for his part has to give himself as a companion, associate, comrade, fellow and helpmate. Humanity lives and moves and has its being in this freedom to be oneself with the other, and oneself to be with the other.

At this fourth stage we are really speaking of the *conditio sine qua non* of humanity, just because we can only talk around the subject,

2. The Basic Form of Humanity

and cannot describe anything, but only point to something hidden. What we have here is not just an optional addition to the whole, a beautiful crown finally adorning humanity but not indispensable. No, if humanity does not consist first and last in this freedom, it does not exist at all. All true openness, and reciprocal speech and hearing, and mutual assistance, has its basis and stability in this dynamic thing, and all that can be described in this indescribable. If the encounter of I and Thou lacked the secret of this freedom, if its whole realisation were merely external and in some sense hollow, how could it be genuine and effective? From the very outset we have tried to represent it in its genuineness and force, and not as a mere mechanism or empty form which might have another content than true humanity. We must now expressly add that the presupposition, if we have not described an empty form, is that which we have finally indicated with our reference to freedom as the secret of being in encounter and therefore the secret of humanity. What we have described—openness, and speech and hearing, and mutual assistance—can be real only when there is also this discovery between man and man, and the necessity of this " gladly," this freedom, rules in their seeing and being seen, their speech and hearing, their reciprocal help. This is not merely the crown of humanity, but its root.

But this means that if we are to embrace human nature as such, as created and given by God, then we must grasp as its motivating element the decisive point that man is essentially determined to be with his fellow-man gladly, in the indicated freedom of the heart. By nature he has no possibility or point of departure for any other choice. If we have to maintain that he has this choice in fact, it does not derive from his nature. For we cannot make God his Creator responsible for this fatal possibility. And it is even worse if we praise the Creator for obviously giving man the possibility of a different choice. For this is to praise Him for allowing and enabling man to choose in his heart inhumanity as well as humanity, and therefore to be in his heart inhuman as well as human, or both perhaps alternately. And we then ascribe to human nature the strange distinction of a freedom for its own denial and destruction. We should not call this freedom nature, but sin. And we should not connect it with God the Creator or the creaturely essence of man, but with man's irrational and inexplicable apostasy from God and from himself. It is the man who has fallen away from God and from himself who thinks that he can find his essence in that false freedom and therefore himself in an original isolation from which he emerges either gladly or reluctantly to be with his fellow-man. Real man as God created him is not in the waste of isolation. He does not have this choice. He does not need to emerge from this waste. It is not just subsequently, and therefore not with final seriousness, that he is with his fellow-man. His freedom consists from the very outset in his intending and seeking this other, not to be his tyrant or slave, but his companion, associate, comrade, fellow and helpmate, and that the other may be the same to him. As we call this humanity, and say that everything which belongs to humanity has both its culmination and root in this one thing, we must call this human nature. Human nature is man himself. But man is what he is freely and from the heart. And freely and from the heart he is what he is in the secret of the encounter with his fellow-man in which the latter is welcome and he is with him gladly.

We have now reached a provisional conclusion in our investigation. What we shall have to say in our third sub-section will not add anything material to it. All that we can do is to establish a definite and unequivocal form of being in the encounter of I and Thou, namely, being in the encounter of man and woman. But first, in relation to our present theme, we must fill out what we have said on the fourth and final level of humanity by a critical observation. At this final level of the concept of humanity we have not been speaking about Christian love.

In the light of the Word of God and on the presupposition of the given divine reality of revelation, i.e., of the humanity of the man Jesus, we have been speaking about the creaturely essence of man, human nature. On this basis, we could not say anything other or less of man than that by nature he is determined for his fellow-man, to be with him gladly. It would be inadmissible to describe man as a being to which this determination does not radically belong but is alien. A being to which it was alien would be different by nature from the man Jesus. If man were a being of this kind, we should either have to say that only the man Jesus was real man as God created him, or that Jesus was not a real man at all, but a being of a different order. If, however, there is similarity as well as dissimilarity between him and us, to His being *for* others there must correspond as at least a minimum on our side the fact that our human being is at root a free being *with* others. This is what we have maintained as the secret of humanity.

We do not associate ourselves, therefore, with the common theological practice of depreciating human nature as much as possible in order to oppose to it the more effectively what may be made of man by divine grace. Orientation by the picture of the man Jesus shows us a very definite way from which we must not be frightened by the danger of meeting the false propositions of Roman Catholicism, humanism or natural theology. If we accept this orientation, what we think and say cannot be false. But it may well be so if we arbitrarily try to avoid certain conclusions. That there is a human nature created by God and therefore good and not evil must be accepted as we see man against the background of the man Jesus. It is not by nature, but by its denial and misuse, that man is as alien and opposed to the grace of God as we see him to be in fact. But rightly to appreciate this corruption brought about by man, and therefore the sin of man, we must quietly consider what is corrupted, and calmly maintain that all the corruption of man cannot make evil by nature the good work of God. It is because the secret of humanity remains even when it is shamed by man that sin is always such an inconceivable revolt, and never loses the character of a crime, or becomes a kind of second natural state which is excusable as such. But this enables us to see and understand why the mercy of God to man is not an act of caprice but has its sure basis in the fact that man is not a stranger or lost to his Creator even as a sinner, but in respect of his nature, of the secret of his humanity, still confronts him as he was created. Becoming a sinner, he has not vanished as a man, or changed into a different

2. The Basic Form of Humanity

being, but still stands before God as the being as which he was created, and therefore as the being whose nature consists in that freedom. And as God makes Himself his Deliverer, He merely exercises His faithfulness as the Creator to His creature, which has not become different or been lost to Him by its fall into sin. This does not mean that by ascribing to man this secret of his humanity as an indestructible determination of his nature we concede to him a power to save himself or even to co-operate in his salvation. This is where the false propositions of Roman Catholicism and humanism arise, and we must be on our guard against them. How can it save a man, or what can it contribute to his salvation, that even as a sinner he is a man, and therefore has the manner of a man ? God alone saves and pardons and renews him, and He does so in free mercy. Yet we have still to point to the fact that that secret is proper to man as an indestructible determination of his nature, for to deny this truth would be to deny the continuity of the human subject as a creature, a sinner, and a sinner saved by grace. Our christological starting-point gives us no reason to make this denial. In what we have said, we do not ascribe to man more than belongs to him on this basis. To contest what is proper to him on this basis is hardly to magnify the glory of God and His grace.

But we have not been speaking of Christian love. New Testament ἀγάπη is not a determination of human nature as such. It is the action and attitude of the man who only becomes real and can only be understood in the course of his history with God. Love is the new gratitude of those who have come to know God the Creator as the merciful Deliverer. As such it is the gracious gift of the Holy Ghost shed abroad in the hearts of Christians convicted of sin against God and outrage against themselves, and to that extent lost, but assured of their justification and preservation in faith in Jesus Christ (Rom. 5[5]). In love they respond to the revelation of the covenant fulfilled in Jesus Christ, in which God comes to them as their merciful Father, Lord and Judge, and they see their fellow-men as brothers and sisters, i.e., as those who have sinned with them and found grace with them. It is thus the turning to them of this particular love of God which in Christian love binds and keeps men together in common life and action. Christian love is humility before Him, obedience to Him, hope in Him, the commonly received freedom of those who know that they are born and created anew as His children and are called as His community to the common proclamation of His name. It is another matter that in love that freedom of the human creature and therefore the secret of humanity is also honoured. But the honour which it receives is a completely new one. In it, it is like a brand plucked from the burning. And it is seen in an unexpected and completely new light which has fallen upon it from above, from the God who has dealings with man, when it was previously wrapped in darkness through the sin of man. Christian love is the determination of the man who in the fulfilled covenant of God is snatched from the depth of his guilt and the misery of his consequent isolation from his fellow-man and exalted to life in fellowship with Jesus Christ as his Saviour and therefore to fellowship with his fellow-man. Love itself, and in love man, lives with his fellow-man on the basis of the revelation and knowledge of what God has done for His human creature ; on the basis of the forgiveness declared to and received by him, and his sanctification as it takes place in this justification. But it is not of this Christian love that we have been speaking.

On the contrary, we have been speaking of the nature of the human creature. The same man who in the course of his history with God, in the fulfilment of his fellowship with Jesus Christ, will also participate in and be capable of Christian love for God and his fellow-men as brothers, is as such this creature whose manner is that which we have come to know as humanity. Humanity, even as we finally spoke of it in the secret of that free co-existence of man and man, is not Christian love, but only the natural exercise and actualisation of human nature—something which formally is on the same level as the corresponding vital functions and natural determinations of other beings which are not men. The fact that a stone is a stone involves a definite nexus of chemical, physical and mathematical conditions and determinations. The fact that a plant is a plant involves a specific organic process. The fact that an animal is an animal involves a particular consciousness and spontaneity in this vital process. But the fact that a man is a man involves freedom in the co-existence of man and man in which the one may be, and will be, the companion, associate, comrade, fellow and helpmate of the other. This is human nature, humanity. Down below, in and for himself, the man who is determined from above as the covenant-partner of God is the creature fashioned and determined and existing in this way. For all the differences in detail, he always lives with varying degrees of consistency and perfection the life characterised by this nature. It is to be expressly noted that we do not have here a gracious gift of the Holy Ghost for the possession of which he must be a Christian, or an operation of the Word of God directly proclaimed to man and directly received and believed by him. What we have called humanity can be present and known in varying degrees of perfection or imperfection even where there can be no question of a direct revelation and knowledge of Jesus Christ. This reality of human nature and its recognition are not, therefore, restricted to the Christian community, to the "children" of light, but, as we are told in Lk. 16[8], the "children of this world" may in this respect be wiser than the children of light, being more human, and knowing more about humanity, than the often very inhuman and therefore foolish Christians. Of course, there is no reason why Christians too should not be human and know about humanity. But this is not what necessarily distinguishes them from other men. In this respect they may be at a disadvantage as compared with other men. At bottom, they are at one with them in this. Hence the totality which we have described as humanity is the determination of human being as such irrespective of what may become of man in the course of his history with God. We cannot, therefore, expect to hear about Christian love when the reference is to humanity in the Christian doctrine of the creature.

"Love never faileth" (1 Cor. 13[8]). It is the life of those who after the fall are restored by the grace of God, and as such a life which cannot be destroyed again, and is not threatened even by death and the end of the world. This is something which cannot be said of humanity and that secret of humanity. Humanity might fail. When man sins, his humanity does not disappear, but it is sick and blurred and perverted and destroyed and unrecognisable. And when man falls victim to death, a term is put even to his life in that freedom. If there were no deliverance from sin and death, if God would not acknowledge the creature in His mercy and keep it from destruction, the end of man would inevitably entail the end of his life in that secret and therefore the extirpation of that freedom. Only as love is shed abroad in our hearts as the love of God can humanity as the nature of man receive new honour and acquire a new stability. As it participates in love, it can and will never fail. We have not, therefore, spoken of that which in itself and as such, as the determination of man, is eternally secure even though man and the world perish. In the history of the covenant between God and man there are two determinations of man which do not belong at all to his creatureliness and therefore to his nature. The one is his determination by the inconceivable act of his own sin, and the other is his determination by the even more inconceivable act of the divine mercy. In his humanity as such there is to be found neither the reality nor even the possibility of his sin, and neither the reality nor even the possibility of divine grace. Hence even in the deepest secret of humanity to which we must continually point there cannot be ascribed to it what may be ascribed only to love.

Yet we must not cease to point to this secret. And it would be highly inappropriate if, to make the distinction between humanity and Christian love even clearer, we adopted a perverse standpoint in defining the concept of

2. The Basic Form of Humanity

numanity, making no use of the Christian judgment, and therefore describing humanity perhaps in the sense of Idealism as humanity without the fellow-man, or as a mere co-existence of man and fellow-man, and therefore excluding from the concept that freedom of the heart in which man and fellow-man are together gladly, as though this freedom could arise only in the sphere of Christian love. To do this is not honest dealing. For how can we fail to see that even outwith the Christian sphere and quite apart from the concept of Christian love humanity is not necessarily present in that perverse and unfounded way, but for all the perverse and unfounded interpretations it is genuinely there, and is to be sought and found in the direction which we have taken. It would fare ill with theological anthropology if it were to fail to keep pace with attempts at something better as they have actually been made outside the sphere of the Church altogether; if in its anxiety not to depreciate grace and Christian love it were to propose a concept of humanity the falsity and untenability of which were immediately apparent even to the decided non-Christian. Surely nothing but the best and most securely grounded is good enough to describe the nature which God Himself has given to man. There is no reason for surprise that in the light of the divine grace shown in the existence of the man Jesus there has to be ascribed to human nature as much as we have actually ascribed to it in the development of our doctrine of humanity. Half-measures are obviously illegitimate at this point, and we are justified least of all by anxiety lest too little will remain for divine grace if we concede too much to human nature. In this respect theological anthropology has to go its own way, and as it pursues it resolutely to the end it is led to statements which are very similar to those in which humanity is described from a very different angle (e.g., by the pagan Confucius, the atheist L. Feuerbach and the Jew M. Buber). But does this constitute any good reason why we should not make them? Of course, if we look carefully, there can be no question of an exact correspondence and coincidence between the Christian statements and these others which rest on very different foundations. We need not be surprised that there are approximations and similarities. Indeed, in this very fact we may even see a certain confirmation of our results—a confirmation which we do not need and which will not cause us any particular excitement, but of which, in view of its occurrence, we shall not be ashamed. Why should there not be confirmations of this kind? In this context we are not speaking of the Christian in particular but of man in general, and therefore of something which has been the object of all kinds of "worldly," i.e., non-Christian wisdom. And surely it need not be, and is not actually, the case, that this worldly wisdom with its very different criteria has always been mistaken, always seeking humanity in the direction of Idealism and finally of Nietzsche, and therefore establishing and describing it as humanity without the fellow-man, the humanity of man in isolation. It would be far more strange if not the slightest trace had ever been found of fellow-humanity, of the humanity of I and Thou. Since we ourselves have reached the conclusion that the nature of man in himself and in general is to be found in this conception of humanity, we shall not take offence, but quietly see an indirect confirmation of our assertion, if we find that a certain knowledge of this conception was and is possible to man in general, even to the pagan, atheist and Jew, and that as *figura* shows it has actually been represented outwith Christian theology. Even with his natural knowledge of himself the natural man is still in the sphere of divine grace; in the sphere in which Jesus too was man. How, then, can he lack a certain ability to have some better knowledge of himself as well as a good deal worse? But theological anthropology has the advantage over this better knowledge of the natural man that it possesses a criterion—its knowledge of divine grace and the man Jesus—which allows and commands it from the very outset and with final resoluteness and clarity to turn its back on that worse knowledge and ignorance, and from the very first and necessarily and therefore with final consistency to move in the direction of the conception of humanity and therefore of human nature according to which man as such and radically is not without but with the fellow-man, and his humanity at its deepest and highest level consists in the freedom of his heart for the other. As we quietly rejoice in the fact that in the general direction of our investigation and presentation we find ourselves in a certain agreement with the wisest of the wise of this world, we can equally quietly leave it undecided whether and to what extent they for their part follow us even to the final and decisive consequences of this conception, namely, to that " gladly," to that freedom of the heart between man and man as the root and crown of the concept of humanity. If they did not do this, as they surely seem to do in the case of Confucius, Feuerbach and Buber, it would certainly be made clear that *duo cum faciunt idem non est idem*. The difference between a Christian and every other anthropology would then emerge in the fact that even in respect of human nature we finally and decisively reach different conclusions. But we do not insist that this is necessarily so. We should not and do not take offence—" Is thine eye evil, because I am good ? "—if Confucius, Feuerbach and Buber finally had in view this freedom of the heart, and only failed by accident to tread it to its ultimate consequences, and thus to come to this final conclusion. What else can they have meant, or what other goal had in view, once they had taken the right direction of human duality ? At any rate, we have no reason not to welcome the proximity to some of the wiser of the wise of this world in which we in some degree find ourselves in this respect, and therefore we have no reason to allow this proximity to deflect us from the consistent pursuit of our own way.

But this brings me to the real point of this final critical observation. The Christian Church, Christianity, has every reason to take note of the reality which we have discovered in treading our own way of theological anthropology consistently to the end. Properly and at its deepest level, which is also its highest, human nature is not isolated but dual. It does not consist in the freedom of a heart closed to the fellow-man, but in that of a heart open to the fellow-man. It does not consist in the refusal of man to see the fellow-man and to be seen by him, to speak with him and listen to him, to receive his assistance and to render assistance to him. It does not consist in an indifference in which he might just as well be disposed for these things as not. But it consists in an unequivocal inclination for them. Man is human in the fact that he is with his fellow-man gladly. But in Christianity there is an inveterate and tenacious tendency to ignore or not to accept this ; not to know, or not to want to know, this reality of humanity. The reason is obvious, and has been mentioned already. It is thought that the grace of God will be magnified if man is represented as a blotted or best an empty page. But in the light of grace itself, of the connexion between the humanity of Jesus and humanity generally, this representation cannot be sustained. Man cannot be depicted as a blotted or empty page. The fatal consequence of this representation which we have seen to be theologically untenable is that real man as he is and is sometimes known to himself is not known in the Church, but in preaching, instruction and the cure of souls a picture of man is used which does not correspond to the reality, but to an erroneous figment of the imagination. And the consequence of this consequence is that real man cannot normally be reached from the Christian side either with what has to be said to him concerning the grace of God or with what has to be said concerning his own sin, because he simply does not recognise himself in the portrait held up to him on the Christian side. And then in what is said about the grace of God and especially Christian love there will probably be brought in that which was ignored and unrecognised as an attribute of human nature. That is to say, under the title of divine grace and Christian love there will probably be proclaimed the humanity which has to come in somewhere, and which will do so all the more forcefully if it is ignored and suppressed at the

2. The Basic Form of Humanity

point where it ought to be mentioned. And the final result will be that the man addressed will conclude that he does not need the Christian Church and its message to know this, because he can know it of himself, or learn it from some of the wiser of the wise of this world. He will then either not hear at all the new and different thing which he ought to be told as that which is Christian, or he will not receive it as such, and either way he cannot take up the corresponding attitude in relation to it. It is no doubt right and good and even necessary that the Church should call him at least to humanity, but in so doing it does not discharge its real task. And it does not do this because it has failed to see that there is a humanity common to the Christian and non-Christian to which it must relate itself, which it must presuppose, which it must take into account in its message, with which it must contrast its message, and which it must above all know and take seriously as such. And if this humanity is overlooked or denied, when reference is made to sin man is probably accused at a point where he knows that he is fallible and imperfect but cannot honestly see himself as truly and radically evil in the Christian sense of sin. It may then be overlooked that even evil man in the Christian sense, the sinner, is capable of humanity in the sense of that freedom of the heart for others, and in a way which puts many Christians to shame, and that he does not really need to be shown from the Christian pulpit that he finds too little place for this freedom. Or it may happen, as it does, that from the pulpit an attempt is made to blacken even that which is human in him for all his wickedness, and with a more or less clear awareness of the truth he is forced to resist this attack. How can he accept a serious accusation in this respect, as the message of the Christian Church seems to demand? He will rightly defend himself against what he is told. He will not be convicted of his sin if he is uncharitably—and falsely—addressed concerning his humanity. Just because humanity even at its root and crown is not identical with Christian love, and yet has its own different reality with this root and crown, Christianity has every reason to seek and tread other paths in this respect, and, in order to be able to do so, not to close its eyes any longer to the necessary insights.

I shall try to make this clear by reference to a point which has played a certain role in recent theological discussion and which is of supreme significance in relation to what has here been called the root and crown of humanity, namely, that " gladly," that freedom of the heart between man and man. No inconsiderable literature is now available on the contrast between *eros* and *agape*. The two can easily be played off the one against the other in history. In Greek religion, mysticism and philosophy, and above all in the ancient Greek feeling for life (cf. for what follows the article ἀγαπάω in *TWBzNT*), *eros* was the sum of the human fulfilment and exaltation of life, the experience, depicted and magnified with awe and rapture, of the end and beginning of all choice and volition, of being in transcendence of human being, of that which can take place in sensual or sexual (and thus in the narrower sense erotic) intoxication, but also in an inner spiritual encounter with the suprasensual and suprarational, with the incomprehensible yet present origin of all being and knowledge, in the encounter with the Godhead and union with it. *Eros* is humanity as dæmonism in both the lowest and the highest sense, and as such it is a kind of supreme divinity. According to Euripides it is the τύραννος θεῶν τε κἀνθρώπων. According to Aristotle it is the power of attraction by which the original principle of all being is maintained in order and in motion. That is to say, it moves all being as it is itself that which is moved by it, the ἐρώμενον. *Eros* is the " universal love seeking satisfaction now at one point, now at another." It is the indefinite impulse, with no taint of decision or act, for an indefinite object, now one thing and now another. In its purest form it is an impulse from below upwards, from man to what is above him, to the divine. In any case, however, it is not a turning to the other for the other's sake, but the satisfying of the vital hunger of the one who loves, for whom the beloved, whether a thing, a man or the divine, is only as it were consumer goods, the means to an end. It needs little wit to see, or skill to prove, that this *eros* is very different from Christian love. That the realities denoted by the two terms are to be sought at very different levels emerges at once from the fact that the words ἔρως and ἐρᾶν are never used at all in the New Testament. We need not pursue this point in the present context. But because the insight and proof are easy, we are ill-advised to make the contrast a reason for not pressing on to a deeper knowledge of human nature or a more true and valid definition of the essence of humanity. From the fact that *agape* is not to be defined as *eros* it does not follow that humanity, the manner of the natural man, is to be defined as *eros* in this historical sense of the term. This is the conclusion on the basis of which there has been set up on the Christian side a picture of man which has nothing whatever to do with the reality of the natural man, and in which the latter finds it impossible to recognise himself. If Christian love cannot be seen in *eros*, it is also difficult—we naturally have to use a more cautious expression—to see humanity in it. In this *eros* of the Greeks there thrusts unmistakeably into the forefront of the picture Dionysius-Zarathustra, the superman, the man without his fellow-man, the great solitary, who at the peak of his aspiration must inevitably make the mistake of regarding himself as God and thus forfeit his humanity. In him, of course, the supreme freedom of man has already become tyranny and therefore slavery. According to our deliberations, a definition of humanity on the basis of its identification with this *eros* could only be called a bad definition. We make a bad start if we accept this bad definition, equating the being of natural man with this dæmonic form, and in this form contrasting it very rigidly but also very unprofitably with Christian love. Even natural man is not yet the Christian man, the man renewed by love as the gracious gift of the Holy Ghost. But does this mean that he is necessarily the man of this Greek *eros*? As we have seen, *tertium datur*. The real natural man is the man who in the freedom of his heart is with his fellow-man. It is bad to be fascinated and transfixed as it were by the picture of erotic man in the Greek sense to which the picture of Christian man can be so easily—indeed, far too easily—opposed. The remarkable consequence of this far too simple opposition has been that in whole spheres of Christendom Christian love has been far too unthinkingly accepted merely as an antithesis to Greek *eros* and thus unconsciously depicted and extolled in the contours and colours of the original. At a first glance it is not easy to tell which of the two figures in Titian's famous painting is supposed to be heavenly love and which earthly. For the two sisters are so much alike. And in whole spheres of meditation and speculation on the part of Christian mystics, who have made so liberal a use of Plato and Plotinus, do we not have to ask seriously whether what is called *agape* is not really a spiritualised, idealised, sublimated and pious form of *eros*, an *eros* which was unacceptable in its original form, but from which it was impossible to break free, and which asserted itself all the more strongly? In face of this repressed eroticism we do well to remember that there is a third factor, something which is neither *agape* nor *eros*, from which there can be a genuine reference to *agape*, and yet in the light of which there can also be done to *eros*, even to the *eros* of the Greeks, the justice which is surely due to so powerful a historical phenomenon, and of which it is not perhaps altogether unworthy, even in substance.

We shall first try to draw an upward line from the concept of humanity discovered and indicated by us, namely, in the direction of Christian *agape*. Humanity as the freedom of the heart for the fellow-man is certainly not Christian love. Man can indeed, not on the basis of a possibility of his nature, but in its inconceivable perversion, fall from God and become sinful man. This does not rob him of his humanity. But what, then, becomes of this humanity, of the freedom of his heart? What does it mean that even in this state essentially,

2. The Basic Form of Humanity

properly and inwardly he is still undeniably with the other " gladly," and still uses as the vital and indispensable element in his life the mutual vision, speech, hearing and assistance of man and man? What is man—still and perhaps for the first time genuinely in the freedom of his heart—if his heart, not by nature or divine creation, but in evil factuality, is evil from his youth up? What does it really mean that he is " gladly " with his fellow-man? What takes place in this free co-existence? This state of real man is the one with which we have actually to reckon and in which he really exists in his history with God. He exists against his nature in this state, this state of sin, which is not really a standing but a falling against which he has no safeguard in his nature, but in which his nature develops, so that his nature becomes a fallen nature. He exists under the negative sign of his antithesis to God, and this is also to be said of his humanity. If he is held, upheld in his fall, and thus kept from plunging into the abyss, this is by the fact that God His Creator intervenes for him in Jesus Christ, making his cause His own, and thus being gracious to him afresh. And if his nature, his humanity, now acquires a positive sign and content, if the freedom of his heart for the fellow-man is for himself and the other a saving, upbuilding, beneficial and helpful freedom, if he is together with his fellow-man not just with a formal " gladly," but gladly in the good sense, i.e., in common thankfulness, in praising the divine mercy, this is not due to himself or his human nature, but this fulfilment of the natural is the gracious gift of the Holy Ghost, and Christian love. God as his Saviour from sin and death has said a new Yes to him in his humanity, a Yes which was not spoken in the fact that he was created in his humanity and therefore in that freedom of the heart, and which he, man, could not speak of himself in his humanity. If he lives in Christian love, he lives in the power of this new divine Yes which frees and saves himself and his humanity from sin and death. He owes it to the faithfulness and constancy of the covenant which God made with the creature if his heart is not merely free for this or that togetherness with the other, but free in the peace and joy and holiness and righteousness of a commonly obligatory service to be together with him in the community of those who may live by the forgiveness of sins and therefore for the magnifying of this grace. Hence humanity and Christian love are two very different things. We may thus speak quite calmly of a gulf between them. But even though the gulf cannot be bridged (except by God alone), there is also an unmistakeable connexion. In humanity, even as it falls through human sin and is thus perverted and brought under that negative sign, it is still a matter of the freedom of one man for another. It was in this freedom, even if in its corruption, that the first men sinned. It is in the wickedness of our heart, which as such, as our own true and essential human being, is still determined for this freedom, in an evil use of this freedom which is not instrinsically evil, that we are evil. Even if we mean it wrongly, we still like to be, and are in fact, with the other " gladly." Highly unnaturally and artificially, we pervert the " gladly " into a " reluctantly." And this " reluctantly " is set aside by Christian love, in which human freedom finds its true exercise. This perversion is reversed in Christian love, in the knowledge of the forgiveness of sins, and in the summons to gratitude by the gracious gift of the Holy Ghost. But it must also be said of Christian love that in it and it alone is it a question of the freedom of the one for the other. This is the new co-existence of man and man which is not merely formal but filled out with positive content. In it, then, humanity is not shamed but honoured. The faithfulness and constancy of the covenant, to which man owes wholly and exclusively the gracious gift of the Holy Ghost, is simply the faithfulness and the constancy of God the Creator acknowledging His work by saving it, and by renewing it as its Saviour. It is again a matter of the heart of man, of his true and essential human being, of his own heart, though new in relation to his evil and corrupt heart, even in the Christian love in which man loves God instead of hating Him and may thus love his neighbour instead of hating him (and thus denying his own nature). What would Christian love be if in it there did not become true and actual what man cannot make true and actual of himself even though his nature is determined for it, namely, a co-existence of man and fellow-man " gladly " fulfilled in freedom. What would be the good to the Christian of all his knowledge of forgiveness and the necessity to be thankful for it, of all the holiness and righteousness of his restored and reconstituted life, of all his praise of God and zeal in His service, if he lacked this element of humanity, and he were not present gladly and in freedom, which means concretely in the freedom of the one man for the other, in the freedom of the heart for the fellow-man ? Where in Christian faith and hope there is no awakening, i.e., no positive fulfilment of humanity, there is no real faith or hope, and certainly no Christian love, however great may be its inward and outward works. And if I am without love I am nothing. For love alone—the love in which there is an awakening and positive fulfilment of humanity, and the Christian is displayed and revealed as real man—is the fulfilment of the Law, because this human and therefore Christian love, the love which includes humanity, is the life of man in the power of the new and saving divine Yes to the creature. This is the connexion between humanity and Christian love.

But now the question seriously arises whether it is not possible and necessary that there should also be a downward connexion in the direction of the world of Greek *eros*, thus enabling us to find a calmer and more objective solution to the dilemma of *eros* and Christian *agape* than that to which Christians far too hastily rush, but without the power to work it out to the extent that it is justified. We perhaps safeguard ourselves better against the danger of slipping back into *eros* (possibly in the most refined of ways), if we refrain from representing it as the one form of sin, and contrasting it as such with *agape*. When we understand humanity as a third thing between the two, we can be more perspicacious and just in relation to *eros*. It is obvious enough that in the historical form of this reality we have a form of sin, i.e., of the corruption of man occasioned and conditioned by his fall from God. It is perhaps the greatness of this historical phenomenon that it can be called a classical representation of human sin. It was understandable and right that the early Christians should first turn their backs on the whole world of Greek *eros* with horror and relief. Where man seeks his self-fulfilment in a self-transcending attempt to have the divinity, the fellow-man and all things as consumer goods for himself, where his vital hunger leads him to be himself the one in all things, we have to do unequivocally with the evil which can only have its wages in death. It would have been far better if Christianity had not so often had the idea of interpreting Christian love as the true form of this hunger and fulfilment. As we have already said, Greek *eros* is ill-adapted to be a definition of humanity. But in all this we must not overlook the point that for all its obvious sinfulness, and the obscurity, confusion and corruption in which it represents humanity, *eros* contains an element which in its visible form and even in its essence is not evil or reprehensible, but of decisive (and not merely incidental and non-essential) importance for the concept of humanity, and therefore indirectly for that of Christian love. For where else but in the world of ancient Hellenism filled and controlled by this *eros* does there emerge with such vitality and consolation, for all the sinful corruption, that which we have seen and described as the *conditio sine qua non* of humanity, that " gladly," as the true and original motive of human existence, preceding all the choice and volition of man, and limiting and determining all human choice and volition ? Is it a mere accident that the Gospel of Jesus Christ, this seed of Israel, took root in the perishing world of Hellenism ? Has it been a misfortune that this origin has haunted its whole subsequent career ? Is it merely in culpable self-will that we seek in soul the land of the Greeks, and cannot refrain from doing so even to-day, when we see so clearly that the

2. The Basic Form of Humanity

necessary reformation of the Church cannot be the same thing as a renaissance of Greek antiquity ? Is there not here something obligatory, which it is better to see and accept than to ignore and deny, if we are ready and anxious to understand the Gospel of Jesus Christ in the full range of its content ? And is not this factor to be found in the " gladly " which incontestably has a basic significance for the Christian concept of man and his humanity (and therefore indirectly for that of Christian *agape*) ? We see the whole distortion of this " gladly " in Greek eroticism. The freedom of this highly-extolled man-god is only too easily seen and stated to be tyranny. It recognised itself to be such—to be a dæmonism. But there is more to it than that. We cannot ignore it merely because it originally and properly maintains and actualises in a way which is still unmistakeable the tyranny of freedom. It is not finally for nothing that it was in the atmosphere of Greek *eros* that for the first time in the West, and perhaps over the whole earth, human freedom in the co-existence of man and man attained a noteworthy and unforgettable form for every age and place. This does not mean that we can despise the barbarians who knew nothing of this freedom. Paul mentioned them together with the Greeks (Rom. 1^{14}), and declared that he was under a similar obligation to both. But this can hardly mean that as Christians we have to champion the barbarians against the Greeks, or that we should ignore the superiority of the latter to the former. The Early Church certainly did not do this, for all its differentiation of itself from Hellenism. We might almost wish that it had done so more, and that its differentiation had been more radical. But again this cannot mean that we can or should fail to see what is so clearly to be seen. The violence displayed against Hellenism in recent theology is not a good thing, and its continuation can only mean that in a short time we shall again be exposed to the Greek danger. The Greeks with their *eros*—and it was no inconsiderable but a very real achievement—grasped the fact that the being of man is free, radically open, willing, spontaneous, joyful, cheerful and gregarious. The shadow of conflict and suffering, of resignation, pain and death, of tragedy, must and does always fall on them as they can give it only the form of a basically erroneous yearning for an object and a radically capricious and finally disillusioning wandering from one object to another, being unable to realise it except in the dæmonism and hybris of psychical and physical, ideal and only too real intoxication. The imagination which created the Homeric Olympus and its inhabitants is one of the strongest proofs of the fact that the heart of man is evil from his youth. Yet for all that the Greeks were able to reveal the human heart, to show what humanity is in itself and as such even in a state of distortion and corruption, to bring out the enduring factor in humanity which persists in spite of distortion and corruption, in a way which cannot be said of any other ancient people (and especially Israel, the people of God), and which can to some extent be said of the peoples of later Western history only as and because they have learned concerning *eros* from the ancient Greeks. How these Greeks knew how to see themselves as men, to speak with one another, to live together in freedom, as friends, as teachers and scholars, and above all as citizens ! To be sure, even apart from perversion and corruption, they did so only to a certain degree, but in such a way that this emerged so clearly as the secret centre of their reflection and volition, as the measure of all their virtues, and even as the secret of their obvious mistakes and defects and vices, that other peoples which came in contact with them could not forget it, and even the community of Jesus Christ had to see and take note of it. The Greeks with their *eros* could not be for it a fact of salvation or divine revelation. If it let them be this, it soon found itself on bypaths. The Christian love proclaimed by Paul did not come from the school of the Greeks. And the Christian community could not and cannot learn from them even what humanity is. We ourselves have not gained our understanding of the concept from them. But even though we gain our understanding of the concept of humanity elsewhere, from the one true fact of salvation and divine revelation, yet we cannot fail to acknowledge—and this was and is the basis of the legitimate relationship between Christianity and Hellenism—that our understanding finds in the Greek with his *eros* a confirmation which we have every reason to remember and by which we have good cause to orientate ourselves when it is a matter of understanding Christian love as the awakening and fulfilment of humanity, of the distorted and perverted but not forfeited manner of the natural man, i.e., of man as God created him. The theology of Paul and his proclamation of Christian love derives neither from the Greeks nor the barbarians but from Israel. But when he portrays the Christian living in this love he never uses barbarian or Israelitish colours and contours, but he undoubtedly makes use of Greek, thus betraying the fact that he both saw and took note of the Greeks and their *eros*. Otherwise he could not have added quite so directly to the great saying: " The peace of God which passeth all understanding, shall keep your hearts and minds through Christ Jesus," the remarkable verse which follows : " Finally, brethren, whatsoever things are true, whatsoever things are honest (σεμνά), whatsoever things are just, whatsoever things are pure (ἁγνά), whatsoever things are lovely (προσφιλῆ), whatsoever things are of good report (εὔφημα) ; if there be any virtue (ἀρετή), and if there be any praise (ἔπαινος), think on these things " (Phil. 4⁷⁻⁸). Otherwise he could not have written Philippians with its dominating χαίρετε, or even the great hymn to *agape* in 1 Cor. 13. As love itself primarily and from within itself, as the gracious gift of the Holy Ghost, is an open, willing, spontaneous, joyful, cheerful and gregarious being and action, and all this newly awakened and filled, in a good sense and not in a bad, it is obviously ready and willing to recognise itself and its humanity in everything human as in the good gift of God the Creator, even though it may be actual and recognisable only in that distortion and perversion in the man who is without love. Surely we may and must apply to its relationship to the Greek man and his *eros* the unforgettable words of 1 Cor. 13⁴⁻⁶ : " Love suffereth long (μακροθυμεῖ), and is kind (χρηστεύεται) ; love envieth not (οὐ ζηλοῖ) ; love vaunteth not itself (οὐ περπερεύεται), is not puffed up (οὐ φυσιοῦται), doth not behave itself unseemly (οὐκ ἀσχημονεῖ), seeketh not her own, is not easily provoked (οὐ παροξύνεται), thinketh no evil ; rejoiceth not in iniquity, but rejoiceth in the truth (συγχάρει δὲ τῇ ἀληθείᾳ) " ? It would partly do and partly leave undone all the things said of it if there were no way from it to man, even sinful man, refusing to him the humanity which is also its own instead of recognising, welcoming, acknowledging and respecting it, and declaring its solidarity with it, even where it appears in its most alien garb. It could not be the joy referred to in Philippians if it were unable or unwilling to rejoice in the truth even when it encounters it in sinners, and therefore to " rejoice with them that do rejoice " (Rom. 12¹⁵). It says No to the sin of these χαίροντες, but it says Yes to their χαίρειν as such, because it is not as such something inhuman, but that which is human in all their inhumanity. Love is itself a life in the " gladly," in the holy, righteous and pure " gladly " of the gratitude which binds together brothers and sisters in Christ, and therefore of the supreme " gladly." How, then, can it fail to penetrate to the depths of the fellow-man who is not yet awakened to this thankfulness but still held by the intoxication of *eros*, thus being both permitted and commanded to find and accept even in his foolish, confused and evil " gladly " that which is genuinely creaturely and human ? How can the Christian fail to see that in this respect and on this level too, with the natural bond of the " gladly," he is bound to the non-Christian, with whom he knows that he is primarily connected in a very different way by the judgment and grace of God in Jesus Christ ? And let him finally see to it that the non-Christian finds the same in him—humanity, and therefore this " gladly " ! " Let your moderation (ἐπιεικές) be known unto all men " (Phil. 4⁵, cf. Tit. 3²). It is, of course, quite normal that Christian love should seem

3. *Humanity as Likeness and Hope*

strange and foolish to those who are without, just as the way in which those who are without live to their *eros* necessarily seems alien and nonsensical from the standpoint of Christian love. But it would be quite abnormal if those who are without did not find in Christian love at least the humanity which is their own ; if they did not perceive in Christians at least that life in the " gladly " ; if this did not speak to them and bind Christians to them. The *agape* of the Christians would perhaps not be all that it professes to be if the Greek man with his *eros* could not see that even in the Christian he has to do with a man and therefore with a being with which he can at least feel and proclaim solidarity in respect of that root of his *eros*. If this were not the case, the love of the supposed Christian would surely be a very loveless love. If it is genuine, in this respect and on this human level at least he will be no less perceptible and understandable to the non-Christian that the non-Christian must be to him. The non-Christian may say No or shake his head in face of what makes the Christian a Christian, but there should be no reason in the Christian why he should not at least say Yes to his χαίρειν as such, because this as such is the human element in him too. This downward connexion of love by way of humanity to the *eros* of the Greeks was obviously present in New Testament times for all the differentiation of the spheres, and it is hard to see why the connexion cannot and should not be seen, respected and used in our own day as well. What we have here is a relationship between the Church and the world without which the Church cannot discharge its function in the world because without it it would not be the Church, the Church of Christian love.

3. HUMANITY AS LIKENESS AND HOPE

In its basic form humanity is fellow-humanity. Everything else which is to be described as human nature and essence stands under this sign to the extent that it is human. If it is not fellow-human, if it is not in some way an approximation to being in the encounter of I and Thou, it is not human. But provision is made that man should not break loose from this human factor. He can forget it. He can misconstrue it. He can despise it. He can scorn and dishonour it. But he cannot slough it off or break free from it. Humanity is not an ideal which he can accept or discard, or a virtue which he can practise or not practise. Humanity is one of the determinations with which we have to do in theological anthropology. It is an inviolable constant of human existence as such. An anthropology which ignored or denied this basic form of humanity would be explicable in terms of the practical corruption and perversion of man. But it would fly in face of a fact which the practical corruption and perversion of man cannot alter, let alone a theoretical judgment based upon it and therefore false. Man is in fact fellow-human. He is in fact in the encounter of I and Thou. This is true even though he may contradict it both in theory and in practice ; even though he may pretend to be man in isolation and produce anthropologies to match. In so doing he merely proves that he is contradicting himself, not that he can divest himself of this basic form of humanity.

He has no choice to be fellow-human or something else. His being has this basic form.

That this is the case it is brought before us by the fact that we cannot say man without having to say male or female and also male and female. Man exists in this differentiation, in this duality. It is to be noted at once that this is the only structural differentiation in which he exists. The so-called races of mankind are only variations of one and the same structure, allowing at any time the practical intermingling of the one with the other and consisting only in fleeting transitions from the one to the other, so that they cannot be fixed and differentiated with any precision but only very approximately, and certainly cannot be compared with the distinct species and sub-species of the animal kingdom. In the distinction of man and woman, however, we have a structural differentiation of human existence. Man has this sexual differentiation in common with animals of all species and sub-species. This is the unavoidable sign and reminder that he exists in proximity to them and therefore within the context of creation as a whole; within and not above the boundary of the creature. But his creatureliness is to be male or female, male and female, and human in this distinction and connexion. He certainly exists in other essential and non-essential differentiations. He is necessarily a child, and this individual as opposed to others. But these distinctions as such are not structural in character. On the other hand, he does not need to be father or mother, brother or sister, young or old, gifted or not gifted, endowed in this way or that, a man of this or that particular time or sphere or race. Even if he is, it is again not on the basis of structural distinction. In all these essential and non-essential but secondary relationships and distinctions, however, he is primarily male or female, male and female. And the necessity with which he is a child, and a son or daughter, and this or that particular individual, is bound up with the fact that he is male or female, and the one or the other on the basis of structural differentiation. In and with his existence as man, and as this particular man, he is male or female, male and female. And in and with all the other essential and non-essential distinctions and connexions, this is decisive and in a sense exemplary because this alone is structural and runs through all the others, maintaining, expressing and revealing itself in them. In all the common and opposing features of human existence, there is no man in isolation, but only man or woman, man and woman. In the whole reach of human life there is no abstractly human but only concretely masculine or feminine being, feeling, willing, thinking, speaking, conduct and action, and only concretely masculine and feminine co-existence and co-operation in all these things. There is conflict and fellowship, there is encounter between men and therefore human being, only on the presupposition and under the sign and conditions of this one and distinctive differentiation. These things

3. Humanity as Likeness and Hope

are present only in the encounter of man and woman, but they are present at once, and with particular force, where this takes place as the necessary limitation and determination, whether to the furtherance or the detriment, of the actuality of their co-existence and co-operation. They are present, too, where man encounters man or woman woman, for man remains what he is, and therefore a being which intends and seeks his true partner in woman and not in man, and woman remains what she is, and therefore a being whose true counterpart cannot be found in woman but only in man. And because fundamentally—even though it cannot attain any corresponding form externally, and the counterpart is either absent or unrecognised—human being is a being in encounter, even human being which is temporarily isolated will definitely bear and in some way reveal the character of this one particular distinction and connexion.

Our present concern is not with the physiology and psychology of the sexes, and we shall not attempt to describe their distinctive structure. But we may perhaps be permitted to issue the following warning in respect of the involved psychological question—that it is much better if we avoid such generalised pronouncements as that man's interests are more outward and objective and woman's inward and subjective; that man is more disposed to freedom and woman to dependence; that man is more concerned with conquest and construction and woman with adornment; that man is more inclined to wander and woman to stay at home. Statements such as these may sometimes be ventured as hypotheses, but cannot be represented as knowledge or dogma because real man and real woman are far too complex and contradictory to be summed up in portrayals of this nature. It cannot be contested that both physiologically and biblically a certain strength and corresponding precedence are a very general characteristic of man, and a weakness and corresponding subsequence of woman. But in what the strength and precedence consists on the one side, and the weakness and subsequence on the other, what it means that man is the head of woman and not *vice versa*, is something which is better left unresolved in a general statement, and value-judgments must certainly be resisted. Man speaks against himself if he assesses and treats woman as an inferior being, for without her weakness and subsequence he could not be man. And woman speaks against herself if she envies that which is proper to man, for his strength and precedence are the reality without which she could not be woman. What distinguishes man from woman and woman from man even in this relationship of super- and subordination is more easily discovered, perceived, respected and valued in the encounter between them than it is defined. It is to be constantly experienced in their mutual exchanges and co-existence. Provision is made that it will be experienced here in supreme reality, not in theory, but in the practice of human existence as a being in encounter.

There can be no question that man is to woman and woman to man supremely the other, the fellow-man, to see and to be seen by whom, to speak with and to listen to whom, to receive from and to render assistance to whom is necessarily a supreme human need and problem and fulfilment, so that whatever may take place between man and man and woman and woman is only as it were a preliminary and accompaniment for this true encounter between man and fellow-man, for this true being in fellow-humanity. Why is this the case? Obviously because, however we may describe and represent man and woman phenomenologically, it is only here, where they are structural, that the antitheses between man and man are so great and estranging and yet stimulating that the encounter between them carries with it the possibility of a supreme difficulty otherwise absent, and yet in all these antitheses their relatedness, their power of mutual attraction and their reciprocal reference the one to the other are so great and illuminating and imperative that the possibility also emerges at least of a supreme interest otherwise absent. It is to be noted that the sphere of this special difficulty and interest, of this play and counterplay of the sexes, is much greater than the circle of what is usually understood more narrowly as sexual love in more or less close connexion with the problem of marriage. In the wider circle around the narrower it is to be found in the relationship of fathers and daughters, mothers and sons, brothers and sisters, and in similar relationships it plays its fruitful but perhaps disturbing and even dangerous role in the whole sphere of education and instruction, and the life of churches of all confessions. Indeed, it is the subterranean motive, which has to be taken seriously into account, in all possible forms of fellowship between man and woman, whether in society, industry or life, among which we have to remember, not with malice but with all honour, the innumerable ways in which it finds compensation or sublimation in friendship between man and man or woman and woman. Yet it is obvious that the encounter between man and woman is fully and properly achieved only where there is the special connexion of one man loving this woman and one woman loving this man in free choice and with a view to a full life-partnership; a connexion which is on both sides so clear and strong as to make their marriage both possible and necessary as a unique and definitive attachment. This is naturally the true element of particularity in this intrinsically particular sphere, and constitutes its centre. There takes place here what can only be indicated and prepared in the wider circle, the female becoming to the male, and the male to the female, the other, the fellow-man, which man cannot and will not be without. Here all that we have described as humanity has its proper locus, the home from which it must continually go out and to which it must continually return. Here there is fulfilled first and perfectly the fact that man and man may be companions, associates, comrades, fellows and helpmates.

3. Humanity as Likeness and Hope

Here this is all moved and sustained from within by the clear-cut and simple fact that two human beings love each other, and that in small things and great alike they may will and have the same thing, each other. This capacity, the freedom of the heart for the other, and therefore that " gladly," has here its simplest and yet its strongest form. May it not be that this particular place is attended, at least in the so-called civilised nations, by so much interest and curiosity, but also so much reticence and anxiety, so much phantasy, poetry, morality and immorality, and so much empty talk and sighing and sniggering on the part of the inexperienced, because there are so few who realise that they have to do here with the centre of the human, with the basic form of primal humanity? But whatever we may realise or not realise, in this sphere, with which we gladly reckon the preliminary as well as the inner circle, and therefore the whole field of sexual encounter, we do actually stand before the primary form of all that has occupied us as humanity. To know nothing of this sphere is to know nothing of the I and Thou and their encounter, and therefore of the human. For where else can a man know it if he does not know it here, if he is a man to whom woman as woman (or a woman to whom man as man) is neutral and indifferent, to whom this structurally different counterpart presents neither difficulty nor interest, who does not stand in some relationship to it, however distorted or repressed, clumsy or unfortunate? Provision is made that no men are excluded from this centre of the human. To be sure, there are only a few who can see clearly and calmly at this point, and therefore live comparatively clearly and calmly, whether in marriage or outside it. There are innumerable men and women who theoretically and practically are walking blindly in a mist, and never see what they have missed, whether in marriage or outside it. But there is none who can escape the fact that he is man or woman and therefore in some sense man and woman. There is none who can escape this whole sphere. Man cannot escape his existence, and his existence as such stands under this determination. In the light of this we said at the very outset that man is fellow-human, that he is in the encounter of I and Thou, that humanity is not an ideal or virtue but an inviolable constant of human existence. In the fact of the duality of male and female, which cannot be resolved in a higher synthesis, we have this constant so clearly betore us that we can only live it out, however well or badly. There can be no question of setting this fact aside, or overlooking it in practice. There is no being of man above the being of male and female.

Is not this fact a subsequent confirmation of the decided and apparently " dogmatic " precaution which we took, at the beginning of the previous subsection, of taking up the historically important anthropology of man in isolation only in the form of a delimitation from it *a limine*, and therefore of an outright rejection? We took this path because Christology left us no option, but compelled us to decide for the opposite path. And now we can only add that we were right, and that a little more of the readiness for real life which is so often lacking in the studies of philosophers and theologians would necessarily lead their occupants to the same result. That it has not done so is perhaps due to the fact that for so many centuries the philosophical and theological study of the West was the cloister-cell, from whose distinctive I-speculation in the absence of the Thou it has been difficult to break free even outside the cloister. Nietzsche did not live in a cell. But it is hard to decide where he was most at home, as a prophet of humanity without the fellow-man, in his repudiation of Christianity or in his almost brutal contempt for women (which fortunately was only literary in form). There is a necessary connexion between the two. This ought to have been remembered in the monastic cells where humanity without the fellow-man was not discovered but forcefully advanced and practised. No veneration of Mary or love for God could fill the terrible vacuum in which it was desired to live and a good deal of life was actually lived to the detriment of the Church and the world. But the vacuum is not filled merely by leaving the cloister, just as the external cloister does not necessarily entail the vacuum. It is very possible even for external life in the cloister to be in fact a being in encounter. And it is equally evident that even a flood of love for women such as that which filled the life of Goethe is not strong enough to make impossible a humanity without the fellow-man, or to actualise with certainty a being in encounter. At any rate, it did not prevent Goethe from becoming, if not the prophet, at least the high-priest of this humanity. And when he broke off his deepest and finest love-affair to study Greek antiquity in Italy, there was revealed the fact that his repudiation of humanity was coincident with a repudiation of this nervous centre of humanity, and he gave conclusive proof of an attitude to woman, confirmed rather than altered by his marriage with Christiana Vulpius, which, while it cannot be compared with the scorn of Nietzsche, can only be described as that of the man who is finally emancipated from women. He too, and especially, was finally captured by the secularised cloister. And behind all this there stands the fact that we have here the profoundest symptom of sickness in the world of the Greeks and their *eros* (which only too fully enslaved the West both in real and secularised cloisters). For all the eroticism of theory and practice, it was a man's world in which there was no real place for woman ; and for this reason it was necessarily a world of the I without the Thou, and therefore a world of the I wandering without limit or object, a dæmonic and tyrannical world. It is not surprising, then, that the discovery or the many re-discoveries of the humanity of the free heart present and not absolutely concealed in the Greek world of *eros* were overtaken by such disasters in the narrower and wider Christian sphere, in real and secularised cloisters. The only safeguard against these disasters is Christology, and a little knowledge of life. By a little knowledge of life we mean a placid and cheerful and sure knowledge of the duality of human existence, of the original form of the I and Thou in the continuity of human being as the being of male or female, of male and female. Where Christianity is genuine in the sense that it is not merely theoretical but living wisdom (the biblical *hokma* or σοφία), it unavoidably carries with it a little knowledge of life. This was forgotten in the mediæval cloister, and it has been forgotten in all other studies where its supposedly Christian but inhuman tradition has been continued. But to attain a little knowledge of life Christology must not be despised as has been the case, with equally inhuman results, in secularised, untheological and non-Christian cells, e.g., that of Goethe or Nietzsche. The Christian community, receiving and proclaiming Christian love and Christian theology with its doctrine of man, ought to be secured against those disasters and to be able to pass triumphantly through every cloister, knowing the man Jesus as the man who is for His fellow-man, and therefore knowing man generally, knowing his humanity as fellow-humanity, and this

3. Humanity as Likeness and Hope

fellow-humanity at the point where it is most concretely and incontestably a fact, in the antithesis and connexion of man and woman. But the test of this twofold and at bottom unitary knowledge is whether it can be ruthless enough to turn its back at once and absolutely on the error of the humanity of man without the fellow-man.

The Old Testament Magna Carta of humanity is the J saga which tells us how God completed the creation of man by giving him woman as a companion (Gen. 2^{18-25}). We have already expounded this text in *C.D.* III, 1, p. 288 f., and to establish our present point reference must be made both generally and in detail to this exposition.

The main point may be briefly recapitulated. In Gen. 2 (like Gen. 1), the account of the creation of man as male and female is the climax of the whole history of creation. In both cases it is solemnly emphasised and introduced by the mention of special reflection on the part of the Creator. In this case, the reference is as follows : " It is not good that the man should be alone ; I will make him an help meet for him." In this saying there is a radical rejection of the picture of man in isolation. And the point of the whole text is to say and tell—for it has the form of a story—who and what is the man who is created good by God—good as the partner of God in the history which is the meaning and purpose of creation. This man created good by God must have a partner like himself, and must therefore be a partner to a being like himself ; to a being in which he can recognise himself, and yet not himself but another, seeing it is not only like him but also different from him ; in other words, a "help meet." This helpmeet is woman. With her he is the man created good by God, the complete human creature. He would not be this alone. That he is not alone, but complete in this duality, he owes to the grace of his Creator. But the intention of this grace is as revealed in this completion. And according to the fine declaration of the text its intention is not merely that he should acquire this duality, woman, but, acquiring her from God, recognise and confess her by his own choice and decision as a helpmeet. God the Creator knows and ordains, but He leaves it to man to discover, that only woman and not animals can be this helpmeet. Thus the climax of the history of creation coincides with this first act of human freedom. Man sees all kinds of animals. He exercises his superiority over them by giving them names. But he does not find in them a being like himself, a helpmeet. He is thus alone with them (even in his superiority), and therefore not good, not yet complete as man. In the first instance, then, he exercises his human freedom, his humanity, negatively. He remains free for the being which the Creator will give him as a partner. He waits for woman, and can do so. He must not grasp after a false completion. But who and what is woman ? That man obviously waits for her does not mean that he knows her in advance. She is not his postulate, or ideal, let alone his creation. Like himself, she is the thought and work of God. " And (he) brought her unto the man." She is not merely there to be arbitrarily and accidentally discovered and accepted by man. As God creates both man and woman, He also creates their relationship, and brings them together. But this divinely created relationship—which is not just any kind of relationship, but the distinctive human relationship—has to be recognised and affirmed by man himself. This takes place when he cries triumphantly : " This is now bone of my bones, and flesh of my flesh." Here we have the second and positive step in the act of freedom, in the venture of free thought and speech, of man exercising his humanity in this freedom. At the heart of his humanity he is free in and for the fact that he may recognise and accept the woman whom he himself has not imagined and conjured up by his desire, but whom God has created and brought. With this choice he confirms who and what he is within creation, his own election, the particularity of his creation. He is man in this negative and positive relationship. Human being becomes the being in encounter in which alone it can be good. His last objective assertion concerning another being becomes his subjective confession (as a male) of this other being, this fellow-man, the woman who has her own equal but proper and independent honour and dignity in the fact that she can be his helpmeet, without whose participation in his life he could not be a man, and without whose honour and dignity it would be all up with his own. " Therefore shall a man leave his father and his mother, and shall cleave unto his wife " means that because woman is so utterly from man he must be utterly to her ; because she is so utterly for him he must be utterly for her ; because she can only follow him in order that he should not be alone he must also follow her not to be alone ; because he the first and stronger can only be one and strong in relationship to her he must accept and treat her, the second and weaker, as his first and stronger. It is in this inversion that the possibility of the human, the natural supremacy of the I over the Thou, is developed in reality. It is in this way that the genuinely human declares its possibility. It is in this form that there exists the possibility of man in isolation, but also of all androcracy and gynocracy. " And they were both naked, the man and his wife, and were not ashamed." The human is the male and female in its differentiation but also its connexion. Hence there is no humiliation or shame. The human cannot be a burden or reproach. It is not an occasion for unrest or embarrassment. It does not need to be concealed and hidden. There can be no shame in respect of the human. In the work of God—which is what the human is—there is nothing offensive and therefore no *pudendum*. The work of God is without spot, pure, holy and innocent. Hence man does not need to be ashamed of his humanity, the male of his masculinity or the female of her femininity. There is no need of justification. To be the creature of God is self-justification. Only sin, the fall from God, can shame the human, i.e., the masculine and the feminine, and thus make it an object of shame. And the awful genius of sin is nowhere more plainly revealed than in the fact that it shames man at this centre of his humanity, so that he is necessarily ashamed of his humanity, his masculinity and femininity, before God and men, and every attempt to escape this shame, every self-justification, or concretely every denial and suppression of sexuality can only confirm and increase the shame. It is to be noted carefully that this is the climax of this text, and therefore of the whole biblical history of creation.

The whole of Gen. $2^{18f.}$ points to the man who is fellow-human as such, as the creature of God, in his divinely given nature, and therefore originally and not secondarily. And it speaks of the co-existence of man and woman as the original and proper form of this fellow-humanity. It singles out this among all other possible relationships as the one which belongs to the creation-history preceding all others, and which alone can come into question when it is a matter of describing the nature which man has been given by God. At this point the reference cannot be to parents and children, to brothers and sisters and other relatives, to friends, to Europeans and Asiatics, to Semites and Arians, to old and young, to gifted and ungifted, to rulers and subjects, teachers and scholars, rich and poor, or even the basic distinction of individual and individual. Or rather, this basic distinction, the differentiation and connexion of I and Thou, must be explained as coincident with that of male and female. All other

3. *Humanity as Likeness and Hope*

relationships are involved in this as the original relationship. All other humanity is included in this centre. In this connexion, particular attention must be paid to the fact that in Genesis 2 the reference is to man and woman in their relationship as such, and therefore not to fatherhood and motherhood or the establishment of the family. It is true that in the rest of the Old Testament the relationship is seen almost exclusively from the latter aspect, in the light of the question of progeny, and with the main interest in the conception and birth of children, especially the son. But it is equally true that this is not the case in the present passage. No mention is here made of child or family. The relationship of man and woman has its own reality and dignity. As such it is the basic relationship involving all others. At this point the Bible thinks and speaks far more seriously " erotically " than all Hellenism. In the light of this text it cannot be called arbitrary if, having sketched the basic form of humanity in general terms, we make the reference to this particular relationship the climax of our presentation, and without the usual expansion or restriction that when it is a question of man and woman we are inevitably led to father and mother and therefore child as the third thing proceeding from the other two. If the Old Testament is a commentary on the New, and decisive account has to be taken of an important passage like Genesis 2, we can only say that this weakens and obscures the true situation and is thus to be rejected. But this means that the encounter of man and woman as such is being in encounter and therefore the centre of humanity, so that before we proceed to consider the circumference of this centre it is worth pausing at this encounter, since otherwise we shall probably misinterpret all other encounters, even that of parents and children. For it is here first and decisively that we have to see and learn what is meant by freedom of heart for the other, and therefore what constitutes the humanity of all other encounters. Genesis 2 is imperious in this respect. If it is objected that it is isolated in its reference to man and woman, the answer is that creation is isolated in relation to the rest of the creature's history, and the divinely given nature of man in relation to what this became at the hands of man. But our present question concerns creation and the creaturely nature of man, and we have every reason to put this question even to understand the history of the human creature and man in his corruption as a sinner. If we are to find an answer, we must read this passage in Genesis 2 without subtraction or addition, as we have tried to do. And we must therefore learn from it that man is first and unquestionably and generally man and woman, and only then all kinds of other things, including perhaps father and mother.

And in any case Genesis 2 is not absolutely isolated in the Old Testament. We might almost speak of a second Magna Carta of humanity in this connexion when we remember that at a rather curious point in the Old Testament Canon a place is found for the Song of Songs. We should not wish that this book were not in the Canon. We should not treat it as if it were outside. And we should not spiritualise it, as if what is in the Canon can have only a spiritualised significance. As all honest exposition must admit, and as ought to be recognised gladly rather than with hesitation and embarrassment, it is a collection of genuine love-songs in the primitive sense, in which there is no reference to the child, but only to man and woman in their differentiation and connexion, in their being in encounter. At this point the most natural exegesis might well prove to be the most profound.

It is to be noted that in this second text we hear a voice which is lacking in the first. This is the voice of the woman, to whom the man looks and moves with no less pain and joy than she to him, and who finds him with no less freedom —only the " This " of Genesis is lacking—than she is found. Implicitly, of course, this voice is to be heard in Genesis as well. But it now finds expression in words. And what words ! " Set me as a seal upon thine heart, as a seal upon thine arm : for love is strong as death ; jealousy is cruel as the grave : the coals thereof are coals of fire, which hath a most vehement flame. Many waters cannot quench love, neither can the floods drown it : if a man would give all the substance of his house for love, it would utterly be contemned " ($8^{6f.}$). And so everything is more luminous if not more strong, more direct if not more unequivocal. And all that takes place is sketched and depicted against a background of day and night, of the passing seasons, of the plants and animals of the Palestinian scene. And this is what the Old Testament calls the song of all songs. Again, it is an isolated text, and in its theological assessment we must take the same line as in Genesis 2, except that now we are obviously at the other end of the line, the end and not the beginning. That this song belongs to the so-called Solomonic literature, being attached to Proverbs and Ecclesiastes, reminds us that Solomon the builder of the temple, and his kingdom, glory and wisdom, represent the figure of the King of the last day and His glory. This is how the expected son of David appeared and his kingdom—so powerful, resplendent and wise, and finally so human. And so we must understand eschatologically the songs ascribed to him when we take seriously their very concrete content. On the long line from creation to the last day the Old Testament speaks very differently of man and woman. The dominating question is that of children. The " erotic " notes are few. Everything is controlled by the Law, and especially the danger and prohibition of adultery. In this respect, too, we are in the world of sin and infamy and shame, in which the love-song must always have a rather dubious sound, and the original of the covenant between man and woman, the covenant between Yahweh and Israel, is continually broken on the part of Israel, and has still to be properly constituted. But the beginning and end, the origin and goal, both between Yahweh and Israel and between man and woman, are as depicted in Genesis 2 and the Song of Songs. In retrospect of creation and prospect of the new creation of the last time, we can and may and must speak of man and woman as is done in these texts.

Hence both these passages justify us in speaking of man in this way when we ask concerning his creaturely nature.

In the light of the theological significance of the Song of Songs this is perhaps the point to elucidate an eschatological question which at a first glance might cause considerable difficulty. We read in Gal. $3^{26f.}$: " For ye are all the children of God by faith in Christ Jesus. For as many of you as have been baptised into Christ have put on Christ. There is neither Jew nor Greek, there is neither bond nor free, there is neither male nor female : for ye are all one in Christ Jesus. And if ye be Christ's, then are ye Abraham's seed, and heirs according to the promise." What Paul is saying, and not saying, is quite clear. He is saying that the being of Christians on the basis of the grace of God commonly directed to them and commonly received by them in faith, their being as children of God, the seed of Abraham and heirs according to the promise, their being in correspondence with their baptism, is one which makes impossible any exaltation of the one over the other or hostility of the one to the other, so that in the Christian community there can be no assertion of natural and historical antitheses. For in this community all are one in Christ Jesus in the sense that all live thankfully by the grace which is manifested equally to each of them as mercy. But Paul is not saying that the antitheses are simply set aside and done away by the being of Christians in Christ. *Cest ordre là est inviolable et nostre Seigneur Jésus Christ n'est pas venu au monde pour faire une telle confusion que ce qui est establi de Dieu son Père soit aboli* (Calvin, C.R. 28, 568). Thus the fact that male and female are one in Christ does not mean that they are no longer male and female. Yet it might be asked whether this is the last word. Does it not apply only so long as Christians still share in this present aeon which passes ? In their life which according to Col. 3^3 is hidden with Christ in God, and especially in its future manifestation in the resurrection of the dead, will it not perhaps be the case that they are no longer male or female, but a third thing which is higher and better. The question is an obvious one in view of Mk. 12^{18-27} and *par.*, where in answer to the question of the Sadducees which of the seven brothers should have the woman to wife in the resurrection Jesus said : "For when they shall rise from the dead, they neither marry, nor are given in marriage ; but are as the angels which are in heaven." Does this mean that they will no longer be male and female ? Is A. Oepke right (*TWBzNT*, I, 785) when he says that by proposing for man in the perfected lordship of God a sexless being similar to that of the angels Jesus lifts from woman particularly the curse of her sex and sets her at the side of man as no less justifiably the child of God ? Yet it does not actually say that man and woman will be ἄγγελοι, but ὡς ἄγγελοι (ἰσάγγελοι, Lk. 20^{36}), i.e., those who according to 1 Cor. 13^{12} no longer see God, themselves and all things in a glass darkly but face to face, and are thus liberated from the problematical, burdensome and complicated nature of their existence in the form which they now know (through a glass darkly). To this form there belongs marrying and giving in marriage with such implicated questions as that raised by the Sadducees on the basis of Deut. $25^{5f.}$, and the overriding concern for children. It is not from the insights of the world of the Song of Songs that the Sadducees ask concerning the solution of such complicated matters in the future aeon, and the stern rebuke which Jesus gives them is fully justified : " Do ye not therefore err, because ye know not the scriptures, neither the power of God ? " This, whole concern for marrying and giving in marriage and the raising up of children, says Jesus, can no longer occupy men in the resurrection when according to Lk. 20^{36} they cannot " die any more." God is the God of Abraham, Isaac and Jacob, and therefore the God of the living (θεὸς ζώντων) and not the dead ; the God for whom, and before whose eyes which span the centuries, all men (or they all, Lk. 20^{38}) are alive in their time. As such they will be revealed in the resurrection, and with their death the necessary cares which now lie like a cover over their lives will be lifted and left behind. Thus the fact that that woman had belonged to seven successive husbands, and must still belong to them according to the law of marriage, could cast no shadow on her temporal life as disclosed in the resurrection, nor on the life of the seven men. For the fact that she married and was married will then be a past event with many other happenings and finally with the death of those concerned. The only thing that will count is that like Abraham, Isaac and Jacob they have lived in their time for God, the God of the living, and therefore live eternally. To that extent they will be as the angels of heaven, not in heaven, but on the new earth under the new heaven—new because the cosmos will then be revealed in the form in which there will be no more possibility or place for tears and death and sorrow and crying and pain (Rev. 21⁴). They will thus be as the angels of heaven because this is how it is already with the angels. But there is no reference here, and cannot be, to an abolition of the sexes or cessation of the being of man as male and female. It is worth noting that even Augustine, who must have been tempted to this thought, expressly repudiated it (*De civ. Dei*, XXII, 17). He met it in the distinctive variation that from the saying in Rom. 8²⁹ about our being conformed to the image of God's Son, and the saying in Eph. 4¹³ about our coming unto a ἀνὴρ τέλειος, it follows that woman will rise after the fashion of the male and not the female. But as against this Augustine prefers the view of those *qui utrumque sexum resurrecturum esse non dubitant*. What is to be set aside in the resurrection is not nature itself, but the violation of nature. But the female sex belongs in its particularity to nature. And so he maintains the opinion : *qui utrumque sexum instituit, utrumque restituet*. Thus in this Synoptic passage Jesus certainly tells us that there will be no continuation of marriage but not that woman will not be woman in the resurrection. By His very negation He presupposes that men will still be men and women women. It cannot be otherwise. In the *Syn. Theol. Leiden* (1624, *Disp.* 51, 37) it is rightly observed that this is also demanded by the identity of the human subject in the two aeons. The determination as man or woman is not the least important of the *conditiones individuantes* of the human subject, so that if it were to lack in the resurrection the subject would no longer be this subject, and man would no longer be man. And in this case it would no longer be τὸ φθαρτὸν τοῦτο which in the resurrection puts on ἀφθαρσία, nor τὸ θνητὸν τοῦτο which puts on ἀθανασία (1 Cor. 15⁵³ᶠ·). Man would not be man if he were no longer male or female, if his humanity did not consist in this concrete fellow-humanity, in this distinction and connexion. He has lived in no other way in time, and he can live in no other way in eternity. This is something which he cannot lose. For by it there stands or falls his creatureliness. In relation to the goal of our existence in the future aeon we have thus no cause to doubt a statement which we formulated in relation to creation as its beginning. We have no cause not to see together the picture of Genesis 2 and that of the Song of Songs.

Why does it have to be as we have stated on the primary basis of these passages ? Why do Genesis 2 and the Song of Songs give us this particular picture of man and his humanity ? Our statement would seem at least to be rather fortuitous if we simply appealed to this Magna Carta in its twofold form, accepting the fact that this is what is actually written and not something else. Why do we read particularly that man is male or female, male and female ? In fact, there is nothing fortuitous about it. It belongs to the very centre of Holy Scripture. It is necessarily grounded in the decisive content of the Word of God. We can thus see, and if we are to have a proper understanding we must see, that there can be no question of anything but what is actually there, and that we cannot possibly adopt any other view than that which we have actually adopted. We must now try to show why this is the case.

As concerns the Old Testament, we have already sketched our

answer. Behind the relationship of man and woman as we meet it in the picture of Genesis 2 and the Song of Songs there stands the controlling original of the relationship between the God Yahweh-Elohim and His people Israel. Behind these passages there stands Old Testament prophecy. And according to the insight which continually breaks through, the sum of all truth and actuality, which is thus also the beginning and end of all things, the secret of creation and its consummation, is the very different duality merely reflected in the nature of man—that of God and man in their co-existence in the concrete form of the covenant established by God between Himself and His people Israel. This duality, the covenant, is the centre of the Old Testament. And it is the original of which the essence of the human as the being of man and woman can only be the reflection and copy. Man is primarily and properly Yahweh, and woman primarily and properly Israel. That is why it is necessary, and the Old Testament poets of creation and the consummation are compelled to describe the human as they have actually done. That is why what they say belongs as it stands to the Canon of Holy Scripture. That is why we have to do here with God's Word concerning man, so that we cannot deviate on either side from what is said. We note that Old Testament prophecy everywhere presupposes the sin of man, Israel's apostasy and therefore the Law and judgment of God, but also and more particularly the faithfulness of God. It thus speaks in the light of the shattering of the original on the side of man. It speaks of the covenant broken by Israel, and therefore of the unfaithful wife who has forfeited her rights and dignity. But in contrast it also speaks of the kindness and mercy of the Husband whom she has left and injured but who does not abandon her. It thus speaks with reference to the long period between creation and the end. But with this reference it speaks concerning this relationship. And it counts on the fact that in and in spite of its disruption it is not ended but persists. The covenant remains. Yahweh is faithful to Israel. His betrothal and marriage continue. His love also remains. And because everything remains on His side, this means that there is also an indestructible continuity in the being of Israel. Even in its apostasy and the rejection and abandonment which it entails it is still the people which Yahweh has marked out and sought and loved, and with which He has entered into covenant. And the end and goal of its history will prove this continuity which exists from the beginning. The hope of Israel is that its continuation in the covenant (not in virtue of its own goodness, but of that of Yahweh) will finally be revealed. This immutable covenant relationship between Yahweh and Israel, and therefore the centre of the Old Testament witness, stands dominatingly behind Genesis 2 and the Song of Songs. As this original confronts them, shattered in the middle of the line, but also in its totality at the beginning and the end, the poets dare to speak of man and woman as they do. We must be clear that they were not just speaking symbolically or allegorically; they were speaking directly and concretely of man and woman and their relationship. But they could do as they did because they had before them as a model and final basis of the form of humanity of which they wrote the relationship of Yahweh and Israel. It was an unattainable model of humanity because love such as that of Yahweh for Israel is beyond the reach of a human husband in relation to his wife. On the one hand we have a covenant between Creator and creature; on the other only a covenant between creature and creature. But the latter covenant rests on the former. Because even God, God Himself, the Lord and King of the heavenly and earthly space created by Him, did not will to be alone, but to have His concrete counterpart in the people Israel, man was not to be alone, but to have his helpmeet or counterpart in woman. Hence it is not at all impossible to find the outlines of the covenant of grace between Yahweh and Israel even in the details of the story of the creation of man as male and female. Because this is the case, it is not by chance that this story has its present form in the Old Testament, and there is good reason to claim it as the Magna Carta of a concept of humanity in which the basic relationship of man and woman receives due honour.

But the final and decisive step has still to be taken to establish it on a biblical foundation. A last appearance of fortuitousness might still cling to it so long as we move only in the sphere of Old Testament promise and not of New Testament fulfilment.

The Old Testament shows an amazing knowledge in this whole matter. Without a knowledge of the true and final meaning of the relationship of man and woman it would be quite intolerable to see this intra-creaturely relationship in the holy relationship between Yahweh and Israel. Again, without a knowledge of the menacing and shattering of the relationship between man and woman the Old Testament could not have such a terribly plastic view of the devastation of the relationship between Yahweh and Israel. On the other hand, without the hope of the last time with its divine fulfilment of the covenant with Israel it would be impossible to see the covenant of man and woman with the freedom of Genesis 2 and the Song of Songs. Again, without the strictly eschatological character of this hope it would be hard to understand why this view of man and woman is the exception to the normal rule of the Old Testament, which is not to consider man and woman as such, in their mutual relationship of husband and wife, but as father and mother in the light of their destiny to have descendants. Thus the knowledge displayed by the Old Testament is strikingly unanimous and yet strikingly contradictory. Why does it include the primary statements? How does it know the dignity of the relationship of the sexes? And yet how does it also know that it is menaced and shattered? How does it know of the eschatological fulfilment of the covenant of grace with Israel? And how does it know that this fulfilment is not to be sought in the sphere of vision of the Israelite, but beyond his sphere of vision, as an eschatological event? It cannot be contested that the Old Testament does know this. But it is also incontestable that in this respect it rests on a secret which is nowhere revealed and never even takes concrete shape in its own sphere. Thus if we were restricted to this sphere alone we should have to accept that a certain

3. Humanity as Likeness and Hope

fortuitousness and uncertainty clings to our statement. We could maintain that things are as we have seen them in the Old Testament. But it could not be said or proved that we for our part are forced to see them in this way.

But why should we be restricted to this sphere? The secret on which the unanimous but contradictory knowledge of the Old Testament rests may well be visible and therefore disclosed outwith the witness of the Old Testament if not within it. The witness of the New Testament tells us that this is the case. If we are to take it seriously we are forced to say that the New Testament tells us what the Old for all its knowledge does not know and therefore cannot tell us. It tells us where this Old Testament knowledge of man derives, where it has objectively its origin and basis, and on what grounds things can be only as indicated in the Old Testament. *Vetus testamentum in novo patet.* It is indeed the case that the New Testament reaches back behind the Old, revealing and disclosing the secret presupposed but nowhere revealed or disclosed in the Old, and thus proving what the Old in itself and as such can never prove—that in all its parts it is right and speaks the truth in a way which is normative for us. We can grasp this if we take our previous questions one by one.

How does the Old Testament know the dignity of the relationship between the sexes? How does it have the knowledge which permits and commands it to see this intra-creaturely relationship in the holy relationship between Yahweh and Israel? The New Testament answers that the covenant between Jesus Christ and His community was in the beginning, the first and proper object of the divine will and plan and election, and the internal basis of creation. This covenant is the original of the Old Testament original, the relationship between Yahweh and Israel, and therefore the original of the relationship between man and woman. It is on the basis of this original that the intra-creaturely relationship has its dignity and necessity, and that the Old Testament finds it essential to see this intra-creaturely relationship at the central point in its witness, in the covenant between God and the people.

But again, how does the Old Testament know that the relationship of the sexes is menaced and shattered? How does it have the knowledge which gives to its complaint against Israel its distinctively sharp and drastic quality as an accusation of adultery? The New Testament answers that the covenant between Jesus Christ and His community, which is the secret of creation, is of such a kind that its Lord, Jesus Christ, is the One who for His community—a gathering of sinners who have fallen victim to the wrath of God and their own perdition—gives Himself up to death in order to win it as His own possession. The history of the covenant between Yahweh and Israel must culminate in the crucifixion of the King for the people because it is grounded in this earlier covenant, the covenant of the Holy with the unholy. On the basis of this earlier covenant Israel throughout the history of the covenant between Yahweh and itself has the form of the ungrateful, faithless and adulterous wife. And on this basis the relationship of the sexes is necessarily seen under the shadow which always falls on it in the Old Testament.

How does the Old Testament know of the eschatological fulfilment of the covenant of grace with Israel? How does it have the knowledge which permits and commands it at least occasionally in these supreme passages to see the relationship of man and woman with this great freedom? The New Testament answers that in the covenant between Jesus Christ and His community it takes place that man's apostasy from God is finally cancelled and made good, that fidelity and love between God and man are made reciprocal by the gift of the Holy Spirit, and that the accusation against man, and therefore the Law which accuses, drop away. On the basis of this covenant the hope of Israel is ineluctably necessary and sure, as constantly depicted in the Old Testament. And on this basis it is possible and necessary to give to the covenant between man and woman—this intra-creaturely covenant as such, and quite apart from any question of progeny—the dignity and honour which are ascribed to it in Genesis 2 and the Song of Songs.

But how does the Old Testament know that the fulfilment of the covenant of grace with Israel is a strictly eschatological reality, and therefore to be sought outside the sphere of the Israelite? How does it have the knowledge which compels the Old Testament normally to speak otherwise of man and woman than in Genesis 2 and the Song of Songs, necessarily putting the fatherhood of the man and motherhood of the woman into the forefront of the picture? The New Testament answers that it is in the covenant between Jesus Christ and His community that the divine will and plan and election have their proper object and thus find their fulfilment. This covenant is the goal even of the covenant between Yahweh and Israel as a promise and preparation. The history of Israel as the history of this covenant has its meaning in the appearance of the Son of God and Son of Man as the Head of a people holy by Him and in Him. And on the basis of this first and proper covenant the Old Testament throughout the middle stretch between creation and the end must display that sober interest in man and woman in their quality as father and mother. This is necessary because in Israel, in the whole sequence of its generations, it is a question only of this promise and preparation, which means finally of the miraculous conception and natural birth of the Son and His people gathered from Jews and Gentiles. Thus the picture of man and woman given in Genesis 2 and the Song of Songs could stand only on the margin of the Old Testament witness, but on this margin it had a place which was not just possible but necessary.

Thus the New Testament witness reaches back behind the Old.

3. Humanity as Likeness and Hope

It reveals the source of the knowledge displayed in the Old Testament. It indicates and discloses the secret which does not emerge and is certainly not revealed in the Old Testament. It proves point by point that the Old Testament is right and speaks the truth in a way which is normative for us, and that it does not therefore say fortuitously of humanity that it consists in the co-existence of male and female.

It is only fitting that at this point we should consider the decisive statements of the New Testament independently and in their own context.

We must first remember the general truth that when the New Testament speaks of Jesus Christ and His community it really speaks of the goal (and therefore of the origin and beginning) of all earthly things. Jesus Christ and His community is not an additional promise given to men. The existence and history of Israel in covenant with Yahweh was a promise. The reality of Jesus Christ and His community does not continue this history. It is not a further stage in actualisation of the divine will and plan and election which are the purpose of creation. It concludes this process. It is the complete fulfilment of the promise. It is the goal and end of all the ways of God. It is *the* eschatological reality. It cannot be surpassed, deepened or enriched by anything still to come. It is followed only by its proclamation to all nations and all creation as the task laid upon the community. But the community has not to proclaim a new offer or promise and its law. It has to proclaim the accomplishment of the divine decree as it has already taken place in the appearance of Jesus Christ, in His death and resurrection, and in the outpouring of the Holy Ghost. All that is outstanding is its manifestation as the light of the cosmos which does not yet know it—its manifestation by Jesus Christ Himself. But as the Head of His community He is already the Head of the cosmos (Col. 1$^{17f.}$). Hence His return cannot alter or improve anything, let alone introduce anything new. " If any man be in Christ, he *is* a new creature " (2 Cor. 5^{17}). What is to be proclaimed by the ministry of His community, and finally revealed by Himself, is simply the fact that this is the case. He is a new creature. For God has given Jesus Christ to be the κεφαλὴ ὑπὲρ πάντα to the community which is His body and in which He has His own divine fulness and His whole divine fulfilment (Eph. 1$^{22f.}$). This completed fact is still to be shown to the cosmos. This completed fact must be revealed as the meaning of the whole cosmos. But it is already a completed fact. There is no salvation which has not already come to the world in the death and resurrection of Jesus Christ and the existence of the community which He has purchased by His blood and has gathered and still gathers by His Holy Spirit.

It was on the basis of this insight that Paul treated his communities, and each of them as *the* community of Jesus Christ. A Christian community is not a religious experiment. It is not a fellowship of faith and hope with a more or less distant and exalted goal to which it is directed and towards which it strives as an ideal. It is this as little as Jesus Christ is a prophet pointing to the future and prophesying something which is not yet real. The people Israel waits for the Son. Its whole history is the history of this expectation. But the community of Jews and Gentiles founded by the apostle derives from the Son. It has its history in the fact that it is in Christ and therefore lives in the fulfilment which has taken place in this Head. It belongs to Him, and what belongs to Him belongs as His gift to it. As the apostle proclaimed to it the Word concerning Him, and it received this Word in faith, as Christians were baptised in the name of Jesus Christ, they were united to Him, and with Him they constitute the eschatological reality and the end of all God's ways, so that they can will only that the glory in which they participate in Him and by Him should be revealed among them and through them to others, and they can expect only that Jesus Christ Himself will finally confess them and manifest the glory with which He has already invested them to their own eyes and those of others, in order that the whole world may be radiant and full of the glory of God in this revelation. It is on this basis that Paul addresses the Christian communities, and always in the light of the fact that the fulfilment has taken place in Jesus Christ alone, but in Jesus Christ for them. All the instruction, consolation and admonition which he imparts to them are references back to this completed fact, to the portion which they have in Jesus Christ and therefore in the fulfilment which has taken place in Him. Any deviation from this line, any return to the situation of the people Israel, i.e., to that of the unfulfilled promise, any re-establishment of the Israelitish Law, but also any legalistic demand for faith and hope, would necessarily mean that Jesus Christ Himself is called in question. But someone in whom everything is not fulfilled would not be Jesus Christ. We know how passionately Paul avoided this kind of Christ. And he was not guilty of any such deviation or compromise. The warfare against sin, error and disorder which he waged in the Christian community was conducted solely on the basis of the fact that Jesus Christ and His community in their interconnexion are the reality of the last time beyond which we cannot expect any other, or any other insights, possibilities or powers, but in which God has reached with man the end for which He created heaven and earth and all that therein is. And the whole warfare of the spirit against the flesh, the good fight of faith, to which Paul summons the community and all its members, can only be the battle to maintain the position which has already been captured and allotted to them by the act of God in Jesus Christ, and from which no one and nothing can ever drive them.

It is on this presupposition that Paul addresses the Corinthians, for example, when he writes in 2 Cor. 11$^{2f.}$: " For I am jealous over you with godly jealousy : for I have espoused you to one husband, that I may present you as a chaste virgin to Christ. But I fear, lest by any means, as the serpent beguiled Eve through his subtilty, so your minds should be corrupted from sincerity towards Christ." We do not know in detail against whom or what Paul was jealous. The only thing which is clear (v. 4) is that an attempt had been made in Corinth to preach another Jesus than the One whom Paul had preached. But in relation to the preaching of Paul another Jesus can only be one in whom we can and must believe without living with him in the fulfilment, or finding consolation in the fulfilment, or fighting the battles which have still to be fought on the basis of the fulfilment as it has been accomplished in him. From Paul's standpoint another Jesus can only be a Jesus who is a mere prophet or the mere bearer of a further promise. If Paul says that in this matter he is " jealous with a godly jealousy " for the Corinthians, and the maintenance of fellowship with them, and the constancy of the faith which he has proclaimed to them, it is obvious that this is not the jealousy of an Elijah or any other Old Testament figure for the fidelity of Israel and in face of its infidelity to the promise and the law of the promise which it has been given. It is the jealousy of God which Paul must make his own as the apostle of Jesus Christ ; the jealousy of the God who has brought the history of the covenant to its goal, and who cannot possibly allow what He has done to be reversed even in the name of another Jesus, in the very name of the One in whom it has reached its goal. The true Jesus Himself stands in question. That is why Paul is jealous with a godly jealousy for the Corinthians. For the true Jesus is not alone. They, too, belong to Him, the One who has fulfilled the work of God. For the apostolic word has been heard by them, and received by them in faith. Something irrevocable has thus taken place for them and to them. The death and resurrection of Jesus Christ are the reality which not only refers to them (as to the whole world) but which also embraces them and in which they have their life. To the extent that

3. Humanity as Likeness and Hope

they are the Christian community, they are absolutely from Him and to Him, and therefore they are determined in what they are and do and refrain from doing by the fact that there is accomplished in Him that which God intended for man from the very first. He, Paul, is the witness of this. For he has attested to them the real Jesus as their Lord, and even the witness of their faith belongs to him. He thus knows that in this matter he is responsible both to God for them and to them for God. He cannot be content merely with the fact that they are Christians and accept Jesus as a good man in whom they somehow have dealings with God but concerning whose significance they have another view which has to be tolerated side by side with that of Paul. No, says Paul, this is not another view of Jesus. It is another Jesus. And this we cannot in any circumstances or in any sense admit. Between the real Jesus and the Corinthians something has taken place, a decision has been made, which cannot be reversed. And he, Paul, was present when this decision was made. As the messenger of the Gospel he was the man who sought and brought them from afar (as Eliezer brought Rebekah to Isaac in Gen. 24$^{1f.}$). Indeed, we might almost say that as God brought Eve and showed her to Adam, he brought and showed them to the real Jesus as the one Husband, betrothing them to Him as His bride. Between this one Husband Christ and them there is a legal relationship created by His Word and Spirit and therefore solidly established. He, Paul, can testify that everything has been in order in the establishment of this relationship. He has not brought the community to any other husband. The Christ proclaimed by him was the One in whom everything was accomplished for them, for He is the Head over all things, and there cannot possibly be any other. And He has brought them to this Husband as a chaste virgin. He knew that when he brought them to this Husband their past and its sins would not be remembered; that as the elect and beloved of this One they could come to Him absolutely pure and righteous and holy; that their faith in this One was genuine and sincere; and that their baptism was not merely water-baptism but the baptism of the Spirit (so that there could be no question of this One later repulsing them as unworthy). The relationship between the one Husband Christ and His bride is a definitive relationship which no power in heaven or earth can alter, let alone a change of opinion which they have allowed themselves in the meantime. It is to be noted that the distinctness with which Paul speaks of the definitive character of this relationship is not denied even by what follows. He fears for them. He fears that their thoughts might be led away from sincerity towards Christ, and therefore corrupted. He fears that something might happen to them analogous to what took place between the treacherous serpent and Eve who was so terribly deceived. He starts back from the possibility that they might go this ruinous way even in thought; that even in thought they might try to play the Eve. But he obviously does not believe that he cannot appeal to their sincerity towards Christ as their true position. "Sincerity ($\dot{\alpha}\pi\lambda\dot{o}\tau\eta s$) towards Christ" is the basic knowledge in which, without glancing aside to the right hand or the left, they are content with Christ because all things are given them in Him. He sees the possibility that their thoughts might go astray in spite of this knowledge, as the thoughts of the community of Jesus Christ have often played the Eve in spite of it, and thus been betrayed into error. But even in this danger he still sees it as the community of Jesus Christ which cannot move away from its basis in Jesus Christ, which cannot separate itself from this Head, which cannot be shaken in this basic knowledge. He is not referring to the legal relationship at the establishment of which he was a witness and assistant. He does not question the continuance of this relationship. He would contradict himself if he did. He would be reckoning with another Jesus; with a Christ whose work could be incomplete or futile like that of so many of the prophets; with a covenant to which one would rather be unfaithful after entering into it. The Christ with whom Paul reckons is the One who has acted and spoken conclusively in the name of God, and therefore united Himself conclusively with His community, however dangerously its thoughts concerning Him may oscillate, so that even though its fidelity may seem to stand in jeopardy we can always appeal to its sincerity towards Christ, and the threat to its fidelity is most effectively met by this appeal. This appeal can and may and must be made, not because we can trust Christians as those who are united with Him, but because we can be confident that the Lord whose possession they are has not given them His Spirit in vain. We maintain that Paul regarded it as right in elucidation of this thesis to recall the encounter of bridegroom and bride and therefore the primitive form of humanity as being in encounter.

On the same presupposition he declared in Rom. 7^{1-6} that Christians are those who in virtue of the death and resurrection of Jesus Christ really have the situation of Israel behind them, who are really liberated from the Law which finally can only accuse and condemn them by confirming that they are sinners. For our present purposes the decisive verses are 3 and 4: " So then if, while her husband liveth, she shall be married to another man, she shall be called an adulteress: but if her husband be dead she is freed from that law; so that she is no adulteress, though she be married to another man. Wherefore, my brethren, ye also are become dead to the law by the body (the physical slaying) of Christ; that ye should be married to another, even to him who is raised from the dead." It is to be noted that in this passage the purity of the bride brought to Christ in 2 Cor. 11^2 is interpreted in the sense in which we understood it in the previous reference. It is not intrinsic but is acquired as she is brought to this Husband. As we are now told explicitly, she had previously belonged to another. This other, her first husband, was none other than the man of the first aeon; the man of the world standing under the dominion of the sin of Adam and Eve. This man was under the Law which accused and condemned him, which confirmed the fact that he was a sinner, and in this way provoked and quickened his sin, so that the fruit which he produced (v. 5), the reward which he earned (6^{23}), could only be death. This man was the first husband of Christians. He was their old man under whose law they had necessarily to stand. So long as he lived! Only his death could free them from his law and therefore from the fact that they were accused and condemned as sinners. Every attempt made prior to the death of this man to escape his law, to disregard its accusation and condemnation, to act in an arbitrarily gained or imagined freedom in respect of him, to pretend to be elsewhere than on the fatal middle stretch between creation and the consummation, could only make them genuinely guilty and worthy of death. So long as our old man lives, what can we accomplish in this direction but what the Old Testament calls the adultery of Israel against its God, the service of alien gods and the corresponding practical alienation from the true God, the sin which does not drive out sin but merely reveals it in its true colours? At this point only the intervention of a higher power can save us. Freedom can be legitimately and effectively established only by the death of the old man and the loosing of our connexion with him. And it is on this basis that Christians rest. They no longer belong to the first man because he is no longer alive. He was put to death on Golgotha in the self-offering of the body of Christ. He was crucified and died in and with the slain body of Christ. And with him their sin was also crucified and died (Rom. $6^{3f.}$). The man of the old aeon was there and then destroyed with his aeon. Thus the law of this man, which was binding so long as he was alive, has lost its validity. He cannot accuse or condemn them any more. He cannot confirm or increase their sin. They are free, not with the illusory and evil freedom of adulterous Israel, but genuinely free. They have not accomplished this themselves. They could have won for themselves only that adulterous freedom. But there and then, in the death of Jesus Christ who alone could do it, they have become genuinely free: free to be the wife of this Other, their Liberator,

3. Humanity as Likeness and Hope

Jesus Christ risen from the dead ; and therefore free for life under His law, which according to Rom. 8$^{2f.}$ is the "Law of the Spirit of Life." "There is therefore now no condemnation to them which are in Christ Jesus" (Rom. 8^1). The community may thus be absolutely pure and righteous and holy as His bride and help meet. It is a creature, but a new creature by His death and resurrection and in the power of His Spirit. Thus man and wife again confront one another as man and fellow-man and need not be ashamed—the original of humanity.

But Paul also spoke on the same presupposition in the passages in which he looked at things from the opposite angle. In 2 Cor. 11$^{2f.}$ and Rom. 7$^{1f.}$ he was obviously considering the relationship between Christ and His community in the light of various aspects of that of the relationship of husband and wife, Jesus Christ being the Bridegroom to whom the community was legally brought as a bride, or the other man by whom and for whom the community is legally free although previously married to another. But there are passages in Paul, understandably better known and more frequently cited, in which he is dealing with some form of the reality of the relationship between husband and wife, and in his interpretation of this reality recalls the relationship between Jesus Christ and the community, explaining the former by the latter. Even and especially in these passages it is obvious that in this relationship, in the act of God which took place on Good Friday, Easter Day and Pentecost, he sees the fulfilment and completion of all things, the dawn of the last time which makes quite impossible any return to the economy of the Old Testament.

In I Cor. 6$^{12-20}$ we have a clear warning against $\pi o \rho \nu \epsilon i a$, or sexual intercourse with a $\pi \acute{o} \rho \nu \eta$, i.e., the kind of intercourse in which man turns to woman merely for the satisfaction of his carnal needs and woman is only an occasion and means to provide this satisfaction. The decisive positive statements which serve as the basis of the warning are as follows (vv. 16b–17) : "For two, saith he, shall be one flesh. But he that is joined unto the Lord is one spirit." From what we are told by the second statement, i.e., from the relationship between Jesus Christ and His community, Paul looks back and down on the relationship between man and woman to which the first statement refers. That the Christian is one body with his wife can take place only in correspondence with the fact that he himself is one spirit with the Lord. But in the kind of sexual intercourse referred to there is no such correspondence and therefore it is impossible. It would be wrong to say that it is forbidden. It is not forbidden ; it is intrinsically impossible. The whole purpose of Paul in this passage is to recall to Christians the impossibility. "Know ye not ? " is his insistent question in v. 15, v. 16 and v. 19. It would be wrong to speak of a Pauline prohibition because at the beginning of the passage (v. 12) there stands the impressive and twofold $\pi \acute{a} \nu \tau a$ $\mu o \iota$ $\emph{\'\epsilon} \xi \epsilon \sigma \tau \iota \nu$: "I have power over all things." Behind this passage, too, there stands the Pauline message of the liberation of man in Jesus Christ from the law of sin and death, and if we do not understand this we cannot understand his warning. We certainly cannot understand how categorical it is. For it is the freedom created by Jesus Christ and given to His community which has the power of decision of which the Pauline warning speaks. The " know ye not ? " is a reminder of this freedom. It is the freedom to choose that which helps ($\sigma \nu \mu \phi \acute{\epsilon} \rho \epsilon \iota$) the Christian and to repudiate that which would bring him under the domination of an alien power, involving an $\emph{\'\epsilon} \xi o \nu \sigma \iota \acute{a} \zeta \epsilon \sigma \theta a \iota$ $\hat{\nu} \pi \acute{o}$ $\tau \iota \nu o s$, and thus limiting and even destroying his freedom. Not everything is a help to him. Having power over all things, he has the freedom to reject that which does not help him. And many things would bring him under an alien domination. Having power over all things, he has the freedom to reject them. The connexion between freedom and decision is seen in a different light in I Cor. 10^{23} : $\pi \acute{a} \nu \tau a$ $\emph{\'\epsilon} \xi \epsilon \sigma \tau \iota \nu$, $\mathring{a} \lambda \lambda$' $o \mathring{v}$ $\pi \acute{a} \nu \tau a$ $o \mathring{\iota} \kappa o \delta o \mu \epsilon \hat{\iota}$. We have to remember here too that the freedom of the Christian is the freedom to play his part in the upbuilding of the community. Who is the Christian ? He is a man who " is joined unto the Lord " (κολλώμενος in v. 17 is the same term as that which the LXX uses in Gen. 2²⁴ᶠ· for the cleaving of a wife to her husband). The Christian is dearly bought (v. 20). At the supreme cost of the self-offering of the Son of God he is freed from the powers which determine a whole world which is now past for him. According to Col. 1¹³ he is translated by God into the kingdom of His dear Son. He has thus become His possession. He shares His lordship over these powers. And his freedom rests in this fact. As he lives in this freedom, he lives in the Spirit. And as he lives in the Spirit, he is one with the Lord. The Christian is thus a man who does not belong to himself but to this Lord (v. 19). He is joined to Him. It is not something abstract which is joined to Him (his soul perhaps), but something very concrete, he himself as the soul of his body. He in his totality, and therefore in his corporeality, does not belong to himself but to the Lord. He is a member of Christ, of His body, of His community (v. 15), and thus participates in His lordship and is free for what is helpful to him as a Christian, free from all alien dominion, and free for the edification of the community. The order under which he stands as this concrete being in his corporeality is, however, that " God hath both raised up the Lord, and will also raise up us by his own power " (v. 14). The Lord took to Himself concrete human being, corporeality. He suffered and died in the body. He accomplished that self-offering in the body. And He was also raised from the dead in the body. In this context the last is the decisive point. As certainly as Christ was raised from the dead in the body the Christian is not subject to death in the body. Jesus Christ has drawn him as His member even in his corporeality after and towards Himself to a new life. In his corporeality he is already determined, disposed and organised for this new life as " the temple of the Holy Ghost, which ye have of God " (v. 19). He is thus summoned to glorify God in his corporeality (v. 20). This is how it stands with the Christian. He is free for what is necessary for him in the light of the resurrection of Jesus Christ ; for what helps him in his being on this basis (as the temple of the Holy Ghost and for the glorifying of God) ; for what confirms and increases his freedom from the powers of the old aeon ; for what edifies the community. He is also free to refrain from the opposite of all these things. He would not be what he is if he had a freedom which could be defined in any other way : the freedom to do the latter and not to do the former ; the freedom to do what does not help him but brings him into captivity and destroys the community. But in this being of the Christian—and Paul thinks it quite impossible that the Corinthians should not know this, or that he should have to do more than give them an interrogative reminder—the decision is already taken what is intrinsically possible and what is intrinsically impossible for the Christian in this matter of sexual intercourse. In the first instance, there is a pre-decision concerning the significance of his action as such. In sexual intercourse it is not merely a question—as some at Corinth obviously seem to have thought (v. 13)—of the satisfaction of a physical and in this case sexual need, which can be met without any particular question of the means, like the need of the stomach by eating. In sexual intercourse we do not move within this kind of physical cycle : " meats for the belly, and the belly for meats " ; a need which cries out for satisfaction, and the satisfaction which answers to the need. Ὁ δὲ θεὸς καὶ ταύτην καὶ ταῦτα καταργήσει. When the time of man is up, God will destroy this physical cycle. It belongs to his corporeality, and therefore to himself. Of course, as Paul himself obviously presupposes a few verses later (7¹ᶠ·), even in sexual intercourse there is a question of this kind of cycle of need and satisfaction belonging to the corporeality of man and therefore to himself. But in sexual intercourse it is also a matter of the body itself and as such, and therefore of man in his corporeality. For sexual intercourse means that at the climax and in the completion of their encounter they become **one body**, belonging wholly to one

3. Humanity as Likeness and Hope

another in their corporeality, and mutually attesting and guaranteeing their humanity. In this completion the man no longer belongs to himself, but to the woman ; and the woman no longer belongs to herself, but to the man. In this completion there takes place between them something final and irrevocable. They are both what they became in this completion—a being belonging to this other. This is not, then, a neutral sphere or indifferent occurrence. There is decided here to whom man belongs as in this completion he belongs to another. For the Christian this decision has been made. Belonging to a woman, he cannot contradict but must correspond to the fact that he belongs to Christ. But he would contradict this if he belonged to a harlot and became one body with her. But why is this so total a contradiction ? Why does the " one spirit " with Christ exclude in this way the " one body " with a harlot ? Obviously because Christ is the faithfulness of God in person, whereas the harlot personifies human unfaithfulness against God. He cannot will to become one body with a harlot, or actually become this, in the freedom which is created for and given to him by Christ. In so doing he who is one spirit with the Lord would become something which would not help him, in which he would not be the temple of the Holy Ghost, or glorify God, or edify the community, but merely return to the bondage from which he has been so dearly and definitively ransomed. In sexual intercourse with a harlot there can be only a sorry distortion of the completion between man and woman. For what kind of a completion is it ? The completion of fellowship ? No, it can be only the completion of self-satisfaction, and therefore at the climax of the encounter the denial of any real encounter ; fellowship in the form of the betrayal of fellowship. For in this intercourse man does not seek woman in the totality of her corporeality. He seeks only the sexual being as an occasion and means to the satisfaction of his own corresponding need. He forgets, and wills to forget, that in woman as herself a human being he has to do with the fellow-man ; that as an I he has to do in her with a Thou. He thus denies the humanity of woman, treating her as an It. And the woman does not expect man as a man, or in the totality of his corporeality. He is for her too an It and not a Thou. She does not seek a true and serious and genuine connexion. She merely answers to his sexual impulse, shaming not only her own womanhood but his manhood too. Let there be no mistake—even in this distortion the completion is real enough. There takes place a mutual self-offering. Male and female become one flesh as stated in Gen. 2^{24}. They belong together. Although as betrayers of their humanity, they mutually determine and shame each other. If a Christian seeks intercourse with a harlot, this is not a neutral happening which does not affect the man himself in his being as a Christian. What happens is that he " takes " (ἄρας) his body, i.e., himself in his corporeality, as though it belonged to himself and he could do this with it, and makes it (himself) the member of a harlot (v. 15), thus giving it (himself) a part in that betrayal. His being as a man is thus brought into contradiction with his being as a Christian. He thus sins against his own body (v. 18). That is to say, he does not merely pervert and corrupt something extraneous, but decisively he perverts and corrupts himself. And he perverts and corrupts himself wholly and utterly, and therefore in his relationship to God and his fellow-man. He who in his corporeality is a member of Christ and as such moves forward to the raising of the dead by the power of God pronounces sentence of death upon himself. For if he belongs to a harlot—and this is what intercourse with her means—he can only die totally and with no hope of life. I take it that in the difficult v. 18 Paul is speaking of a sin of which only the Christian is really capable. μὴ γένοιτο, he says to this sin (v. 15), and this is an expression which he usually reserves for the rebuttal of a possibility which is radically excluded. He thinks through this possibility logically and to the bitter end. But he definitely tells the Corinthians that this is a way which cannot be entered. It must be remembered that immediately prior to this passage he had written (6¹¹): "But ye are washed (in baptism), but ye are sanctified, but ye are justified in the name of the Lord Jesus, and by the Spirit of our God." This "ye are" is like a barrier blocking the way. This is what they know according to vv. 15, 16 and 19. This is what Paul has only to remind them in order to say something which is far more powerful than any prohibition. It is the same absolute obstacle to which Jesus Himself referred in Mt. 6²⁴: "No man can serve two masters. . . . Ye cannot serve God and mammon." Paul takes the same line. He does not need to present any law or morality. He has only to show what they can and cannot do. They cannot place themselves afresh under forces which they have once and for all escaped as they belong to Christ in their corporeality. Conversely, they cannot escape the service in which they have been placed once and for all as they belong to Christ in their corporeality. They cannot exist in their corporeality as only the victims of death can exist. They have the risen Christ behind them and before. They cannot make the temple of God a den of thieves. They cannot blaspheme God; they can only glorify Him. They cannot compromise Jesus Christ, with whom they are one spirit, as though He Himself to whom they are joined—in this case they would indeed belong to another Jesus—were one of the powers of the old world and He Himself invited them to do so. They cannot be guilty of that contradiction. For they know perfectly well that that contradiction is itself contradicted, and that it is contradicted victoriously and definitively, so that no option remains. Hence they cannot either seek woman in the form of a harlot, or accept her advances in this form. It is to be noted that this does not merely apply to what is called extramarital intercourse. They cannot make woman a harlot, or accept her as such, either outside marriage or within it. They cannot affirm πορνεία and the πόρνη in any form. They cannot do this because their being excludes this affirmation of the harlot in any form. They can only really do what Paul commands in v. 18: φεύγετε τὴν πορνείαν. Turn your back on it with the firmness and totality which are the only possibility when we have to do with the impossible. What is intrinsically possible to the man who is one spirit with Christ in the relationship of man and woman and therefore in the completion of this relationship can only be, as an exercise of his freedom and therefore his participation in the lordship of Christ, and in his obedience to "the law of the Spirit of life," the intercourse which beyond all need and its satisfaction is the completion of the encounter of man and fellow-man and the fulfilment of full and serious and genuine fellowship. There is thus possible for him only the becoming "one body" in which there is clearly and unequivocally reflected the full and serious and genuine fellowship of Jesus Christ with His community and each of its individual members. There is possible only the becoming "one body" of which he does not need to be ashamed in face of the fact that he is "one spirit" with Jesus Christ, and in respect of which the man and woman have no cause for mutual shame but for rejoicing as in a reflection of light from above. It is on the basis of this positive recognition that the decision goes against πορνεία. At this critical point, therefore, Paul set the anthropological question as that of man's humanity in the light of Christology, and answered it accordingly. All that remains for us is simply to state that this is what happens in the passage. Paul brings the concrete form of the fellow-humanity of man and woman, and sexual intercourse as its most concrete form, into connexion with the relationship between Jesus Christ and His community, and derives his normative concept of the human—not without express reference to Gen. 2—from this basic norm. The necessary stringency is not lacking. But there is none of the papistical severity which is so often encountered in this sphere. Paul knew how to give a categorical and effective warning on the basis of the whole Gospel, and his warning is far more categorical and effective than that of many who before and after him have tackled the problem purely from the standpoint of the Law.

3. Humanity as Likeness and Hope

In 1 Cor. 7$^{1-10}$ and then again in 7$^{25-40}$ Paul took up the question of marriage and celibacy. In 7$^{10-17}$ he dealt with divorce. In 14$^{33-38}$ and 1 Tim. 2$^{8-12}$ he discussed the question of women speaking, or rather being silent, in the ἐκκλησία. We shall not take up these problems here because in these passages (as distinct from 1 Cor. 6$^{12-20}$) there is no explicit reference to the connexion between man and woman on the one side and Christ and His community on the other. To understand these passages we can hardly avoid making this connexion in their exposition. But our present question is not where it can and must be made, but where it is actually made in the New Testament.

The second passage in which this is indisputably the case is 1 Cor. 11$^{1-16}$. As a text for this whole section we might well take vv. 11–12: " Nevertheless neither is the man without the woman, neither the woman without the man, in the Lord. For as the woman is of the man, even so is the man also by the woman ; but all things of God." Man and woman are here considered in relation to a question of liturgical order. It is a small, external and peripheral question. But Paul regards the decision made in its solution as so great, internal and central that he does not hesitate to devote 16 verses to it and to make again the connexion which is our present concern. His aim is to show that because in the Lord and " of God " the woman is not without the man or the man without the woman, a definite course has to be adopted in relation to this peripheral question of order. What was the point at issue ? An enthusiastic attempt was being made to introduce equality where previously the custom had been both at Corinth and in other Christian communities that in their gatherings for worship the men should be uncovered and the women covered. We may well imagine that Gal. 3^{28} (" neither male nor female ") provided either verbally or materially the main argument in favour of abolishing this outward distinction and therefore against Paul, who had given this dictum but now favoured the keeping of the tradition (v. 2). There can be little doubt, as we gather from the earlier chapters of the Epistle, that an attempt of this kind was being made at Corinth, and that it was directed generally against the recognition of the specific authority and office and word of the apostle. Must the freedom won in Christ acquiesce in the irreversibility of the relationship of order and ministry between the apostle and the community ? We learn from 4^8 that the Corinthians were very largely of the opinion that they were full and rich, and had thus attained to a βασιλεύειν independent of the apostle. And it may be gathered from 12^{29} that the slogan " We are all apostles " was only just round the corner. It is certainly no accident that Paul refers briefly to this basic question in vv. 1–2, and even vv. 3–16 with their presentation of the relationship between man and woman (perhaps this is one of the reasons why they are so definite) are to be understood as an indirect elucidation of the relationship between the apostle and the community. The latter is a decisively important derivative of the relationship between Christ and the community. Because it was a matter of the absolute and incomparable authority of the crucified Jesus, Paul as His witness could not yield an inch in the question of his own relative and human authority as an apostle. Without Christ's commission and Spirit there was no apostolic word, but without the apostolic word there was no Christian hearing, no hearing of the Word of Christ, no life in the Holy Spirit. And it was also a question of the relationship between absolute and relative, directly divine and indirectly human order in the problem of man and woman discussed in vv. 3–16. Paul tells us plainly enough in vv. 11–12 that he does not retract anything that he has said in Gal. 3^{28}. In the Lord, " of God," it is just as true that the woman is of the man and the man by the woman. Both are told us by Gen. 2. Woman is taken out of man, but man is man only by the woman taken out of him. Yet only an inattentive enthusiasm could deduce from this that man and woman are absolutely alike, that there can be no question of super-and subordination between them, and that it is both legitimate and obligatory to abolish the distinction between the uncovered and the covered head in divine service. It was the same inattentive enthusiasm which concluded from the fulness of spiritual gifts of which there was evidently no lack in Corinth that there was no further need for the teaching, exhortation and admonition of the apostle. In both cases, as in many other respects, it was forgotten that God (14³³) is not a God of ἀκαταστασία but of peace. But there is peace only if distinctions are observed in the fellowship : in the fellowship, so that the antitheses caused by their misunderstanding and misuse are overcome ; but genuinely observed, so that there is true super-and subordination, and it is seen that we are dealing with two different things and not one and the same when we are told by Gen. 2 that woman is from the man and by Gen. 2 again that man is by the woman. The demonstration of this peace, and therefore of these distinctions in the fellowship of man and woman, is the theme of the present passage. Paul is trying to show that the observance of this relative, indirect and human order is necessary because it rests on an absolute, direct and divine order, so that the denial of the one means the denial of the other. The curious saying about the angels in v. 10 is most simply explained as follows. The angels are generally the bearers and representatives of the relative principles necessarily posited with the work of God, and they are specifically the bearers and representatives of the indirect human orders necessarily posited with the divine work of salvation. They cannot, therefore, see these orders violated without sorrow. This is something which should not happen. Hence διὰ τοὺς ἀγγέλους the woman must bear on her head in divine service an ἐξουσία (a sign of her recognition of the ἐξουσία of the man which she does not possess). But what is the connexion between the divine work of salvation and the order in question ? The decisive statement in this regard is undoubtedly to be found in v. 3 : κεφαλὴ δὲ γυναικὸς ὁ ἀνήρ. If this is accepted as a justifiable assertion, we maintain that it proves both the point and even the necessity of the custom. The uncovered head of the man is the sign that in divine service, in his participation in the act of προσεύχεσθαι and προφητεύειν, he has no κεφαλή over him because he is himself κεφαλή. But the covering of the head of the woman is a sign that in the worship of the community, in her participation in the act of προσεύχεσθαι and προφητεύειν, she has a κεφαλή over her and is not therefore herself κεφαλή. The conclusion is drawn in vv. 4-6 that in the light of v. 3b any other practice dishonours both the head of man and that of woman. The particular honour of both demands this custom. Verse 10 underlines this conclusion by referring to the angels, and vv. 12–15 add that it corresponds to natural sensibility. But the whole argument depends on v. 3b and therefore on whether this assertion is justified. What is its basis ? We might refer to the passage in Eph. 5²²⁻²³, where this assertion is reversed and explained in v. 23 : ἀνήρ ἐστιν κεφαλὴ τῆς γυναικὸς ὡς καὶ ὁ Χριστὸς κεφαλὴ τῆς ἐκκλησίας. On this basis we could argue that the whole point of the statement is that man in his relationship to woman represents Christ in His relationship to the community, and that woman in her relationship to man represents the community in its relationship to Christ, as developed in the Ephesian passage. But in the first instance the assertion in 1 Cor. 11³ᵇ should be evaluated in its own context. It is immediately preceded by 3a : παντὸς ἀνδρὸς ἡ κεφαλὴ ὁ Χριστός ἐστιν, and followed by 3c : κεφαλὴ δὲ τοῦ Χριστοῦ ὁ θεός. On the basis of these three statements in their interconnexion Paul then goes on to say : " But I would have you know. . . ." It is to be noted that he does not ask here as in 1 Cor. 6⁹ : " Know ye not ? " It is obviously presupposed that they ought to know, but it emerges more plainly at this point that they need the apostle to proclaim and interpret what they might basically know of themselves. Above all, the order of the statements is to be noted. They are not arranged as a demand for perspicuity might suggest : 3c, that God is the Head of Christ ; 3a, that Christ is the Head of man ; and 3b that man is the head of woman. Nor do they take the opposite course—

3. Humanity as Likeness and Hope

3b, 3a, 3c. They are necessarily arranged as in the text. They contain neither deduction from above downwards nor induction from below upwards. They are not a scale. They have often been understood in this way, with the absurd result that man is taken to be for woman what Christ is for him and God for Christ, so that it is only indirectly and by way of man that woman is in relationship to Christ and therefore to God. The remarkable position of 3b warns us against this interpretation. Telling us that man is set above woman, it is preceded by the statement that Christ is set above him. And telling us of the subordination of woman, it is followed by a statement which speaks of a subordination of Christ to God. Thus it is grounded and explained in Christ whether it speaks of the superordination of man or the subordination of woman. Both superordination and subordination are primarily and properly in Christ. According to Col. 2^{10} He is ἡ κεφαλὴ πάσης ἀρχῆς καὶ ἐξουσίας. According to Eph. 1^{10} it was the good-pleasure of God ἀνακεφαλαιώσασθαι τὰ πάντα in Him. " πᾶσα ἐξουσία is given unto me in heaven and in earth " (Mt. 28^{18}, cf. also Col. 1^{16}, Eph. 1^{20} and 1 Pet. 3^{22}). He, then, is the Head of every man. That is to say, He is the sum of all superordination, and He stands relatively much higher than man behind his majesty. Whatever may be the ἐξουσία of man in relation to woman, it is legitimate and effective only to the extent that primarily and properly it does not belong to him but to Christ, and can therefore only be attested and represented by man. Conversely, Christ is the sum of all humility before God, of all the obedient fulfilment of His will. He is the One who according to Phil. $2^{6f.}$, although He was in the form of God, did not count it His prey to be equal with God, but emptied Himself, and took the form of a servant, and made Himself equal to man . . . and humbled Himself. He thus enters on His lordship by becoming the slave of God and man. God has made Him— we must not forget this supreme statement—to be sin for us (2 Cor. 5^{21}). Could He stoop any lower before God than this ? He is thus the sum of all subordination, and stands relatively much lower than woman under man. And whatever may be her relationship to the ἐξουσία of man which she lacks, it is sanctified, ennobled and glorified by the fact that her subordination is primarily and properly that of Christ and can only be attested and represented by her. Thus it can really be said between the height and the depth, the lordship and service, the divinity and humanity of Christ : " The head of the woman is the man." So little does this ascribe to man or refer to woman ! So sharply and clearly is it determined and limited on both sides by what is primarily and properly the affair of Christ ! His is the superordination and His the subordination. His is the place of man, and His the place of woman. And what place is there to speak of little or much ? There is assigned to each that which is helpful and right and worthy. If it is no little thing for man to be κεφαλή in relation to woman, i.e., the one who has precedence, initiative and authority, the representative of the order which embraces them both, it is no little thing for woman to take the place which she is assigned in relation to man and therefore not to be κεφαλή but to be led by him, to accept his authority, to recognise the order which claims them both as it is represented by him. In vv. 7–9 Paul refers explicitly to Gen. 2. The determination and limitation of the relationship of man and woman as established in Christ emerge already in the work of creation. Woman is fashioned out of man and for the sake of man. She is not created as he is out of the dust of the earth but (more humanly, we might almost say) out of man himself, in order that he should not be alone but have a helpmeet (vv. 8–9). Thus he is the " image and glory of God," yet not alone or without or against the woman, but together with the woman who is his glory (v. 7). This basic order of the human established by God's creation is not accidental or contingent. It cannot be overlooked or ironed out. We cannot arbitrarily go behind it. It is solidly and necessarily grounded in Christ, with a view to whom heaven and earth and finally man were created. It is so solidly grounded in the lordship and service, the divinity and humanity of Christ that there can be no occasion either for the exaltation of man or the oppression of woman. " If any man be in Christ, he is a new creature." It is the life of this new creature which Paul describes with the saying that the head of the woman is the man. Gal. 3²⁸ is still valid, in spite of shortsighted exegetes, like the Corinthians themselves, who shake their heads and think they can claim a contradiction. The mutuality of the relationship still obtains, as described in vv. 11–12. To that extent there is an equality of man and woman ἐν κυρίῳ in the order in which the one God has with equal directness assigned this place to man and that to woman. Where is there any real knowledge of differentiation and mutuality, and where are the exaltation of man and the oppression of woman radically excluded, except in the community of Jesus Christ, in which His lordship and service are the final word, and the Creator of all things is found and recognised in the baby in the crib, and in the baby in the crib the Creator of all things, no contradiction being seen between majesty and humility, superordination and subordination, lordship and service ? Is not the community of Jesus Christ itself and as such, as adduced in Eph. 5, the model of the woman who has her κεφαλή in the man, and cannot really exist except in subordination to this κεφαλή, but in this way, determined and limited in Him, is exalted above all heavens by His majesty and lowliness, in fellowship with this Head ? It is for this reason that this order cannot be broken in the community ; that the relationship of man and woman established in creation, and the distinctions which it entails, cannot be regarded as transitory and accidental and abolished in Christ, as though Christ were not their meaning and origin. In the community this relationship cannot imperil either man or woman. It can only be their honour and joy and blessing. There is thus no cause to deny or abolish it as though it were a mere convention. On the contrary, dishonour and harm are done both to man and to woman if this clear relationship is abolished. It is quite ridiculous to think that progressiveness should be played off against conservatism in the matter of this relationship. If there is anything which is inwardly necessary and no mere convention, it is this relationship. Progress beyond it can only be regress to the old aeon. It is only in the world of the old aeon that the feminist question can arise. And for this reason the Corinthians should accept the custom. It is a symbolic recognition of the relationship, and therefore of the basis, determination and limitation which it has been given in Christ. This recognition may not be withheld. Self-evidently it might have taken a different form in a different age and place. But in Corinth and all the Christian communities of the time (v. 16) it took this form. And as it was called in question in this form it had to be protected and defended in this form, not for the sake of the form, but for the sake of what was at issue in this form. The fact that it also conformed to natural sensibility, to φύσις (v. 14), was an additional recommendation as Paul saw it. But this statement was only incidental. The decisive point was that the enthusiasm for equality which outran the form was not particularly Christian, but that the custom should be accepted in Christ. We cannot say more than that it should be, for Paul was not arguing from the Law, but centrally from the Gospel. It was not the one who called the Corinthians to order who was thinking legalistically, but the Corinthians themselves, who, armed with a general, liberal, non-christological concept of humanity, thought it their duty to attack this relative and indirectly human order, as though they were all apostles, and as though an apostle were a genius. It was as well for them that they had in Paul a real apostle able to maintain an unruffled front against their impulsive genius ; and they were well-advised to accept his summons to be imitators of him as he himself tried to be of Christ (v. 1).

Our final passage is Eph. 5²²⁻³³, the *locus classicus* for the point at issue. No other passage makes the connexion so emphatically. No other is so primarily concerned to make it. No other is so complete in its exposition of the two

3. Humanity as Likeness and Hope

relationships. And no other refers so solemnly to Gen. 2. From it we can survey the whole landscape which we have traversed : the New Testament relationship of man and woman in the light of the relationship between Christ and the community, and conversely the elucidation of the relationship between Christ and His people by reference to the man-woman relationship ; the Old Testament marriage between Yahweh and Israel and its reflection in the man and woman of the Song of Songs ; and finally our starting-point in Genesis 2, the natural being of man as fellow-humanity, as being in the encounter of I and Thou. Should we really have the courage or find it necessary to consider all these things not only in detail but in their manifold relationships if they were not set before us so authoritatively and perspicuously in Eph. 5 ? But this is an idle question. This passage does in fact make everything clear. And we have only to apply ourselves directly to this text in which everything is set out directly and verbally in an exegetical norm for all other texts. It forms the introduction to the so-called " house-table " of Ephesians, a list of specific admonitions to wives, husbands, children, fathers, slaves and masters among the members of the community, all of which stand under the overriding injunction : " Be filled with the Spirit ; speaking to yourselves in psalms and hymns and spiritual songs, singing and making melody in your heart to the Lord ; giving thanks always for all things in the name of our Lord Jesus Christ ; submitting yourselves one to another in the fear of God " (vv. 18–21). This basic note must be remembered if we are to understand the ensuing injunctions, and especially the first and lengthy admonition addressed to husbands and wives. Be filled with the Spirit, speaking to one another in praise of God, not only with your lips but in your hearts, not ceasing to give thanks, and subordinating yourselves to one another as you are engaged in this thanksgiving to God. Humanity in the New Testament thus derives directly from the practical experience of the Gospel. And we must certainly not forget the negative beginning to this general exhortation : " Be not drunk with wine." We recall from 1 Cor. 11 that the knowledge of the true relationship between man and wife established and determined and limited by the knowledge of Jesus Christ stands in contrast to an enthusiasm for equality which will not accept the fact that they are both allotted to their distinctive place and way in the peace of God. Where it is not a matter of this intoxication but of the fulness of the Spirit, not of the boasting and defiance of man but of the praise of God, not of the establishment of one's own right by one's own might but of constant thanksgiving, there flows from the Gospel the necessity of the reciprocal subordination in which each gives to the other that which is proper to him. This is the meaning of the house-table : *Suum cuique*. It has nothing really to do with patriarchalism, or with a hierarchy of domestic and civil values and powers. It does not give one control over the other, or put anyone under the dominion of the other. The ὑποτασσόμενοι of v. 21 applies equally to all, each in his own place and in respect of his own way. What it demands is ὑποτασσόμενοι ἀλλήλοις ἐν φόβῳ Χριστοῦ ; mutual subordination in respect before the Lord. He is the Exalted but also the Lowly, the Lowly but also the Exalted, who causes each to share in His glory but also His burden, His sovereignty but also His service. And here there is only mutual subordination in full reciprocity. In this way order is created within the creaturely sphere, and humanity established. It is, of course, no accident that more than half of the table is devoted to the relationship of man and woman, and particularly their relationship in marriage. This relationship is typical or exemplary for the whole relationship which has to be estimated in the fear of Christ. In good or evil alike all other relations between the sexes have their fulfilment and norm in the fact that this man finds this woman and this woman this man and therefore man the fellow-man to whom he is referred and with whom he is united. We stated at the outset that expression is given to fellow-humanity as one man looks the other in the eyes and lets himself be seen by the other. The meaning and promise of marriage is that this should take place between man and woman, that one woman should encounter one man as his, and one man one woman as hers. Where it takes place we have a good marriage; the marriage which can only be monogamous. It is from this height that the whole field is surveyed. Again, it is no accident that the list of admonitions opens with that to the wife and not to the husband (v. 22). That the participle clause ὑποτασσόμενοι is naturally continued in this way, and general mutual subordination has its first concrete form in the wife, is explained at once in v. 23 by the comparison: "For the husband is the head of the wife (a statement taken from 1 Cor. 11³), even as Christ is the head of the church: and he is the saviour of the body." Because her subordination stands under this comparison, the woman must see to it that it is not broken but maintained. And therefore the subordination of woman to man is the first and most interesting problem which arises in this field. Not man but woman represents the reality which embraces all those who are addressed, whether they be wives or husbands, old or young, slaves or masters, which claims even the apostle himself in his peculiar position, and from which he thinks and speaks and admonishes them to think and act. They are all the community which has in Jesus Christ its Head. They are all set in this place and called and gathered to this community by baptism. For none of them can there be any question of a higher or better place. None of them can ever think of escaping from or trying to climb above it. In the fulness of the Spirit they can only wish to remain at this place, listening, obedient and therefore subordinate to the One from whom and for whose sake the whole community exists, and without whom it could not continue for a single moment or in any respect, since it is the body which is snatched and rescued from the fire of perdition only in virtue of its union with this Head. The advantage of the wife, her birthright, is that it is she and not the man who, in relation to her husband and subordination to him, may reflect, represent and attest this reality of the community. The exhortation specifically addressed to her is simply a particular form of the basic admonition which applies to all. She is subordinated to her husband as the whole community is to Christ. The whole community can only take up the position in relation to Christ which is proper to the wife in relation to her husband. Even husbands and masters must take up the same position in relation to Christ as the wife in relation to her husband. This is what makes the admonition to the wife so urgent and inescapable. And this is what characterises it as a peculiar distinction for the wife. If she does not break but respects the true relationship to her husband, the wife is not less but greater than her husband in the community. She is not the second but the first. In a qualified sense she is the community. The husband has no option but to order himself by the wife as she is subordinate in this way. The curious wish of Schleiermacher that he had been a woman is not so foolish when it is seen against this background. It is striking that the final statement of the whole passage (v. 33b) repeats the admonition to the wife: "And the wife see that she reverence her husband." Whatever is said to the husband stands within the framework of what has to be said to the wife as wife. She and not her husband is the type of the community listening to Christ and the apostolic admonition. She must be mentioned both first and last, for she may first and last take this admonition to heart, all hearing and obedience being represented in her hearing and obedience. On the other hand, the greater part of the passage (vv. 25-33) is devoted to the particular admonition to husbands. This emphasis is significant. What is meant by the mutual subordination in the fear of Christ expected of all (v. 21) is demonstrated in the attitude of the husband, who in his relationship to his wife is the κεφαλή, the superior, the first, the leader, the bearer of primary responsibility. In this respect he is the type of the κεφαλή of the whole, of the Author and Lord of the community, of the Saviour of the body (v. 23). In the being and action of

3. Humanity as Likeness and Hope

the husband in relation to the wife there is thus decided whether the hearing and obedience of the wife take place in the sense in which they are established; whether she is really subordinated to him ὡς τῷ κυρίῳ and therefore necessarily and not merely in the sense of an androcracy which might easily become a gynocracy. As men in their being and action towards the wife reflect the being and action of the κεφαλή Christ, the community is the community and not merely seems to be or would like to be. How could it be the body of this Head without this reflection ? And it is the particular calling of husbands to produce this reflection. More has to be said to them than to wives because in respect of the life of the community more has to be said about the being and action of Christ than the being and action of the men concerned. There can be no question of anything more than reflection. Men are not the authors, lords and saviours of women any more than they can be their own authors, lords and saviours. Christ stands equally above both husbands and wives as He stands equally below them. But the reflection of His majesty and lowliness in relation to them and their wives, to the whole community, is the particular responsibility of the men. It consists in the fact that they love their wives. For Christ loved the community—it was in this that He became its Author, Lord and Saviour. He gave Himself for it (v. 25). And in this self-giving He made it His community. It did not make itself His community. It did not even make itself ready to be this. He Himself sanctioned it when it was unholy and purified it when it was unclean. He gives it a part in His own Word and Spirit. He invested it with His own glory, and thus made it the counterpart from which He had taken away every spot of reproach or occasion for blame. He Himself prepared it for Himself. He thus made it His own (vv. 26–27). It owes itself to Him and Him alone. This is the love of Christ for His community. This is the original form of the majesty and humility in which He stands in relation to it, and to both husbands and wives within it. There can be no question of repeating the original of this love of Christ. It is unique and once-for-all. But even less can there be any question of living in the light of this original without accepting the summons to a relative imitation and reflection of this original. This once-for-all and unique light does not shine into the void but into a sphere of men and therefore of males and females, i.e., into the sphere described in Gen. 2, where it is decided that it is not good for man to be alone, where he is to recognise himself in another and another in himself, where humanity relentlessly means fellow-humanity, where the body or existence of woman is the same to man as his own body or existence, where the I is not just unreal but impossible without the Thou, and where all the willing and longing of the I— on the far side of all egoism or altruism—must be the willing and longing of the Thou. This is the humanity of man which in the community is set in the unique and once-for-all light of the love of Christ. What else can this mean but that place is found for this fellow-humanity (which is what is meant by the imitation of that image); that man (who is the first to be summoned) takes seriously the " This now " of Gen. 2[33]; that he loves the woman which God has given him as himself, i.e., that he deals with her as with the fellow-man without whom he could not be himself, in whose person he constantly has to do with himself, in whose person he does good or evil to himself, exalting or abasing himself, and whose existence gives humanity to his own. This is what Paul describes as the particular responsibility of men in vv. 28–29a. They may and should and must precede women by accepting and affirming them in such a way that they do what man did at the climax of his creation in Gen. 2. For, as the decisive passage vv. 29b–32 goes on to tell us, what man did at the climax of his creation ; this humanity as the fellow-humanity of male and female ; the purely creaturely happening that a man leaves his father and mother and cleaves to his wife and they become one flesh—this is not a primary thing, the original, but a secondary, the copy. We have to do here with the great mystery and not just the small

(v. 32). For the creation of man and for this climax, for this form of humanity, the normative pattern, the basic decree and the plan of all the plans of God is "Christ and the community." This stands inaccessibly before and above the copy of man and woman. Thus in the little copy, between man and woman, there can be no question of the self-offering of the one for the other, of the one making the other a worthy counterpart by self-offering, and of the other owing itself and all that it is and has to it. Man cannot be the Creator and Saviour of men, or the man of the woman. On the other hand, it belongs to the very essence of the copy modelled on this pattern that the man should be with the woman, that he should not will to be without her, and that he should therefore love her as himself. And that this may and must take place is the admonition which must be given and heard where the light of this original falls into the human sphere, i.e., in the community created by baptism and the Word of Jesus Christ. And it is to the men first that this admonition must be given, and by them that it must first be heard: "Let every one of you in particular so love his wife even as himself" (v. 33), willing and affirming her existence together with his own, and her honour and welfare with and as his own, willing himself only as he wills her too. Wives must and will hear this also. We remember that this inversion takes place in the Song of Songs. There is a love of the community for Christ as well as a love of Christ for the community. But as the love of Christ precedes the answering love of the community, so the love of the husband precedes that of the wife. In imitation of the attitude of Christ the husband may and should precede at this point as the wife may and should precede him in representing the community in its absolute subordination to Christ. But it is to subordination that the husband himself is summoned. That he should love his wife is his particular part or function in the mutual subordination demanded in v. 21.

"This is a great mystery" (Eph. 5^{32}). The saying refers to Gen. $2^{18f.}$. But in Gen. $2^{18f.}$ it is a matter of the creation of man as male and female, and therefore of the basic form of being in the encounter of I and Thou, of humanity as fellow-humanity. In the New Testament a mystery (μυστήριον) is a reality which carries with it a definite message and does so in such a way that it is both concealed and declared. Where the revelation of God does not take place in and with this reality, and in such a way that it evokes the faith of man, and in his faith knowledge, the message is concealed and the mystery undisclosed. It is received, but not revealed. But where in and with it the revelation of God takes place and faith is evoked, it speaks and discloses itself; it is an open secret. The humanity of man is a reality of this kind. "But I speak," says Paul in Eph. 5^{32}, "concerning Christ and the church." If we read Gen. $2^{18f.}$ in the context of the Old Testament "Yahweh and Israel" is the message contained in this matter and both concealed and declared. The New Testament does not exclude but includes this interpretation. But it reaches above and behind the whole of the Old Testament as such. It sees the same reality, the creation and being of man as male and female, his humanity as fellow-humanity. It also sees the "Yahweh and Israel" contained and both concealed and declared in it. But it sees further and deeper. For it even the "Yahweh and Israel," and the whole Old Testament message grouped around this word of the

3. Humanity as Likeness and Hope

covenant, is itself a mystery which has still to be disclosed, a prophecy which has still to be fulfilled, a preliminary history which has still to be followed by the true history. The disclosure, the fulfilment, the true history is "Christ and the community." The New Testament knows that before all time, and in the beginning of time posited by the act of creation, and in the perishing time which stands under the sign of the fall and its penalty, and finally in the new time of freedom which has dawned, the resolve and will of God was and is and will be : "Christ and the community." And for this reason it says of the humanity of man that it is *this* mystery ; that it is the concealed and declared content, undisclosed without the Word and the Spirit and faith but disclosed by the Word, in the Spirit and for faith, of the reality "Christ and the community."

This is the biblical confirmation of the presupposition with which we took up this theme at the beginning of the section. We described the humanity of man as a mystery of faith. We had to deal with it accordingly. We had thus to ask first concerning the humanity of the man Jesus. In answer to this question we found that Jesus is the man who is *for* His fellows. We descended from this height to the lower question of humanity generally, and we found that man is the man who is *with* his fellows, the I with the Thou, the male with the female. We could not say more than "with." To say "for" would be to make the false assertion of a general anthropology. It would be to say too much. It can and must be said of the man Jesus, but of Him alone. Yet on the other hand we could not say less. For man without the fellow-man would be a creature which has nothing in common with the man Jesus, and with which the man Jesus has nothing in common. We had to turn our back resolutely on the idea of a man without the fellow-man and the ensuing anthropology. Setting our aim neither too high nor too low, we had thus to interpret humanity simply as fellow-humanity. And we had finally to realise that in this fellow-humanity we are not dealing with an ideal or law or anything of that kind, but with the normative and natural determination of man. For in the co-existence of man and woman at least we have a difference and fellowship given to man in and with his existence, so that in it he is fellow-human quite apart from his own thought or volition. This I-Thou relationship in its distinctive factuality and necessity is thus characteristic of his whole being, controlling it and giving it its character as fellow-humanity. We also saw that in this fellow-humanity, and at the very point where it emerges unequivocally as a natural fact of creation, i.e., in the co-existence of man and woman, the New Testament finds a great mystery. And the New Testament explanation of this mystery is as follows. What is contained and both concealed and declared in this reality, what everyone can receive but not everyone can know because its recognition is conditioned by God's revelation and the obedient faith which it evokes, is "Christ and His community." It is obvious that this brings us back to the starting-point and beginning of our whole investigation and presentation. We have here a confirmation of the fact that to understand what humanity is we had to look first at the man Jesus, the man *for* the fellow-man, and that on this basis we could come to see in man generally only man *with* his fellow-man. According to the main passage in Ephesians 5, but finally in all the relevant New Testament texts, Christ *and* the community means quite unequivocally Christ *for* the community. This dualism stands in clear distinction to that of man and woman and every human I and Thou denoted and controlled by that of man and woman. For the One who takes the place of man—and in this He differs from every other man or I—does not exist and act for Himself or for His own sake, but absolutely for others, for those who are united with Him as His community. He is their Head and Saviour. He is the One who takes away their sins and conquers their death. He is the One who lifts from them the yoke of the corresponding and confirmatory law of their sin and death. He is the One who brings and guarantees their freedom. He is the pledge of the eternal life promised to them. He is wholly for them and not for Himself; Jesus, the man for His fellows. And the co-existence of man and woman, humanity as fellow-humanity, is a great mystery because it contains and both conceals and discloses this fact that Jesus is the man for His fellows, both hiding and disclosing it, so that it can be received by everyone but not known by everyone. In this reality we have the witness of the creature itself to this truth. The Old Testament plainly attests it with its Yahweh and Israel. In the fact that it does so it is itself a mystery, prophecy and preliminary history, which must speak of man exactly but exclusively in the way in which it actually does in Genesis 2 and the Song of Songs. If, then, humanity as such, as a purely natural and creaturely determination of man, is this mystery, this real witness, disclosed and received or concealed and rejected, to this first and final element in the will and decree of God, it must be seen as we have tried to see it, and we have no option but to resist any idea of man without his fellow-man, and to understand humanity as fellow-humanity. As fellow-humanity, in the form of the co-existence of man and woman, it is this real witness. The general "with" corresponds to the unique "for" of Jesus from which all the plans and ways and works of God proceed and to which they move. If we accept Ephesians 5 and the New Testament view of this matter, we see that the circle closes at this point, that this is the end, and that we could not begin at any other point than that at which we did, or move forward from that point in any other way. Against this background the basic thesis of theological anthropology, that human being is a being in encounter, loses every shred of similarity with a mere hypothetical assertion. It acquires an axiomatic

3. Humanity as Likeness and Hope

and dogmatic quality. In the Christian Church we have no option but to interpret humanity as fellow-humanity. And *si quis dixerit hominem esse solitarium, anathema sit.* We can now regard this as secured and demonstrated. And the future history of humanity may well depend to some extent upon whether the Christian Church can agree to recognise this as secured and demonstrated, and thereafter assert that anathema with a stringency for which it has so far lacked both the perception and the resolution. It is to be noted, however, that this is possible only on the basis of Ephesians 5.

We have still to draw a concluding line. It is no accident that in this whole sphere we have had to make such ready use of terms like image, original, copy, correspondence, analogy, parity, likeness, similarity, and finally mystery. The title which we have given to the whole section is : " Man in his Determination as the Covenant-partner of God." Our starting-point was that man is determined in and with his creation and existence to be the covenant-partner of God. Our problem was how far he is this ; how far his creation and existence, his nature, must correspond to this determination. Our interest has been focused upon man below, in his reality distinct from God, in his creaturely nature in relation to that for which he was created, and may exist, and is summoned to exist from above. We have thus been concerned with the inner relationship between this being and his destiny. We have seen that this relationship is not one of contradiction but of correspondence. Man is orientated towards that for which he is determined. Even when he sins, he can deny and conceal but he cannot remove or destroy the fact that he is orientated in this way. Even as a sinner he remains the creature of God and therefore the being whose orientation is to be the covenant-partner of God. He can give himself up for lost. But he cannot escape God, or lose his being as the creature of God, or the nature of this being. He can trifle with the grace of God, but he cannot make himself wholly unworthy to be in covenant with God. He does this too. But he is found and rescued by the free and totally undeserved grace of God as the creature which even when it gave itself up for lost did not escape God, but whose being in all its perversion and corruption remained a being in correspondence with its determination as the covenant-partner of God. God is faithful. God acknowledges and confesses Himself the Creator by reconciling the world to Himself in Christ, in the One for whom and with a view to whom He created it. He thus proves true that which we contested but which did not in any way cease to be the truth because we did so, but was always the truth even in the form of our lie, namely, that our orientation is to be the covenant-partners of God.

And now we have investigated and described what we are, what our humanity is, in what way we are orientated to be God's covenant-partners in spite of our perversion and corruption, in what our correspondence to this determination consists. Our corresponding being is a being in the encounter of man and fellow-man. In this being we are covenant-partners by nature. This does not mean that we are the covenant-partners of God by nature. This is the determination under which we are created and exist. This is the particular plan and will of God operative and executed in our creation. This is the gracious meaning of our existence and nature. But it is not a human attribute. It does not belong to us in virtue of the fact that as men we are the creatures of God. We are not created the covenant-partners of God, but to be His covenant-partners, to be His partners in the history which is the goal of His creation and in which His work as Creator finds its continuation and fulfilment. That this is achieved, that we fulfil this determination, that this history is in train and moves steadily to its goal, is a matter of the free grace with which God deals in sovereignty with His creature, of the Word and Spirit with which He has intercourse with His creature, of His good-pleasure which we cannot control but must always acknowledge that we do not deserve. Yet the fact remains—and this is something which belongs to us as the creatures of God, which is part of our human essence, which can rightly be called a human and even the typically human attribute—that we are covenant-partners by nature and in our mutual dealings, the man with the fellow-man, the I with the Thou, the man with the woman. This is something which is our own, and is inviolable and indestructible. This constitutes the unbroken continuity of human existence. In this we correspond to our determination, and cannot cease to do so. In this there is a positive relationship between our being and our destiny. In this we ourselves, whether we know and accept the fact or not, are in sheer fact a sign and witness of our determination. We are created as mutual partners. And this leaves open the further possibility that we are created to be the partners of God. The latter statement speaks of the free grace of God in relation to man created with a specific nature. But it does undoubtedly speak of this human nature as such. And the content of the two statements makes it clear that the first is a reflection of the second, its truth being a likeness of that of the second.

It is to be noted that the *tertium comparationis*, the feature common to both likeness and reality, to both copy and original, consists in both cases, between man and his fellow-man on the one hand and God and man on the other, in an indestructible connexion and fellowship between two subjects which are indestructibly distinct. The only point of comparison is that on both sides there is a firm and genuine covenant. A covenant means co-existence for better for worse. It is genuine if it is between two partners who are obviously not identical. And it is sure if there is no question of the dissolution of the relationship between the two partners. More than this cannot be said. For apart from this common feature everything is different.

3. Humanity as Likeness and Hope

On the one side we have a union of creature with creature in virtue of the creaturely nature which they do not owe to themselves but to their Creator ; on the other we have a union of the Creator and His creature, in which the Creator is the free Lord of the covenant, and His mercy is its basis and goal, His wisdom the power of its initiation and execution, His faithfulness the guarantee of its continuance, and finally His own person its fulfilment. On the one side we have reciprocity, the giving and receiving of two partners of equal essence and dignity ; on the other everything is one-sided—the authority, the rule and the judgment, the plan and the work, being all of God, and His, too, the gift which makes it possible for the human partner to have a part in the covenant. On the one side man is with man ; on the other, God is with man but also for him in a way in which man can never be for God. On the one side there is an obvious and necessarily two-sided need ; on the other all the need is on the side of man but on God's side there is the sheer sovereignty of a grace which knows neither internal nor external compulsion but is wholly free, its address to man being an overflow of the inconceivable goodness of God. In our consideration of the man and woman on the one side and Christ and the community on the other, we have seen how great are the differences between the two relationships. But we have to remember that even the autonomy of the two partners is different in the two cases. In the one case it is only the relative and parallel autonomy of two creatures, but in the other we have the absolute autonomy of God on the one side and the relative autonomy of the creature on the other. And we have to remember that the firmness of the covenant differs in the two cases. In the one case it is that of the factuality which man cannot escape because he has this nature and no other ; but in the other it is that of the constancy of God which cannot turn from man because it is the free mercy of God which will not let go of man. It is, therefore, with this disparity that the being of man corresponds to the fact that man is ordained to be the covenant-partner of God. And this means that the correspondence of his nature does not give him any right or claim, any power to decide either to be or not to be the covenant-partner of God. It is no merit if he is ready to become this. He can only magnify the grace of God if he may do so. For it is only the grace of God if he is called and enabled to do so. It thus follows that natural theology cannot find here a point of contact for the proclamation of the grace and revelation of God. For if it is true that man in his humanity is himself a purely factual sign and witness of his determination, this can only mean that he is himself a mystery, a reality which encloses the declaration of his ordination to be with God, but only encloses it, and therefore conceals no less than discloses it, and discloses it only when it is expressed by the grace and revelation of God, and in the knowledge of faith thereby awakened. If this does not happen, it is of no help to man that he is himself a sign and witness. He is dumb even in relation to himself. The declaration of his determination takes place—he is in fact a man with the fellow-man—but he does not receive it. It does not tell him that God is with him and for him; that he is not merely the covenant-partner of the fellow-man, but of God. This is something which man cannot tell himself. He cannot even prepare himself to receive it. Only the Word and Spirit of God can tell it to him. Only subsequently can the proclamation of the grace and revelation of God draw his attention to the fact that it cannot be anything strange or unnatural for him to be called and set in covenant with God and gathered to the people of God.

And this is the positive thing which results from the fact that for all the dissimilarity there is similarity. This is the firm and genuine covenant in which man finds himself by nature in virtue of the fact that his humanity as such is fellow-humanity—corresponding to the firm and genuine covenant with God to which he, the creature to whom this nature is intrinsic, is summoned by the grace and revelation of God. If this takes place, this calling, this actualisation of his determination, finds him in the deepest sense at home. The Word of God really applies to him, this creature. The Spirit of God really speaks to his spirit. For as God discloses Himself to him, there is also disclosed to him the mystery of his own human reality, the meaning of the fact that he is man with his fellow-man, man with woman. If God comes to man, He comes to His possession which He has already marked as such in creating it. And what man may discover by the Word and Spirit of God as God comes to him is that God has not created him as a being alien to Himself, but as His neighbour and confidant. He has marked his nature, himself in his humanity, with the mark of one who is His neighbour and confidant. Man bears the sign of the firm and genuine covenant in which he may find and have his fellow-man, the I the Thou and man woman. He may recognise and find confirmed in this sign the fact that God really intends and seeks him when He calls him to covenant with Himself, to this covenant which is firm and genuine in a different way because grounded in and maintained by His grace. This sign and likeness, this reality full of declaration, the mystery of his own reality, is no longer dumb but eloquent. His humanity can no longer be a mere fact—a matter of accident or caprice. As the reflection of the light of grace which lay on it even when he did not know it, marking his existence as such, his humanity becomes the task and problem and content of his own action. Now that the meaning of his being is no longer unknown or obscure, he will now will, and will to practise and actualise, what he is by nature. In order that the fact of the human nature of man may be actualised, there is needed the grace and revelation of the covenant which God has concluded with the man created for this purpose. On the side of man there is needed his hearing of

3. Humanity as Likeness and Hope

the Word of God, his calling by His Spirit, his awakening to faith, his accepting and occupying his place and status as God's partner in this covenant. There is thus needed for the human willing and actualising of humanity the fact that this humanity, which in the first instance is a mere fact and as such a mystery, should be inwardly illumined and made transparent by the free act of God from above. There is needed what takes place in Ephesians 5—that the relationship of husband and wife should be lit up by that of Christ and His community. "In thy light shall we see light." But humanity, the human and natural relationship which is made clear and transparent in this way, itself becomes light. It is the fact of humanity which, giving light and speaking as a sign and mystery, becomes the task and problem and content of human action and therefore, as in Ephesians 5, the theme of Christian admonition. And conversely this fact presupposed in all human action and grounded in the nature of man is as such the sign and witness that as man lives in the human covenant he is obedient to his calling to be the covenant-partner of God and thus participates in this covenant-fellowship. That the covenant between God and man is the original of that between man and man means, therefore, on the one side that the latter covenant may and should be lived out in human action ; and it means on the other side that in its actual existence it is the hope that may also live in covenant with God and live this out too in his own action. This sign given him in and with his own nature tells and assures him that he is the neighbour and confidant of God, that he has not slipped from Him, that marked in this way he has always been regarded by God as His own, and always will be. It tells him that in this nature of his he who stands in this temporal covenant is also called to the eternal, that he may take comfort in and hold to the fact that he is called in this way, and that the Creator is faithful by whom he is called.

It must be pointed out in conclusion that if the being of man in encounter is a being in correspondence to his determination as the covenant-partner of God, the statement is unavoidable that it is a being in correspondence to God Himself, to the being of His Creator. The Initiator, Lord and Sustainer of the covenant between God and man is God Himself, and He alone. If man is ordained to be God's partner in this covenant, and if his nature is a likeness corresponding to this ordination, necessarily it corresponds in this respect to the nature of God Himself. God has created him in this correspondence, as a reflection of Himself. Man is the image of God. This is not an arbitrarily invented statement. In relation to the man Jesus, by whom we are impelled already to this conclusion, it is clear and necessary as a final definition. But in Gen. 1[26f.] the Old Testament also makes it in relation to man generally. I refer to my discussion of this text in *C.D.* III, 1, pp. 191 f., and believe that the present train of thought yields exactly the same results. Man generally, the man with the fellow-man, has indeed a part in the divine likeness of the man Jesus, the man for the fellow-man. As man generally is modelled on the man Jesus and His being for others, and as the man Jesus is modelled on God, it has to be said of man generally that he is created in the image of God. He is in his humanity, and therefore in his fellow-humanity. God created him in His own image in the fact that He did not create him alone but in this connexion and fellowship. For in God's action as the Lord of the covenant, and even further back in His action as the Creator of a reality distinct from Himself, it is proved that God Himself is not solitary, that although He is one in essence He is not alone, but that primarily and properly He is in connexion and fellowship. It is inevitable that we should recall the triune being of God at this point. God exists in relationship and fellowship. As the Father of the Son and the Son of the Father He is Himself I and Thou, confronting Himself and yet always one and the same in the Holy Ghost. God created man in His own image, in correspondence with His own being and essence. He created Him in the image which emerges even in His work as the Creator and Lord of the covenant. Because He is not solitary in Himself, and therefore does not will to be so *ad extra*, it is not good for man to be alone, and God created him in His own image, as male and female. This is what is emphatically said by Gen. 1^{27}, and all other explanations of the *imago Dei* suffer from the fact that they do not do justice to this decisive statement. We need not waste words on the dissimilarity in the similarity of the similitude. Quite obviously we do not have here more than an analogy, i.e., similarity in dissimilarity. We merely repeat that there can be no question of an analogy of being, but of relationship. God is in relationship, and so too is the man created by Him. This is his divine likeness. When we view it in this way, the dispute whether it is lost by sin finds a self-evident solution. It is not lost. But more important is the fact that what man is indestructibly as he is man with the fellow-man, he is in hope of the being and action of the One who is his original in this relationship.

INDEXES

I. SCRIPTURE REFERENCES

GENESIS

CHAPTER	PAGE
1	161
1:26f	193
1:27	194
2	161, 163, 164, 166, 167, 168, 183, 185, 188
2:18-25	161, 162, 176, 186
2:24f	176, 177
24:1f	173

DEUTERONOMY

25:5f	165

SONG OF SONGS

8:6f	164
in general	164, 166, 168, 170, 183, 186, 188

DANIEL

7	80

MATTHEW

6:22	122
9:36	81
18:27	81
20:34	81
22:38-39	86
28:18	81

MARK

1:15	82
1:41	81
8:2	81
9:22	81
10:44-45	83, 85
12:18-27	163
12:29-31	86
14:24	84

LUKE

2:11	80
7:13	81
10:29f	80, 81
15:20	81

CHAPTER	PAGE
16:8	146
20:36-38	165

JOHN

1:1	91
1:14-18	56
3:16	83
6:39	81
6:51	83
10:11	83
10:30	91
10:38	91
11:51	83f
12:28	90, 91
12:26	81
14:2f	81
14:10	91
14:20	91
14:26	91
15:9	91
15:13	83
16:27	91
17:3	91
17:5	90
17:6	80
17:8	91
17:10	81
17:11	91
17:14-16	91
17:18	91
17:19	83
17:21	91
17:22	91
17:23	91
17:24	81
17:26	91
18:9	81
20:17	81

ACTS

10:38	80

ROMANS

4:25	84, 86
5:5	145
6:3	174

CHAPTER	PAGE
7:1-6	174, 175
8:1f	175
8:29	80, 166
8:31	83
8:32	83
8:33	84
12:15	154
14:15	93

I CORINTHIANS

6:12-20	175
7:1-40	179
8:11	93
10:23	175
11:1-16	179, 184
11:24	84
11:26	84
13	154
13:4-6	154
13:8	146
13:12	165
15:3	83
15:47	80
15:53	166

II CORINTHIANS

4:16	80
5:14-15	83
5:17	171
5:21	84, 181
8:9	80
11:2f	172, 174, 175

GALATIANS

2:20	83
3:20f	164
3:28	179, 182

EPHESIANS

1:4	80
1:10	181
1:20	181
1:22	191
4:13	166
5	182, 188, 189, 193

CHAPTER	PAGE
5:2	84
5:22-33	83, 180, 182, 186

PHILIPPIANS

2:6f	80, 181
4:6-8	154

COLOSSIANS

1:13	175
1:16	181
1:17f	80, 171
2:10	181
3:3	165
3:9f	80

I TIMOTHY

2:6	83

TITUS

3:2	154
3:4	88

HEBREWS

1:6	80
2:9	83
2:14	80
2:17	80
4:15	80
6:20	84
7:25	84
9:24	84
12:2	80

I PETER

3:18	83
3:22	181

I JOHN

2:2	83

REVELATION

21:4	166

II. NAMES

Anselm, St., 2, 64, 68
Aristotle, 149
Augustine, 5, 101, 166

Ballenstadt, Kurt, 2
Barbour, Ian, 67
Berdyaev, Nicholas, 2

Indexes

Berger, Peter, 58
Berkouwer, G. C., 20
Blumhardt, 63
Bouillard, Henri, 4
Brunner, Emil, 62
Buber, Martin, 2, 39, 40, 60, 147, 148
Bultmann, Rudolf, 60
Busch, Eberhard, 69, 81

Calvin, John, 5, 83, 165
Cobb, John, 20
Come, Arnold, 20, 44, 53, 60, 61, 68
Confucius, 39, 147, 148
Congar, Yves, 4

Dante, 103
Dehn, Gunter, 64
Deschner, John, 69
Dionysius, 102, 105, 107, 108, 110, 111, 150

Ebner, Ferdinand, 2
Ehrenburg, Hans, 2
Ehrenburg, Rudolf, 2

Feuerbach, Ludwig, 67
Freud, Sigmund, 67

Godsey, John, 52
Goethe, 102, 110, 160
Gogarten, Friedrich, 2
Grisebach, Eberhard, 2

Hamer, Jerome, 4
Harnack, A., 1
Hartshorne, Charles, 20
Hegel, G. W. F., 12
Herrmann, W., 1
Hitler, Adolf, 62, 64
Hunsinger, George, 62, 68, 69

Kant, I., 110
Kuhn, Thomas, 50
Küng, Hans, 4

Litt, Theodore, 2
Löwith, Karl, 2

Luckmann, Thomas, 58
Luther, Martin, 5

Marcel, Gabriel, 2
Marx, Karl, 67
McConnachie, J., 8
McLean, Stuart D., 67
Mozart, W. A., 4, 5

Niebuhr, H. Richard, 20, 68
Niebuhr, Reinhold, 3, 62, 69
Nietzsche, Friedrich, 52, 101, 112, 147, 160

Oden, Thomas, 20
Overbeck, Franz, 101

Pepper, Stephen, 67
Proudfoot, Wayne, 60, 61, 68

Ritschl, A., 1
Röpke, Wilhelm, 69
Rosenstock-Huessy, E., 2, 8
Rosenzweig, Frans, 2

Schleiermacher, F., 1, 20, 110, 184
Schopenhauer, 102
Shakespeare, 103
Skinner, B. F., 6, 9, 28
Stahmer, Harold, 8
Strauss, 110

Thomas, Aquinas, 5
Thurneysen, 69
Titian, 150
Torrance, Thomas, 7, 8, 12, 20
Troeltsch, Ernst, 1

Voltaire, 105
von Balthasar, Hans Ur, 4, 20
von Rad, Gerhard, 8
von Weizsäcker, Victor, 2

Wagner, 102, 103
Weismantel, Leo, 2
West, Charles, 62
Willis, Robert, 7, 20
Wittig, Joseph, 1

III. SUBJECTS

Abraham, 57, 79, 165
act(s), 14, 15, 18, 31, 32, 40, 41, 44, 45, 51
act of being, 40, 41
action, 9, 12, 14, 15, 18, 19, 27-29, 31-33, 36, 41, 46, 48, 51, 53, 59, 61
action-relationship, 18, 45, 50

actional, vii, 34, 37, 38, 50-52, 56
active being, 47, 49
activity, 20, 35, 36, 42, 44
address, 30, 41, 56, 126, 127, 129
addressed, 27, 30, 31, 38
agape, 19, 42, 53, 145, 149-155
alienation, 35, 86

analogia entis, 4, 37, 90, 194
analogia fidei, 2, 4
analogia relationis, 2, 4, 15, 36-38, 43, 51, 58, 90, 91, 194
analogy, 58, 64, 189, 194
anthropology, vii, 6, 24-26, 28, 34, 50, 71, 74, 76, 77, 78
anthropology, theological, 96, 98, 99, 101, 147, 148, 155, 188
assistance (aid), 41-43, 60, 124, 132-134, 138, 148
atomistic, 13, 20, 24
awareness (sensing), 45, 46, 48, 49, 60

Barmen Conference, Declaration, 69
basic form of humanity, 39, 41, 42, 52, 95, 135, 136, 155, 159, 186
being, 4, 16, 18, 23, 45, 51, 82, 84, 136
  for God, 36, 37
  for man (his fellows), 36, 38, 52, 92, 113
  in-encounter, 39-43, 58, 71, 117, 119, 120, 122, 135, 136, 157, 160, 162-164, 186, 188, 190, 193
  in-fellowship, 113
  in-gratitude, 26, 29, 31, 32
  in-relationship, 43
  in-responsibility, 26, 32
  in-togetherness, 37
  of the man Jesus, 80
  with Jesus, 29, 30
  with/for the other/others, man, 39, 58, 92, 113, 130, 194
body, 16, 23-25, 43-46, 171, 185
body-soul, 12, 25, 46-49, 60, 71, 76
bureaucracy, 122

call, called, calling, 14, 17, 29, 30, 32, 33, 41, 42, 193
Christ, see Jesus Christ
Christian community, community of Jesus Christ, 8, 14, 15, 43, 44, 171-179, 182-188, 191, 193
church, 1, 3, 4, 7, 13, 14, 16, 17, 59, 148, 155, 160
co-existence, 37, 39, 43, 88, 142, 151, 156, 157, 162, 187
co-inherence, 37, 38
communism, 3, 62, 66
community, 1, 4, 7, 8, 13-15, 17, 24, 43, 44, 56, 61, 66, 145, 165, 175, 184, 185, 187
companion (associate, comrade, fellow, & helpmate), 43, 141, 142, 144, 146, 158
conditio sine qua non, 42, 136, 142, 152
conflict, 56, 57, 123, 156
connexion, 75, 89, 114, 158, 161, 162, 164, 190, 194
contract metaphor, 56-58, 67, 71
conversation, 11, 12, 14, 56, 58

cooperation, 123, 156
copy, 88, 139, 186
correspondence/similarity, 36-38, 75-77, 89-91, 94, 95, 113, 131, 132, 135, 141, 189-193
cosmic, 35, 45
cosmic being, 74, 79
cosmos, 24, 30, 40, 73, 82, 86, 87, 171
covenant, 14-16, 18, 19, 24, 29, 30, 36-38, 42, 43, 45, 53, 56, 57, 59, 68, 69, 73, 75, 77, 84, 87, 88, 94, 145, 151, 164, 167, 169, 170, 187, 190-193
  broken, 164
  eternal, 36, 37, 88, 193
  partner, 16, 20, 34, 42, 73-76, 87, 88, 91, 94-96, 113, 135, 146, 189-193
  partner of God, vii, 34, 37, 39, 43, 164
  temporal, 193
covenantal, iv, 6, 15, 18, 30, 57, 58, 61
  metaphor, 20, 56, 58, 65-68
created, creating, 32, 33, 42, 44
creation, 4, 5, 13-19, 23, 24, 28-30, 43-45, 53, 74, 79, 82, 156, 161, 167, 181, 187, 189
  doctrine of, 12, 17
Creator, 31, 36-38, 44, 45, 53, 90, 93, 94, 142-145, 151, 154, 161, 182, 189, 191, 193, 194
creature(s), 2, 5, 11, 16, 18, 19, 23-25, 27, 29-31, 36, 43-45, 74, 90, 145, 146, 156, 191
creaturely being, 46
  essence, 38, 144, 163, 164
  form, 12, 18, 35, 38, 42, 74-76
  life, 46
crucified God (crucifixion), 109, 169
culture, cultural, 1-5, 12, 19, 34, 40, 59, 62, 65, 66, 68, 71, 78

death (power of), 79, 82, 146, 165, 172, 188
decision, 30, 33, 36, 51, 56, 77
deliverance (divine), 26-28, 30, 78, 80, 85, 87, 146
Deliverer, 23, 35, 53, 79, 82, 83, 92, 95, 97, 145
delivers, 32, 35, 53
desire, desiring, 44, 45, 48, 49, 60
determination, 50, 74-77, 85, 91, 95, 113, 135, 144, 157, 159, 189, 190, 192
devil, 79, 80, 82-84
dialectic, 12, 20, 43
dialectical, 1, 12-14, 18-20, 24, 34, 49, 50, 63, 67
dialogue, 2, 3, 7, 8, 62, 129
dialogical, 7, 18, 19, 43, 59, 61
dialogical-dialectical, vii, 6, 12, 13, 15, 18, 19, 27, 38, 40, 43, 44, 48, 49, 56
differentiation, 13, 48, 156, 162, 164, 182

Dionysius, 102, 105, 107, 108, 110, 111, 150
distinction and connexion, 115, 116, 156, 157
divinity, 77, 80, 86, 87, 89
divinity of the man Jesus, 77, 78
dogmatic, 1, 8, 12
dualism, dualistic, 46, 75
duality, 52, 121, 122, 138, 148, 156, 160, 161, 167
dyad, dyadic, 29, 38, 56, 60, 61
dynamics, 18, 19, 36, 37, 52, 56, 61

Ecce homo, 101, 105-108, 110
ecology, 13, 20
economics, 3, 4, 40, 62, 65, 69
  capitalism, 3
  socialism, 3, 62-64, 66, 69
elected, election, 26, 29, 30, 32, 42, 51, 142, 169
empirical analysis, 62, 64-66
  evidence, 19, 45, 50
  sciences, 28, 29, 50
encounter, 2, 14, 39-41, 60, 116-118, 120, 123, 129-131, 136, 138, 140, 143, 144, 156, 157, 163
Epistle to the Romans (der Romerbrief), vii, 1, 67, 69
equality, 80, 162, 182
eros, 19, 149-155, 160, 163
eschatological, 57, 62, 164, 168, 170, 171
eternity, 12, 15, 18
ethical, 5, 6, 20, 50
event, 12, 13, 18, 27, 123
exchanges (ing), 56, 61
existentialism (ists), 2, 9, 23, 60
external basis of the covenant, 14, 15, 24, 29
eye, 120-122, 183

father/mother, 168, 170
feeling, 39, 46, 104
fellows, 28, 35, 36, 43, 85
fellow-humanity (man), 23, 35, 38-43, 45, 78, 79, 82, 85, 92, 95, 98, 117, 128, 131, 138, 139, 144, 145, 147, 148, 150, 155, 158, 162, 178, 183, 185-189, 190, 192, 194
fellow-men as brothers and sisters, 43, 53, 145
fellowship, 156, 194
fellowship with Jesus Christ, 43, 145
field, 40, 119, 120, 123
for and with God, 35, 36, 51, 61, 73, 86, 87, 88
for and with man, 35, 36, 38, 41, 45 (others), 61, 79, 80, 86-88, 93, 113, 144, 187, 188
for us, 83, 84
forgiveness, 57, 61, 145, 151, 152, 173

form, 12, 13, 35-39, 41-43, 51, 52, 56, 95, 144
formal, formal basis, 26, 29, 38, 50, 87
free co-existence of man with man, 145, 146
freedom, vii, 4, 5, 8, 13, 14, 17, 18, 26, 27, 29-37, 42, 53, 57, 73, 82, 115, 137, 139-155, 161, 174-176, 187
  of God, 4, 13-17, 26, 27, 30, 31, 36, 37, 44, 45, 51, 56, 80, 88, 90, 191
  of man, vii, 4, 5, 13, 14, 17, 18, 26, 29, 32, 33, 35, 42, 49, 55, 60, 87
freedom of the heart between man and man, 149, 150, 159, 163
from, to and with God, 29, 36, 74
from, to and with his fellows, 35, 36, 86, 162
functions, functional, 47-49, 58

gestalt, 23, 25
gift (giving) 82, 142
gladly, gladness, 40-43, 135-137, 139-144, 147-155, 159
glory of God, 27, 77-80, 82, 87, 145, 171, 172, 176, 181
God, vii, 1-3, 6, 8, 11-19, 23, 24, 64, 71, 145
  action, 1, 15, 18, 27, 33, 56
  Father, 15, 16, 18, 19, 37, 38
  freedom (decision), 4, 13-18, 26, 27, 30-32, 36, 37
  -God, 37, 43
  for us, 83
  Immanuel, 55
  initiator, 193
  is dead, 108
  Lord, Lordship, 14, 16, 24, 26, 27, 193
  -man, 1, 6, 7, 12, 13, 18, 23-29, 34, 37, 42-44, 56, 58, 67, 71
  revelation, 3, 11, 13, 14, 16, 19, 43
  so loved the world, 83
  sustainer, 193
  with and for man, 2, 14, 25, 36, 37, 55, 57, 88, 135, 191
  Word of, 1, 8, 11, 77, 79, 80
  work of, 162
Godhead, 15, 78
grace, 1, 14, 15, 20, 27, 30-33, 44, 60, 73, 77, 79, 146, 148, 191
gracious, 31-33, 145
gratitude, 32, 33, 145, 151
Greek, 108, 150-153, 160, 163

harlot, 177, 178
harmony, 56, 57
head, 80, 173, 184, 188
hear, hearing, 13, 14, 29, 41, 122, 128, 129, 193
help, 78, 80, 129
helpmate, 43, 141, 161, 162, 168, 181

history, 2, 12, 15, 18, 19, 26-32, 39, 40, 43, 73, 77, 80, 85, 118, 120, 145, 146, 190
Holy Spirit (Ghost), 14-19, 53, 145, 146, 150, 151, 154
hope, Christian, 17, 63, 145, 154, 167, 168, 170, 193
human condition, 31
 constructs, 12
 existence, 6
 finitude, 12
 nature, 144-147, 155, 156, 159
 reality, 79, 81
 sciences, 23, 49
 word, 32
humanist, humanism, 42, 145
humanistic insights, thought, 5, 6, 49
humanity, vii, 5, 8, 11, 18-20, 23, 25-27, 34-44, 49, 51, 52, 60, 61, 71, 74-80, 82, 84-89, 91, 93, 98, 117, 120, 121, 125, 129, 131, 134, 136-138, 141, 142, 144-155, 158-163, 183, 186-191, 194
 as likeness and hope, 155
 of Jesus, 92, 97, 113, 114, 144, 187
 without the fellowman, 52, 102, 114, 147
humility (childlikeness), 7, 129, 145, 181
humor, 8
Hungarian revolt, 3, 62
husband and wife, 168, 183, 185, 193

I, 35, 37, 39, 40, 48, 49, 114, 115
I am, 99-104, 113, 115-117
I am as thou art, 118-121
I am in encounter, 117, 128
I-Thou/thou, 2, 3, 35-43, 52, 56, 73, 85, 86, 88, 92, 114-119, 122-131, 134-139, 144, 149, 155, 159, 160, 162, 183, 185-188, 190, 192
I-it, 114, 117
idealism, 52, 146, 147
idealistic, 41, 50
image of God (imago Dei), 15, 37, 38, 52, 89, 91, 92, 95, 96, 181, 185, 189, 193, 194
immanent, 34, 62, 115
in their place, 82-84
incarnation, 17, 58, 87, 88
independence, vii, 43-46, 60
individual, 13, 16, 23-25, 34, 43-46, 60, 162
individualism, 52, 55, 60, 66
individuality, vii, 18, 23, 61, 114
inhumanity, 39, 76, 97, 98, 111, 121, 133, 154
interactional, vii, 12, 18, 33, 34, 43, 50, 53, 56, 58, 59, 61
interconnexion (and particularity), 45-47
intercourse, 123, 126, 127, 178, 190
interdependence, 49, 60

internal meaning of creation, 15, 24, 29, 34, 169
intersubjectivity, 31
isolation, 52, 61, 120, 127, 128, 130, 132, 143, 145, 147, 155, 159, 162

Jesus is with/for his fellows, 93, 172, 187, 188
Jesus Christ, 1, 2, 7, 11, 13-16, 18, 19, 21, 23-31, 33-39, 41, 43-45, 55, 56, 58, 59, 62, 65, 67, 73, 77, 92, 144, 145, 165
 divinity, 13, 25, 26, 29, 34-36, 41
 manhood, 2, 13, 15, 26, 27, 29-31, 34-39, 41, 92, 97, 113, 114, 144, 160, 187
 revelation in/of, 1, 11, 13, 14, 18, 24, 26, 43
joy, joyful, 5, 8, 19, 21, 42, 84, 87
judgment, 1, 4, 12, 14, 15, 17
justification, 4, 14-16, 84, 145

Kingdom of God, 27, 58, 63, 83
knowledge of God, 26, 32, 77, 191

language, vii, 2, 12, 13, 18, 33, 34, 38, 59, 68
law, 37, 57, 137, 138, 164, 165, 167, 170, 174, 188
logos, 56, 58-61, 67, 68
Lord as servant, 14, 16
love, 12, 14-16, 18, 19, 21, 32, 33, 36-38, 42, 43, 50, 51, 53, 61, 64, 86, 88, 90, 145, 146, 159, 185
love, Christian, 42, 43, 53, 144-148, 150-152, 155, 160

man-woman, male-female, 156-163, 165, 166, 168, 179, 185-188, 190-192, 194
man, men, person, vii, 1, 6-8, 11-19, 21, 23, 24
 for God, 25, 35, 73, 78
 for man, vii, 6, 12, 13, 23, 25, 29, 37, 44, 49, 51, 56, 57, 67, 78
 for other man, 35, 38, 73, 82, 190
 real, 19, 20, 23, 25-34, 37, 43, 44, 49, 71, 73, 74, 77, 84, 98, 113, 136, 143, 145
 whole, 25, 43, 44, 81
marriage, 158, 165, 166, 167, 184
Marxist, 3, 112
material, 26, 29-32, 36-38, 46, 50, 52, 87, 89
mechanistic root metaphor, 9, 13, 58, 65, 67, 69
metaphor, root, 6, 20, 56, 59, 65, 67-69, 71
method, methodology, 1, 11, 13, 28, 29
Mozart, 4, 5
 mutual 123, 129, 137, 182
 assistance, 40, 41, 130-132, 141, 143

Indexes 201

attack, 141
attraction, 158
constraint, 140
dealings, 190
determination, 138
exchange and co-existence, 157
expression and address, 130
joy, 142
limitation, 138
look, 122
partner, 190
recognition, 141
speech and hearing, 40, 58, 122
summons, 131
vision, speech, hearing and assistance, 58, 151, 157, 158
withdrawal, 141
mystery, 76-78, 88, 135, 136, 142, 185, 188, 189, 192, 193

nature of man, vii, 28, 29, 33, 39, 43, 46, 145
Nazism, 62, 64, 66, 106
needs, 127, 129, 134
neighbor(s), 79, 80, 86, 192

obedience to God, 26, 29, 32, 33, 87, 145
one and the many, 52, 114
ontology, 68, 80
open, openness, 43, 120-123, 143, 148
oppression, 3, 64
order, 47-49, 80, 162
organic metaphor, 20, 56-58, 66, 67, 69, 71

part-whole, 13, 14
particularity, 47, 120, 139, 156, 158
Patmos Circle, 2
Paul, the apostle, 154, 171-186
perceiving, percipient being, perception, 44, 46-49
philosophy, 1, 8, 11, 19, 25, 39, 49, 50, 68
political, politics, 3, 4, 55, 58, 62, 64-66, 71
poor, weak, alienated, 3, 4, 64, 66, 79
power metaphor, 58, 65-68, 175
praxis, 62-64, 71
proclamation, 1, 17, 55, 59, 83, 145
promise making and keeping, 57, 165, 171
providence, 4, 14, 16, 44, 45, 47, 53
psychological, 5, 6, 11, 13, 23, 24, 45, 49, 50, 62, 65, 157

qualitative, quantitative, 65, 66

reality, 12-16, 18, 19, 23, 25, 33, 38, 43
reason, 18, 45, 56, 61
reciprocal address, 41, 123, 137
    expression, 41, 123, 137

hearing, 131
    openness, 41, 123, 137
    reception, 41, 123, 137
    sight, 131
    speech, 131
    visibility, 130
reciprocity, 37, 80, 88, 113, 129, 130, 131, 137
reconciliation, reconciling, 14-17, 23, 27, 34, 61, 65, 170, 183, 189
redemption, 16-18, 27, 34, 43-45
related, relates, relating, 8, 13-15, 23-25, 44, 45
relational, vii, 13, 33, 34, 38, 56, 61
relationship(s), vii, 2, 3, 12-15, 18, 19, 23-27, 29-31, 33-38, 40, 43-45, 50, 51, 56, 58, 59, 61, 79, 135, 194
relative, 28, 57
representative of guilt and punishment, 35, 85, 93
responsibility, 2, 25, 26, 29, 32, 41, 51, 82
resurrection, 63, 64, 83, 165, 166, 172, 175, 176
revelation, 1, 16-18, 27, 29, 30, 43, 44, 50, 55, 56, 58, 59, 61, 65, 76, 87, 144, 145, 154, 186, 191
Roman Catholicism, 4, 13, 61, 144, 145

Safenwil, 1, 62
salvation, 13, 30, 35, 85, 154, 180
sanctification, 14-16, 145
save, saved, 32, 82, 145
saving work, 36, 80, 82, 87
saviour, 77, 79, 80, 92
scripture, 1, 3-5, 14, 17, 55, 58, 59, 74
secret, 42, 43, 81, 135, 137, 139, 141-146, 167, 168, 171, 186
    great, 42, 135, 146
    lesser, 42, 135
see, seeing, seen, 40, 42, 43, 60, 123, 148
self-
    activity, 46
    alienation, 136
    consciousness, 46, 47
    declaration, 124-126
    determination, 45, 46, 49, 53, 66
    expression, 124-126
    interpretation, 123, 124, 183
    justification, 162
    knowledge, 28, 46
    sufficient, 133
senses, 46, 48, 85, 87
servant as Lord, 14, 16, 181
service of God, 79, 182
sexual encounter, intercourse, 159, 176
sign, 190, 192, 193
similarity & dissimilarity, 26, 36-38, 56, 76, 77, 96, 192, 194
sin, 6, 25, 26, 32, 53, 73, 75, 76, 82, 84, 98, 143-146, 148, 149, 151, 152,

162-164, 167, 169, 172, 174, 177, 181, 188, 189
sinful, sinfulness, 6, 14, 57
sinner, 1, 82, 145, 192
social, 4, 7, 12, 29, 50, 60, 71
social science(s), vii, 5-7, 19, 23-25, 28, 34, 39, 49, 50, 64, 65, 69, 71
society, 2, 3, 23
sociology(ies), 11, 13, 23, 49
solidarity, 80, 81
Son of God, 14-16, 18, 19, 32, 37, 38, 41, 73, 80, 83, 84, 132
Son of man, 14, 16, 83
soul, 16, 18, 23-25, 42-46, 48
sovereignty, 27, 50, 64, 183
spatial, 13, 14, 46
speak and listen, 12, 41-43, 60, 122, 123, 128-130
speech, 12, 41, 42, 53, 56, 59, 124, 129, 143
Spirit (Holy), 18, 23, 32, 33, 44, 45, 80, 183-185, 187, 190, 192, 193
spontaneity, spontaneous, 32, 33, 123, 137, 139, 153
structure-event, 16, 18, 52, 61
struggle, 11, 56, 57
subject, 14, 31, 32, 39, 45, 46, 57
subordination, superordination, 51, 57, 125, 157, 162, 179-186
superman, 105, 107, 109
symbolic interactionist, 67

technological, 3, 13, 20
temporal, 13-15, 46
tertium comparationis, 36, 86, 190
thanksgiving, 15, 29, 31-33, 56, 73, 151, 154, 165, 183

theology, theological, vii, 1, 2, 5-8, 11-21, 23-25, 27, 33, 34, 36, 39, 40, 50, 58, 59, 62, 64, 66, 71
thinking, thought, vii, 1, 2, 5, 6, 12-14, 19, 20, 23, 24, 34, 43-47, 60
time and space, 7, 46, 57
to, with, and for man, 18, 19, 23, 35, 47
transcendence, transcendent, 11, 12, 19, 31, 34, 62, 64, 71
Trinity, triunity, 1, 16, 18, 19, 37, 55, 88, 194

unity, 13, 19, 20, 25, 44, 46-49, 56, 57

victory, 41, 82, 132
visual, 13, 14, 120
vocation, 14, 15

whole man, 23, 34, 43, 45, 47, 49, 71
whole-part, 13, 14, 49
wholly other, 1, 2, 34
will, willing, 18, 27, 30, 36, 37, 41, 44, 45, 48, 49, 60, 87, 142
with and for man, 18, 35, 41, 52
with and for God, 29, 30
with Jesus, 29
Word of God, i, 8, 11, 13, 16-18, 20, 21, 23, 27, 29-34, 55, 57, 59, 62, 66, 78, 92, 144, 146, 166, 185, 187, 190, 192, 193
work, saving, 27, 36, 38, 39

Yahweh and Israel, 167, 169, 183, 186

Zarathustra, 103-105, 110, 111, 150